DATE DUE

GAYLORD			PRINTED IN U.S.A.

Color, Hair,
and Bone

Color, Hair, and Bone

Race in the Twenty-first Century

Edited by

Linden Lewis and Glyne Griffith
with Elizabeth Crespo-Kebler

Lewisburg
Bucknell University Press

© 2008 by Rosemont Publishing & Printing Corp.

Associated University Presses
2010 Eastpark Boulevard
Cranbury, NJ 08512

The paper used in this publication meets the requirements of the American National Standard for Permanence of Paper for Printed Library Materials Z39.48-1984.

Library of Congress Cataloging-in-Publication Data

Color, hair, and bone : race in the twenty-first century / edited by Linden Lewis and Glyne Griffith with Elizabeth Crespo-Kebler.
    p.   cm.
Selected papers from a conference held Sept. 26–28, 2002, hosted by the Race/Gender Resource Center at Bucknell University.
Includes bibliographical references and index.
ISBN-13: 978-0-8387-5668-3 (alk. paper)
ISBN-10: 0-8387-5668-9 (alk. paper)
1. Race—Congresses. 2. Race in literature—Congresses. I. Lewis, Linden, 1953– II. Griffith, Glyne A. III. Crespo Kebler, Elizabeth. IV. Bucknell University. Race/Gender Resource Center.
HT1505.C5 2008
305.8—dc22

2007008080

PRINTED IN THE UNITED STATES OF AMERICA

Contents

Acknowledgments

THE EDITORS AND THE CONTRIBUTORS OF THIS VOLUME WOULD like to acknowledge the support of Jim Rice of the Office of Academic Affairs and Development at Bucknell University, who offered encouragement and financial support for the conference from which this volume is made possible. We would also like to thank Renée Gosson, Pawan Dhingra, Glyne Griffith, Elizabeth Crespo-Kebler, and Linden Lewis—the members of the organizing committee for the conference—for their work in the planning and organization of this event. The contribution of Academic Assistant Martha Shaunessy is particularly recognized also for much of the behind the scenes logistics and publicity of the conference. The then Race/Gender Center (now the Center for Race, Ethnicity, and Gender), and its former director, Elizabeth Crespo-Kebler, are also hereby acknowledged for agreeing to host this conference and for providing some of the human and financial support for this event. Lastly, we would like to thank all the participants, contributors, and colleagues who attended the conference and helped it to be a success.

Color, Hair,
and Bone

Transcending the Grosser Physical Differences of Race in Contemporary Society: An Introduction

Linden Lewis

W. E. B. DU BOIS'S FAMOUS PRONOUNCEMENT IN *THE SOULS OF Black Folk,* that the problem of the twentieth century was the problem of the color line, seems eerily appropriate, at least in this first decade of the twenty-first century. Inasmuch as social science theorists would advance arguments that suggest we abandon the concept of race because of its imprecision or because it is ethically indefensible,[1] the material effects of this phenomenon are as visible today in the United States as they were during slavery, Reconstruction, Jim Crow, and sadly, in much of the post–civil rights era. Gerda Lerner's argument against abandoning the concept of race at this stage is powerfully stated: "But the arbitrary, socially constructed designation "race" cannot be simply dropped from our language. Although there are no biologically definable, essential races, the term "race" has become reified in law, custom and historical practice to such an extent that it has acquired a historical existence."[2] In addition, the classification of the U.S. population by race had both sociological and policy implications from the outset, the impact of which has lasted through the twentieth and into the present century.[3]

The persistence of race in the twenty-first century can be seen through the lenses of a number of violent racial attacks on African Americans and people of African descent in the United States. Nineteen ninety-seven was the year of the vicious assault on Abner Louima, the Haitian man who was arrested outside of a nightclub, handcuffed, and taken to the Seventieth Precinct in Brooklyn where he was sodomized with a broomstick while in police custody. In 1998 in Jasper, Texas, James Byrd Jr., an African American man, was tied to a pickup truck and dragged for some distance until his death, for no apparent reason other than the fact that others hated him because of his race. A year later, in

11

1999, the tragic death of Amadou Diallo occurred in New York—shot forty-one times by four white police officers. Along the way there was the death of Anthony Baez, the result of an illegal choke hold, and the similar fate for Anthony Gammage, who died of suffocation while in police custody, and more recently the beating of Donavan Chavis, who was slammed onto the hood of a car in Inglewood, California, like a crash dummy. These incidents bring us back to the reality of the concept of race, which though arguably not real, has real consequences, and is firmly rooted in the social experiences of people. These events, horrific as they appear, are not the peculiar expression of the American racial order or landscape. The consequence of race and racial thinking is as pervasive in Europe as it is in the United States.

England, for example, has its own history of racial incidents involving the police. The deaths of Stephen Lawrence, Brian Douglas, Joy Gardner, Ibrahima Sey, and Shiji Lapite, are all cases that raise the specter of race that hangs over Europe. More recently the racially motivated killing of Zahud Mubarek, the Asian youth, by his white supremacist cellmate, Robert Stewart, and the clashes of Asians and African Caribbean groups in cities such as Manchester and Liverpool, are testimony to the persistence of race providing the backdrop to a continuing drama of identity, belonging, and social exclusion.

The more recent explosion in the suburbs of Clichy-sous-Bois, outside of Paris, called into serious question the French official *modèle républicain d'intégration*. Many called for its overhaul. The challenge to the French republican model arose in the aftermath of the death by electrocution of two French teenagers of African descent who were hiding from police in a substation. This event set off approximately thirty days of rioting and vandalism by alienated youth in France that went way beyond the suburb of Clichy-sous-Bois. In writing about the series of incidents, Naima Bouteldja observed: "But the reason for the extent and intensity of the current riots is the provocative behavior of the interior minister, Nicolas Sarkozy. He called rioters "vermin," blamed "agents provocateurs" for manipulating "scum" and said the suburbs needed "to be cleaned out with Karsher" (a brand of industrial cleaner used to clean the mud off tractors)."[4] Sarkozy's comments appealed to the sentiments of some of his right-wing supporters and to other xenophobic elements in French society, but they also outraged some who were rioting and those who were more sensitive to issues of exclusion and discrimination in that society. The issue of race in France has always simmered in that society but was brought to a boil by the recent events, exposing a long-term problem, which has persisted despite all efforts to manage the racial order. In similar fashion, the recent racial clashes in the suburbs of Australia between Lebanese Australians and surfers and residents of Cornulla, deeply disturbed and surprised nationals of this continent, even though such tensions have existed for several years, and despite increasing anti-immigration sentiments articulated even in governmental circles.

Whereas in the United States it is uncommon to declare one's self a racist, European racism has become "electoral."[5] There is an active and growing extreme right-wing parliamentary presence that is visibly a part of the political landscape of Norway, Denmark, France, Italy, and Germany. There is, for instance, the rather unabashed statement from the former finance minister in Germany, Theo Waigel, who held a hard line against immigrants, that: "We are not a multicultural society, we remain a German nation."[6] Unstated in the above comment is exactly how membership in the nation is to be determined, who could join in this exclusive club, and whose blood and belonging render them ineligible for inclusion in the national community.

One of the most dramatic recent examples of racism in Europe took place on the soccer field in November 2004 at the Bernabeu stadium in Madrid. On that occasion, thousands of Spanish soccer fans made monkey noises and gestures whenever England's black players touched the football. Of course, this was hardly the first time that such an incident had taken place in Europe; similar spectacles have occurred in Slovakia, Macedonia, and Greece. Prior to the Madrid incident, however, there was the unbelievable outburst by the Spanish soccer manager, Luis Aragones, who described one of the most brilliant players of the game, Arsenal's Thierry Henry, as that "black shit."

More recently, in June 2005, the Mexican government issued a postage stamp depicting a cartoon character called Memín Pinguin. Memín Pinguin appears to be a little boy with the face of a monkey. The cartoon in which Memín appears has been published in Mexico since 1940. The boy has exaggerated facial features, such as large, bulging eyes and large lips, images reminiscent of the racist stereotypes of African Americans in the American Jim Crow era and beyond. If there were any doubt about the racist intent of these stamps, there is an Aunt Jemima type, a heavyset black woman in the background of the picture, seemingly looking on as a mother would after a child who is going off to school. There is therefore a connection drawn between the images of the woman and the boy, which disrupts any naïve or innocent reading of the boy as a so-called lovable character, as Mexican officials have tended to argue. Moreover, the speech and mannerism of Memín

Pinguin are subject to mockery by the white characters in the comic book. Some 750,000 stamps were printed and as an index of insensitivity to racial offense in Mexico, these stamps were quickly sold out.

Interestingly enough, the president of Mexico, Vicente Fox, remarked: "Frankly I don't understand the reaction."[7] Perhaps Mr. Fox's befuddlement serves only to underscore a more profound problem of racial insensitivity in Mexico, which would prompt him just a few weeks prior to the publication of the Memín Pinguin stamps to state without apology that Mexicans cross the border to take jobs that "not even blacks" want. Perhaps also Mr. Fox did not understand that his statement was insulting to his own people and to all African Americans. Regardless of the lack of clarity on the racial issue by the head of state of Mexico, the fact remains that black visitors to Mexico are often referred to as Memín, and to the extent that this is done, it signifies that blacks are marked as other, and their difference is viewed in negative terms. In a country in which Mexican-born blacks are often viewed as foreigners, and in which people of African descent are a tiny minority, the publication of the Memín Pinguin stamp and the remarks of the president can only serve to fuel the insecurities associated with the experience and memory of race in the contemporary society.

The persistence of race is an issue that troubled W. E. B. Du Bois all his life. He noted: "All my life I have been painfully aware of the dichotomy between American freedom for whites and the continuing subjection of Negroes."[8] Du Bois saw very little hope for optimism at the time. In 1953 he argued that the color barrier in the United States would not be broken soon. He explained that even as it yielded in certain areas, the insult and memory of what remained would be felt perhaps more deeply.[9] At times Du Bois seems to locate race as the principal agent of history: "The history of the world is the history, not of individuals, but of groups, not of nations, but of races, and he who ignores or seeks to override the race idea in human history ignores and overrides the central thought of all history."[10]

Du Bois was not merely concerned with the issue of race, however. The issue of social class seemed quite central to his thinking in this regard also. "When the whole caste structure finally does fall, Negroes will be divided into classes even more sharply than now, and the main mass will become a part of the working class of the nation and the world, which will surely go socialist."[11] Though his socialist vision did not materialize, and "socialism would have had little more than a casual appeal for most of his readers,"[12] his comments here represent a full appreciation of the dialectical relationship between race and class for which he is often not given sufficient credit.

Moreover, Du Bois's apparent emphasis on the biological and physical characteristics of race in "The Conservation of Races" was very much tied up with a project "to correct the systematic erasure of black people from history."[13] Du Bois was indeed wrestling with the views extant at the time about the purity of the white race on the one hand, and the insufficiency of scientific knowledge about black people on the other, which combined to imply for him that black people had no history.[14] "Rather than allow the erasure of black people from history on racially biased, but nonetheless technical scientific grounds, he employed scientifically defined racial categories to establish their presence."[15]

The background provided above is therefore crucial to an understanding of the views expressed in "The Conservation of Races." Bernard Bell's observation is particularly germane to this effort of contextualization. Bell argues that Du Bois's views were expressed one year after the *Plessy v. Ferguson* Supreme Court decision, and two years after Booker T. Washington's Atlanta Cotton Exposition speech, both of which clearly supported the notion of separate but equal racial policies.[16] The emphasis on the biological here is therefore understandable. It is within this discourse therefore that one must read Du Bois's comment in his 1897 essay on "The Conservation of Races," from which the title of this volume has been culled:

Although the wonderful developments of human history teach that the grosser physical differences of color, hair and bone go but a short way toward explaining the different roles which groups of men have played in Human Progress, yet there are differences—subtle, delicate and elusive, though they may be—which have silently but definitely separated men into groups. While these subtle forces have generally followed the natural cleavage of common blood, descent and physical peculiarities, they have at other times swept across and ignored these. At all times, however, they have divided human beings into races, which, while they perhaps transcend scientific definition, are clearly defined to the eye of the Historian and Sociologist.[17]

It should be pointed out that Du Bois did not at the time have access to a language and theoretical framework of social constructionism; nevertheless, as indicated above, he was mindful of the prevailing biological thinking and the way he wanted to position himself in that discourse while also being cognizant of the forces of history as well as considerations of culture and spirituality. Not only, therefore, does race persist in the twenty-first century but so also do efforts to explain the phenomenon conceptually, theoretically, philosophically, and in terms of policy. Noticeably missing from this reflection, though present in other parts of Du Bois's writing, is an explicit articulation of the role of power in the meaning and experience of race in society. One could argue, however, that given Du Bois's objective in "The Conservation of Races," his concerns had more to do with the connection of knowledge to a particular form of power whose primary function was to provide scientific legitimation or delegitimation. It is, however, in the realm of political economy that the lived experience of race is more generally recognized. It is in the determination of access to valued resources, the acquisition of privilege and the capacity to have a material effect on the lives of others that the real impact of race is experienced. What is argued in the essays in this volume in one form or the other is that race is a socially constructed phenomenon, based on physical characteristics, which are interpreted culturally to have significance for nonphysical attributes. In short, like Du Bois, we contend that one cannot reduce the concept of race to the physical differences of color, hair, and bone. Rather, we argue that race is a complex, multilayered phenomenon that requires considerable unpacking.

As with all social phenomena, race is a dynamic concept, not one that is fixed and etched in stone. The idea and meaning of race is one that is contingent, and can only be properly understood within a given historical context. Understandably then, as history is being made or as it marches on, the meaning of race, or more specifically the discourse on race, moves right along with it. In the contemporary era, beginning in the closing decade of the twentieth century and continuing to the present, is the emergence of a shifting discourse from an explicit formulation and expression of race, to one in which race resides within the mystical shell of culture. The shift in the terminology and conceptualization of race to one of culture, especially the organization of culture, allows many to talk about race without even mentioning the word. Culture of course has always been a medium through which race is understood; however, what has changed is the emphasis or the way culture is used to deemphasize the real impact of race and racism. Some have begun to address this semantic and conceptual transformation, exposing its hidden agenda. Eduardo Bonnilla-Silva has called it color-blind racism, or racism without race.[18] Many remain unconvinced by these arguments about a color-blind society or policies that are putatively color-blind. "I do not think we are headed toward a policy regime that is 'color blind' and that will prevent the government from collecting data about race, ethnicity, or national origin. Powerful constituencies, notably in the public health and education fields, join with civil rights groups to contest such policy changes. They will prevail because the politics behind the color-blind movement are viewed, fairly or not, as a throw back to the policies of exclusion that the majority of Americans have firmly rejected."[19] Kenan Malik has spent considerable time in his book, *The Meaning of Race*, discussing this development of the appropriation of the language of a color-blind society.

For Malik this new discourse about race has essentially co-opted the language of cultural pluralism and reconfigured it so that it became a language of cultural exclusion. "Politicians and academics alike now look at clashes between cultures of civilizations as the real root of human difference. Culture, history, tradition—these are the means of delineating one people from another."[20]

In his most recent work Samir Amin goes even further by adding: "The discourse on the 'clash of civilizations' is completely intended to cement 'Western' racism and cause public opinion to accept the implementation of apartheid on a world scale."[21] The subtext of the new discourse is grounded in considerations of race but in a language that is essentially diversionary. In short this new emphasis in the discourse stresses that cultures are incommensurable, and since different peoples have different cultures, it is virtually impossible to bridge the cultural divide, particularly when one culture attributes superiority to itself. Put differently, in the new discourse on race, culture becomes particularistic and exclusivist, establishing a common past to which some may or may not belong.[22] According to Thomas Holt: "It is clear that through the "culture" concept biology in fact often reasserts itself. Conceptually culture sustains an aura of voluntarism and mutability that biology forecloses, but in the practical discourse of ordinary folk it carries much the same signification."[23]

The new discourse allows both liberals and conservatives to talk in a coded language about "urban types" when it is clear that a reference is being made to African American youths. The language of religious difference and clash of culture used in the aftermath of the tragedy of September 11, 2001, was remarkable for its ability to invoke fear, suspicion, and even hatred directed at Arab Americans and Arabs in general, all under the guise of further threats to national security but without any mention of race in that public discourse. However, this is not merely an issue of semantics but a specific and novel strategy for imposing silence on the concept of race, and in the process sanitizing any unpleasantness that such discourses may occasion. The switch from race to culture makes it infinitely harder for people to be accused of racism because their prejudices can be subsumed under concerns over national identity, cultural values, and other retrospective illusions. Despite its apparent new orientation, however, Holt provides an incisive note of caution, which is worth pondering. "Part of the solution is to adopt a conception of historical transformation, in which we recognize that a new historical construct is never entirely new and the old is never entirely supplanted by the new. Rather the new is grafted onto the old. Thus racism, too, is never entirely new. Shards and fragments of its past incarnations are embedded in the new."[24]

It is precisely this dialectical process that allows race to persist in one form or the other by virtue of adapting to the historical and social conditions within which it operates. The contemporary context also permits the articulation of certain fictions about race, which masquerade as truth and idealism, and often go unchallenged.

In his recent inaugural address on the occasion of the beginning of his second term of office as president of the United States, George W. Bush made a pronouncement about race and racism whose inaccuracy seems to have gone largely unnoticed. President Bush claimed: "And our country must abandon all the habits of racism, because we cannot carry the message of freedom and the baggage of bigotry at the same time" (Inaugural address, January 20, 2005). On its face this statement appears quite laudable; however, this is a contradiction, which the United States has been able to pull off quite successfully since the Declaration of Independence. As Eric Foner has pointed out rather clearly, "Slavery for blacks did not necessarily contradict white American's understanding of freedom."[25] The cold reality, however, is that at the time of the Declaration of Independence in the United States, when the founding fathers were articulating and embracing the ideal of freedom and equality, there were 650,000 slaves living in the colonies, 250,000 indentured workers, and 300,000 Native Americans, consideration of whose unfreedom did not seem to bother the signers of the independence document. In fact, of the first sixteen presidential elections held in the United States between 1788 and 1848, only four of those elections did not result in the White House being occupied by a Southern slave owner.[26]

The contradiction involved in espousing the ideals of freedom while embracing bigotry was spectacularly demonstrated in 1906 in Springfield, Missouri. Among the many lynchings that took place there that year, a white mob that had falsely accused three black men of rape, "hanged them from an electric light pole, and burned their bodies in a public orgy of violence. Atop the pole stood a replica of the Statue of Liberty."[27] Foner very perceptively notes that given their historical experience, African Americans were understandably suspicious of the way the notion of freedom was articulated in the United States because they have grown accustomed to ways in which "symbols of liberty could coexist with brutal racial violence."[28] The historical experience in the United States is that racial difference, in addition to other differences such as gender and sexual orientation, has led to the denial of freedom for many, but this form of prejudice has never really interfered with the articulation of the message of freedom in this country.

In reflecting on issues such as that expressed in the preceding paragraph, the pre-eminent African American novelist and writer Richard Wright noted:

> We black folk, our history and our present being, are a mirror of all the manifold experiences of America. What we want, what we represent, what we endure is what America is. If we black folk perish, America will perish. If America has forgotten her past, then let her look into the mirror of our consciousness and she will see the living past living in the present, for our memories go back, through our black folk of today, through the recollections of our black parents, and through the tales of slavery told by our black grandparents, to the time when none of us, black or white, lived in this fertile land.[29]

If Wright forces us all to confront history in attempting to understand the role of race, he is no less persuasive in getting us to contemplate what the alternative could have been if we had the courage to fashion a society that was truly built on racial equality. "If we had been allowed to participate in the vital process of America's national growth, what would have been the texture of our lives, the patterns of our traditions, the routine of our customs, the state of our arts, the code of our laws, the function of our government! Whatever others may say, we black folk say that America would have been stronger and greater!"[30]

In recent years many students of race have come to realize that race does not operate in a vacuum. It cannot be divorced from other social relations. Very often, race occupies the same habitus as that of gender, sexual orientation, and social class. The more sophisticated treatment of race in contemporary discourses on the subject take as their point of departure the intersection of these other social phenomena. Indeed, this intersection of race and other social relationships is consistent throughout this book, whether it is the convergence of race and masculinity, as in the essay by Linden Lewis, or the relationship between race and the marked body, as addressed by Carmen Gillespie, or the connection between race and the cinematic representation of Asians. In addition, Griffith, for example, explores this connection with race in relation to literature, while Raina demonstrates a similar point in relation to the development of archeology, anthropology, and German identity in the Andes.

Recognizing the polyvalence of the discourse on race has to extend beyond the mere notion of intersectional or interconnected forms of oppression. Its significance is not simply conceptual and theoretical but programmatic. This recognition of race in relation to other social phenomena allows us to appreciate that those who practice various forms of racism are also likely to be homophobic, xenophobic, and anti-Semitic. Both Jean-Paul Sartre and Frantz Fanon have spoken eloquently on this matter. Sartre, for example, notes for the anti-Semite, "the Jew only serves him as pretext; elsewhere his counterpart will make use of the Negro or the man of yellow skin."[31] Fanon was more expansive in his own comment: "At first though it may seem strange that the anti-Semite's outlook should be related to that of the Negrophobe. It was my philosophy professor, a native of the Antilles, who recalled the fact to me one day: 'Whenever you hear anyone abuse the Jews, pay attention, because he is talking about you.' And I found that he was universally right—by which I meant that I was answerable in my body and in my heart for what was done to my brother. Later I realized that he meant, quite simply, an anti-Semite is inevitably anti-Negro."[32] It was, however, W. E. B. Du Bois who had earlier made a similar point about the intersection of these social forces more explicit in relation to the African American attitude toward Jews that is very compelling here.

> The source of anti-Semitism for American Negroes is not far to seek. It is simply slavish imitation of the whites. It is the feeling that if we agree with powerful white groups in their prejudice and hatreds we shall in that way be brought closer to them and in wider sympathy. The cowardly and short-sighted attitude is then rationalized and strengthened by the knowledge which Negroes think they have of Jews. In truth the knowledge which one persecuted minority has of the other is seldom truth. They see each other through the eyes and hear of each other with the ears of the persecuting majority.[33]

This thinking led Du Bois to conclude in similar fashion to Sartre and Fanon noted above: "We have got to realize that the forces in the world back of anti-Semitism are exactly the same facts that are back of color prejudice."[34]

Programmatically, therefore, strategies of resistance must also operate on all fronts, forging alliances between constituencies of the oppressed, and establishing a more generally inclusive type of politics. These alliances ultimately serve to reinforce each other, ensuring a greater degree of success in the process of social transformation.

Recognition of the complexity of the concept and experience of race requires an additional awareness—a certain vigilance that eschews being co-opted by the very trajectory of the hegemonic discourse itself. Andrea Herrera raises a similar point in this book, specifically in relation to the U.S. context of the civil rights struggle. Gramsci (1980) of course first warned against this possibility in his *Prison Notebooks*, but Sartre raises the issue to another level. In discussing the inauthentic Jew, Sartre describes a scenario in which such a Jewish person becomes, in effect, anti-Semitic. "He [the inauthentic Jew] is so afraid of the discoveries the Christians are going to make that he hastens to give them warning, he becomes himself an anti-Semite by impatience and for the sake of the others."[35] Sartre also notes that this anti-Semitism of the inauthentic Jew "is an effort to make himself an objective witness and judge, and thus escape liability for the faults ascribed to his "race."[36]

Building on the above theoretical formulation, David Theo Goldberg has reintroduced this idea of "anti-racist racism." He argues that race can be mobilized for anti-racist purposes only to a limited extent. "In invoking the very terms of subjugation, in 'standing inside of them' to transformative purposes, racial invocation likely reinscribes elements of the very presumptions promoting racist exclusions it is committed to ending."[37] The problem as Goldberg sees it is that anti-racist racism creates a binary system, which reifies the process of assimilation and integration, while inadvertently stimulating the growth of separatism, Black Nationalism, and other types of racially essentializing ideologies.[38] Vigilance against the derailing of the process of racial transformation leading to racial equality by the practice of anti-racist racism should be a central mission of any progressive strategy of anti-racist struggle. In addition, the conceptual clarity to which Goldberg's argument points has implications for the practice of the anti-racist struggle in so far as it should move us beyond mere consideration of a new category of discourse—often a fundamentally rhetorical and liberal project—and lead to political action that avoids limitations of racial and narrow nationalist thinking. The idea here is to be able to engage in political action against anti-racist racism, rather than to be seduced by purely discursive practices, which disable political agency. These issues about how we approach and conceptualize race are too important to the lives of people, too fundamental to the way they experience privilege and marginalization, and too crucial to the way people navigate the terrain of power relations, to be relegated to the realm of discourse and academic rhapsodizing. The goal of the anti-racist struggle after all has to be one in which race becomes untethered from the apparatuses of power and hierarchical social arrangements, and where in the words of Hardt and Negri, there emerges "a process of liberation based on the free expression of difference."[39]

On September 26–28, 2002, the Race/Gender Resource Center at Bucknell University hosted an international conference on race whose title was "Color, Hair and Bone—The Persistence of Race into the Twenty-first Century." Pursuant to an earlier discussion in this introduction, the Bucknell faculty who were involved in the planning and organization of this conference chose to invoke W. E. B. Du Bois's reflection on what he described as the grosser physical differences of color, hair, and bone, to address the issue of the persistence of race at the dawn of the new millennium. Many of us felt that it was certainly a propitious time to reflect on Du Bois's formulation, while simultaneously providing an opportunity for those of us at Bucknell who had worked and published in the areas of race, class, and gender for many years, to engage in a wider dialogue with colleagues from other universities on some of these issues.

In keeping with the understanding articulated at the beginning of this introduction, we solicited papers for the conference that moved beyond, in the words of Du Bois, what human history had taught us and that address the intersections in which race continues to play a pivotal role. Our success in this regard was seen in the broad range of papers presented that examined issues of hybridity and the diaspora, race, nationality and sovereignty, popular culture, and colonial and postcolonial relations. This book therefore, is a product of what we considered a successful conference on race and race related matters not only at the national but international level. The essays assembled in this volume represent the selected papers from the conference. A wide range of topics is addressed here from different disciplinary perspectives that include literature, sociology, anthropology, and history.

In a very interesting literary, philosophical, and discursive approach, Glyne Griffith, building on Toni Morrison's *Playing in the Dark*, addresses the way racial "blindness" and race itself, function to limit people's understandings and possibilities. He looks at the role played by literature in the discourse of race and more specifically the experience of blackness and of black identity formation. In reading Morrison in conjunction with Du Bois, Griffith concludes that American canonical literature cannot be fully understood without due consideration to African and African American contributions to the American literary imaginary.

The representation of black masculinity in the United States has long been an arena of contestation particularly since black men did not have control over their own images. The travails of black manhood in America are essentially an important narrative of the history of racism, the denigration of personhood, and the erasure of a strong masculine identity. The essay by Linden Lewis examines the ways in which Gloria Naylor constructs different understandings and interpretations of the black male in her most recent novel, *The Men of Brewster Place*. This chapter seeks to explore the extent to which gender and race intervene in the formulation of the black male identity in America.

Isabell Cserno's work uses iconography to explore the meaning attributed to certain well-known German artifacts pertaining to black people. Her work points to a different racial discourse that is rooted in the cultural imagination of the German nation. She employs images to show their cultural construction of meaning, as well as the way these meanings change over time. Cserno's work is a creative effort to approach the discourse of race using different lenses. Continuing to understand the formation of German identity and attitudes toward race, Uta Raina examines identity formation and racial construction through imperial anthropological investigations of Germans in the Andes. She ties their research in Peru to the invention of notions of superiority and to the idea of a unifying national German identity. Raina makes an important contribution by documenting the role played by anthropology and archaeology in shaping perceptions of the other in Germany and in demonstrating how this research served to construct a national identity and reinforce social hierarchies.

The range of the interest in the construction of race is further expanded by Lan Dong's essay on the cinematic representation of the yellow peril. Her work focuses on the way Asians are represented in American film and the media in general. She uses D. W. Griffith's *Broken Blossoms* as her point of departure for addressing the stereotype attributed to Asian men in film and in the wider society. Her essay also shows how the so-called yellow peril can be problematized, reinterpreted, and co-opted by Asian American film producers.

Returning to the literary approach, Carmen Gillespie offers a comparative analysis of two Jamaican authors, Michelle Cliff and Margaret Cezair-Thompson, who describe and reinterpret the body within the Jamaican context. Gillespie argues that their reading is a postcolonial attempt at critiquing the authorial voices of British writers such as Richard Ligon. This essay raises some important issues about the discourse on colonialism, postcolonialism, race, and the body as text.

Sarah Daynes's essay is another perceptive analysis of race in an international context. Her concern is with the construction of race through the prism of the religious culture of Rastafari. The more immediate project was an analysis of discussions among Rastafarian women in an Internet club. In the process of dialogue among Rastafari women, issues of the shifting meaning of race add important nuances to our understanding of the same. Here race and cosmology merge, in which Rastafarian women struggle to balance the globalization of this religious culture with forms of inclusion and exclusion. In this discourse then, notions of authenticity are never far away and become more pronounced in the context of race and desire—an issue always fraught with controversy and contestation.

Norlisha Crawford brings into focus the intersection of race and class in African American literature. Her work revolves around the detective fiction of Chester Himes from the 1920s to the 1950s. In this essay she examines the socioeconomic stratification found in Himes's work on Harlem—one of the most important locations of black culture and struggle in the United States. Crawford unpacks Himes's work on Harlem, concluding that in his removal of the distinction between the licit and the illicit, the same patterns of rugged individualistic capitalism and its corresponding emphasis on entrepreneurship can be discerned among the characters in his Harlem, except that race renders their contribution suspect and unworthy of notice in the broader tenets of the American dream.

Theda Wrede's chapter re-centers the focus of the thoughts and ideas of W. E. B. Du Bois. In her essay on the cultural consciousness in August Wilson's *Joe Turner's Come and Gone*, Wrede draws on Du Bois's notion of the double consciousness in *The Souls of Black Folk* to interpret August Wilson's play. Wrede locates this double consciousness in the migration of African Americans from the South to the North where they encountered disappointments and frustration born of the similar experiences of race they thought they were leaving behind. This chapter attempts to contextualize and chronicle the experiences of these recent transplants to their new location using the play as a sounding board for the analysis that forces these essentially displaced people to negotiate new social relations and new lives in an often unfriendly and unwelcoming environment.

Finally, from pulpit to podium, is a reflection on the conjuncture of racial practice and racial discourse. Herrera examines the way racial discourse has formed the basis of liberation theories that contribute to the anti-racist struggle. She raises the difficulty of seeking to end racism while having to operate within the context of racist structures and institutions. The author looks at the role played by racial discourse in U.S. religious and academic discussions and its implications for racial transformation. She argues the case for the development of an alternative discourse that merges the activist orientation to race and race matters, with that of academic theorizing about the same. Herrera views this approach as important to the anti-racist struggle and as having significant implications for the development of an alternative pedagogy of liberation in the classroom.

This collection of essays represents not merely the product of an academic conference on the various dimensions of race, but it is also intended to contribute to an understanding of the existential realities of those lived experiences of a phenomenon, which impinges on all aspects of our lives. Race is everywhere and nowhere. No one is immunized from the intrusions of the discursive practices of race, even at the most quotidian level. Yet, depending on the way one stands in relation to the effects of the ensemble of power relations, some appear to become anaesthetized by the very pervasiveness of race. This point brings us back to the position alluded to earlier in this essay that the concept of race is constituted in the field of power relations and other social practices and cannot be separated there from.

Du Bois more than most people of his time understood the complexity of the notion and lived experience of race in the United States. It was recognition of the polyvalence of race that led him to examine the totality of the lives of African Americans and the impact of capitalism on them not only as black people but also as working class subjects. It was this realization, in conjunction with his socialist commitment, that led him to speculate about the future of African Americans in a post-segregation era. As indicated earlier, Du Bois felt that when the burden of race was eased, issues of class would emerge much more fiercely among African Americans. Race for the mature Du Bois was part of a complex ensemble of social practices that had to be understood in its totality. Race evidently continues to matter, but issues of class, gender, sexual orientation, and national origin have all risen to positions of equal concern in the contemporary United States. It is for reasons such as these developments that our analysis of race has to be more nuanced and polyvalent.

One of the important contributions of this volume is the confluence of newer and more experienced voices, all searching for new ways of mapping these continuing discourses and complexities of race. These essays are thoughtful and engaging interdisciplinary reflections on a familiar and enduring human experience, and should be read widely by all students of race and race relations everywhere. In addition, it stands as a testimony to an effort to engage in a wider discourse on race and to provide a forum for new and creative ideas on America's most enduring problem.

NOTES

The author would like to thank Collins Airhihenbuwa, Jim Rice, and Glyne Griffith for their comments and suggestions on an earlier draft of this chapter.

1. See Paul Gilroy, *Against Race*.
2. Gerda Lerner, *Why History Matters*, 188.
3. See Kenneth Prewitt, "Racial Classification in America," 7.
4. Naima Bonteldja, "Explosion in the Suburbs," November 11–17, 2005.
5. See Liz Fikete, "Popular Racism in Corporate Europe," October 1998–March 1999.
6. Ibid.
7. *Washington Post*, July 2, 2005, A26.
8. Quoted in Eric Foner, *The Story of American Freedom*, 172.
9. See W. E. B. Du Bois, "Negroes and the Crisis of Capitalism," April 2003.
10. Cited in David Levering Lewis, *W. E. B. Du Bois*, 171.
11. Du Bois, "Negroes and the Crisis," 39.
12. Lewis, *W. E. B. Du Bois*, 338.
13. Tommy Lott, "Du Bois's Anthropological Notion of Race," 71.
14. See ibid.
15. Ibid.
16. Bernard Bell, "Genealogical Shifts in Du Bois's Discourse," 91.
17. Du Bois, "The Conservation of Races," 73.
18. Eduardo Bonilla-Silva, *Racism Without Racists*.
19. Prewitt, "Racial Classification in America," 14.
20. Kenan Malik, *The Meaning of Race*, 182.
21. Samir Amin, *The Liberal Virus*, 26.
22. See Malik.
23. Thomas C. Holt, *The Problem of Race*, 14.
24. Ibid., 20.
25. Foner, *The Story of American Freedom*, 32.
26. Ibid., 36.
27. Ibid., 173.

28. Ibid., 172.
29. Richard Wright, *12 Million Black Voices*, 146.
30. Ibid., 145.
31. Jean Paul Sartre, *Anti-Semite and Jew*, 54.
32. Fanon, *Black Skin, White Masks*, 122.
33. Cited in Phil Zuckerman, ed., *The Social Theory of W. E. B. Du Bois*, 63.
34. Ibid., 64.
35. Sartre, *Anti-Semite and Jew*, 103.
36. Ibid., 104.
37. David Goldberg, *The Racial State*, 114.
38. Ibid., 115.
39. Michael Hardt and Antonio Negri, *Multitude*, 224.

BIBLIOGRAPHY

Amin, Samir. *The Liberal Virus*. New York: Monthly Review Press, 2004.

Bell, Bernard. "Genealogical Shifts in Du Bois's Discourse on Double Consciousness as the Sign of African American Difference." In *On Race and Culture*, edited by Bernard Bell, Emily Grosholz, and James Stewart. New York and London: Routledge, 1996, 87–108.

Bonilla-Silva, Eduardo. *Racism Without Racists: Color-Blind Racism and the Persistence of Racial Inequality in the United States*. New York: Rowman & Littlefield Publishers, 2003.

Bouteldja, Naima. "Explosion in the Suburbs," *The Guardian Weekly* 173, no. 21 (November 11–17, 2005): 6.

Du Bois, W. E. B. "The Conservation of Races," *American Negro Academy Occasional Papers* no. 2 (1897). Reprinted in *W. E. B. Du Bois Speaks, Speeches and Addresses 1890–1919*, edited by Philip Foner. New York: Pathfinder Press, 1970, 73–85.

———. "Negroes and the Crisis of Capitalism in the United States." *Monthly Review*, 54 (April 2003): 34–41.

———. *The Souls of Black Folk*. New York and London: Penguin, 1995.

Fanon, Frantz. *Black Skin, White Masks*. New York: Grove Press, 1967.

Fikete, Liz. "Popular Racism in Corporate Europe," *Race and Class* 40 (October 1998–March 1999): 189–97.

Foner, Eric. *The Story of American Freedom*. New York: W. W. Norton, 1998.

Gilroy, Paul. *Against Race: Imagining Political Culture Beyond the Color Line*. Cambridge: Harvard University Press, 2001.

Goldberg, David. *The Racial State*. Oxford: Blackwell Publishers, 2002.

Gramsci, Antonio. *Selections from the Prison Notebooks*. New York: International Publishers, 1980.

Hardt, Michael, and Antonio Negri. *Multitude: War and Democracy in the Age of Empire*. New York: Penguin, 2004.

Holt, Thomas C. *The Problem of Race in the 21st Century*. Cambridge: Harvard University Press, 2000.

Lerner, Gerda. *Why History Matters.* Oxford: Oxford University Press, 1997.

Lewis, David Levering. *W. E. B. Du Bois: Biography of a Race, 1868–1919.* New York: Henry Holt, 1993.

Lott, Tommy. "Du Bois's Anthropological Notion of Race". In *Race,* edited by Robert Bernasconi. Oxford: Blackwell Publishers, 2001, 59–83.

Malik, Kenan. *The Meaning of Race.* New York: New York University Press, 1996.

Prewitt, Kenneth. "Racial Classification in America: Where Do We Go from Here?" *Daedalus,* 134 (Winter 2005): 5–17.

Sartre, Jean-Paul. *Anti-Semite and Jew: An Exploration of the Etiology of Hate.* New York: Schocken Books, 1976.

Washington Post. "Mexicans Flock to Buy Stamp criticized in U.S.," *Washington Post,* July 2, 2005: A26.

Wright, Richard. *12 Million Black Voices.* New York: Thunder Mouth Press, 1988.

Zuckerman, Phil, ed. *The Social Theory of W. E. B. Du Bois.* California: Pine Forge Press, 2004.

Reading in the Dark: Race, Literature, and the Discourse of Blackness

Glyne Griffith

WHETHER ONE IS FOR OR AGAINST RACE, RACE IS A SOCIAL CATE-gory that continues to have material and cultural consequences in the Unites States, as elsewhere. In the United States, public discourse around race still tends towards strategies of evasion that fall, generally speaking, into two broad categories: (1) representations of avoidance regarding the long historical, philosophical, and institutional nature of race and racism in the Americas, and (2) what one might refer to as the rhetoric of exceptionalism and individuality regarding race and racism. The first category of evasion is exemplified, inter alia, by the tendency in some quarters to attribute racism to ignorance and to the realm of emotional response. Thus, we hear or speak of this or that person's racist attitude and behavior as a sign of his ignorance. We refer to criminal acts motivated by racism as "hate crimes," locating the source of the act in the emotional response. However, when one considers the lengthy philosophical and discursive nature of race and racism in the modern period, racism is more properly located in the realm of the rational and the institutional than in the too readily dismissed category of ignorance.

Regarding the notion of racism as necessarily linked to an emotional response, it is highly conceivable that a so-called hate crime could occur with absolutely no hatred toward the victim being registered by the perpetrator. One does not have to hate the "other" to behave in a racist manner toward "otherness." It is quite possible that one could be dispassionate in determining that "otherness" needs to be controlled or eradicated from the body politic as a social good. As such, "hate crimes" might more properly be labeled "crimes against humanity" in order to shift the discourse on racism away from the emotions and place it squarely back in the realm of the rational and philosophical where it discovered its epistemological and institutional growth and development. In addition, the emphasis on the victim's humanity focuses attention on the very category that is often philosophically and ideologically at stake as a result of racism, that is to say, the individual's or group's humanity

The second broad category of discursive evasion linked to the idea of exceptionalism and individuality might be illustrated, for example, by the response of several media persons commenting on Shani Davis's gold medal win at the 2006 winter Olympic games in Turin, Italy. As the first African American to win individual gold at a winter Olympics, interviewers' questions and comments invariably turned upon Davis's exceptionalism—the fact that his achievement marked "a first." There was no contemplation, at least no obviously public contemplation, of the long institutional and systemic nature of racism and the inequities resulting from it that might have made a Shani Davis individual Olympic gold medal seem like an exceptional occurrence. One commentator, an assistant professor of Communication at Marist College, appeared to invoke the "credit to one's race" idiom when he suggested in an NPR interview that in the apparent personality conflict between Shani Davis and fellow U.S. skater, Chad Hedrick, Davis carried a greater burden than Hedrick, as the first African-American individual speed skating medalist, and therefore should have been more gracious in his public remarks about his fellow teammate. He even suggested that Davis "robbed the world of what could have been a defining moment."[1] Thus, the burden of a long history of institutionalized racism was yet again individualized rather than conceptualized as institutional and systemic, and the onus of appropriately representing a historically misrepresented race was again placed on an individual from that racial group rather than referred to the group that has historically benefitted from the systemic misrepresentation that is institutionalized racism. It is against this background of a general discursive tendency to separate, compartmentalize, and individualize analyses of race and racism that Toni Morrison's regard of the U.S. literary landscape is instructive.

The first part of my title, "Reading in the Dark" is an amended borrowing from Toni Morrison's *Playing in the Dark: Whiteness and the Literary Imagination*. In this collection of essays, Morrison examines the intricate relationship, within conservative literary practice, between a peculiar sort of racial "blindness" and the exegetical "insight" of literary historians and critics regarding American literature. As Morrison indicates:

For some time now I have been thinking about the validity or vulnerability of a certain set of assumptions conventionally accepted among literary historians and critics and circulated as "knowledge." This knowledge holds that traditional, canonical American literature is free of, uninformed, and unshaped by the four-hundred-year-old presence of, first, Africans and then African-Americans in the United States. It assumes that this presence-which shaped the body politic, and the Constitution, and the entire history of the culture—has had no significant place or consequence in the origin and development of that culture's literature. Moreover, such knowledge assumes that the characteristics of our national literature emanate from a particular "Americanness" that is separate from and unaccountable to this presence.[2]

Morrison's text examines this conventional racial blindness that is germane to conservative literary insight in order to reveal the exegetical possibilities for a literariness, which would seek to incorporate rather than exclude the centrality of race in its regard of American literature.

Following a similar line of analysis and argument, I wish to examine some of the ways in which racial "blindness" on one hand, and racial discourse, on the other, function to limit hermeneutic as well as ontological possibilities. Thus, the first part of my title, that is to say, "Reading in the Dark," is meant to signal both the type of discursive blindness of which Morrison speaks in her text, as well as the interpretive and ontological possibilities that reveal themselves when we read *in* the dark, that is to say, when we incorporate rather than exclude race and "blackness" as a crucial exegetical element in literary and ontological readings.

Significantly, in the quotation taken from Morrison's text and cited above, she places the word "knowledge" in quotation marks. That is, when she speaks of her concern with "the validity or vulnerability of a certain set of assumptions conventionally accepted among literary historians and critics," she refers to the circulation, dissemination and consolidation of such assumptions as "knowledge," and she places the word in quotation marks. I take her quotation marks to be indicative of an inherent contradictoriness in the existence of this set of assumptions in the world. In other words, these assumptions, at least from Morrison's careful reading of them, are epistemologically flawed, yet this does not substantially curtail their function as knowledge in the world of literary criticism.

In a similar manner, although it has become commonplace in a world that has embraced the etiquette of "political correctness" to speak of obviously racist beliefs and practices as a sign of ignorance, perhaps it might be more useful to locate such practices in the context of a historical knowledge. We can, if we want, place the term "knowledge" in quotation marks to indicate the inherent contradictoriness therein and to register our own ambivalence toward such representation. At the same time, however, reading racist ideas and practices as participating in struggles for the constitution of knowledge, rather than simplistically dismissing such as mere ignorance, might provide us with a keener sense of the complex ways in which such conventional assumptions function in the world.

"Knowledge," in this sense, has less to do with the idea of some irrefutable truth with a capital "T," and more to do with conventional assumptions and practices that participate in the exercise of power in culture and society. Thus, the "knowledge" of which Morrison speaks participates, to some degree, in the authority and legitimacy of literary studies in the academy. In a similar manner, the conventional assumptions established around the idea of race in the Americas also participate in authorizing and legitimating certain attitudes and practices in culture and society. As such, these conventional assumptions are characteristic of a historical body of knowledge; they speak of institutionalized and systemic ideas and practices rather than individual ignorance and idiosyncrasy. Viewed in this manner, we recognize that the struggle against racist beliefs and practices is not really a matter of filling an empty vessel with the gift of knowledge. Rather, the struggle is characteristic of competing knowledges engaging each other in an arena in which the rewards are intersected by power. Ignorance is not the problem; the problem is the body of knowledge established around the idea of race, a body of knowledge that locates its modern genesis in the late fifteenth century and Columbus's entry into the so-called New World.

Let us briefly consider, for example, Columbus's response to the Taino peoples he met in the Caribbean when he made landfall in October 1492. In his journal entry dated Sunday, October 14, the admiral writes: "I went along the island in a north-north-easterly direction, to see the other part, which lay to the east, and its character, and also to see the villages. And soon I saw two or three, and the people all came to shore, calling us and giving thanks to God. Some brought water, others various eatables. . . . Many came and many women, each with something, giving thanks to God, throwing themselves on the ground and raising their hands to the sky, and then shouting that we should land."[3] Columbus observes that the people he encounters are friendly and hospitable, yet, only a few lines later he writes:

I saw a piece of land, which is formed like an island although it is not one, on which they were six houses; it could be converted into an island in two days, although I do not see that it is necessary to do so, for these people are very unskilled in arms, as your Highness will see from the seven whom I have caused to be taken in order to carry them off that they may learn our language and return. However, when your Highnesses so command, they can be carried off to Castile or held captive in the island itself, since with fifty men they would be all kept in subjection and forced to do whatever may be wished.[4]

Thus, despite acknowledging the friendly hospitality and gentleness of the people he has just encountered, Columbus orders the capture of seven Taino who will be taken back to Castile to learn "our language and return," and then his thoughts shift to the subjugation of those others who remain on the island. I do not cite this passage to indulge in retrospective moralizing or recrimination, but to suggest that this initial encounter between Old World and New, and the response it would elicit from Columbus and his men, provided a kind of preface to a modern discourse on race and the power relations therein. We know that this European encounter with the peoples of the so-called New World would quickly lead to religious and philosophical discussions about the nature of humanity. In 1525 the ecclesiastic Thomas Ortiz addressed the newly established Council of the Indies on Spain's Indian problem and argued that: "They [the Taino] are incapable of learning . . . They exercise none of the humane arts or industries . . . The older they get the worse they behave. About the age of ten or twelve years they seem to have some civilization, but later they become like real brute beasts . . . God has never created a race more full of vice . . . the Indians are more stupid than asses and refuse to improve in anything."[5]

The royal historian Gonzalo de Oviedo and Juan de Sepulveda, the influential scholar who garnered many of his ideas from Aristotelian philosophy, both concluded that the Indians were "so backward and bestial that they should be converted by force of arms and made to serve the Spaniards as natural slaves, according to the dictates of Aristotle."[6] We begin to see, therefore, that this European encounter with the putative New World does not merely produce a vulgar and brutish conquest and plunder. It also produces the seeds of a modern discourse on race and humanity, and it establishes a context in which these non-European peoples would not only serve their conquerors as slaves, but also as a kind of ontological canvas upon which Europeans could further explore their ideas regarding humanity and being. The Taino would come to have a metaphysical, as much as a material, value for the Europeans, and it is conceivable that they provided greater value in terms of the former rather than the latter. They provided living evidence in the "New World" of the noble savage, that pre-human or would-be-human, by means of which the European philosophical mind could chart and establish its own humanity, civility, and advancement. Having encountered and subdued or exterminated the noble savage in the "New World," European "knowledge" of non-European savagery soon consolidated itself into a set of assumptions that, for the most part, would become conventionally accepted among learned minds of the day.

Thus, just three generations or so later, we observe eighteenth-century philosopher Jean-Jacques Rousseau, for example, setting much of his philosophical argument regarding inequality among men against the backdrop of the idea of the noble savage. Rousseau does not need to establish the logic and validity of his concept of savage man. He can take it for granted because the idea has been long consolidated in European thought. It is quite interesting to discover that all of Rousseau's examples of noble savagery are discovered among those whom we would nowadays refer to as "people of color." Arguing that savage man has little fear of wild beasts because he can choose to fight or flee, and no animal naturally makes war against him, Rousseau states: "These are, without doubt, the reasons why Negroes and savages trouble themselves so little about the wild beasts they may encounter in the woods. In this respect the Caribs of Venezuela, among others, live in the most profound security and without the slightest inconvenience."[7] Rousseau's noble savages are narrative creations, fictitious creatures, but they are given a racial and geographical specificity even as they are dehistoricized. Thus he continues: "I would note that, in general, the peoples of the North are more industrious than those of the South because they can less afford not to be, as if nature thereby wanted to equalize things by giving to minds the fertility it refuses the earth."[8] And he establishes the indifference of the savage by claiming that: "His soul, agitated by nothing, is given over to the sole sentiment of its present existence without any idea of the future, however near it may be, and his projects, as limited as his views, barely extend to the end of the day. Such is, even today, the degree of foresight of the Carib: in the morning he sells his bed of cotton and in the evening he comes weeping to buy it back, for want of having foreseen that he would need it for the coming night."[9] Again, Rousseau provides his savage with racial and ethnic specificity; he is a Carib, and according to Rousseau's narrative, the Carib lacks foresight. Yet the Caribs are known to have engaged the

European conquistadors in some of the fiercest battles as they sought to defend their territory and way of life. Indeed, even the supposedly more peaceful Arawaks had produced pockets of resistance to Spanish conquest under such leaders as Guacanagari, Anacaona, and Enrique, before they were finally decimated. The Caribs endured much longer against the Spanish, and as Louis Allaire tells us, "Caribs appear by name throughout the sixteenth century in connection with enduring hostilities toward the Spanish colony in Puerto Rico, when the island of St. Croix seems to have been used as a base for their raids.[10] In addition, we learn that "The Caribs were essentially a farming people. They planted small manioc and sweet potato gardens in the surrounding rain forest near their villages, which consisted of a series of round huts for the women built around a larger rectangular men's house."[11]

Surely the historical presentation of the Caribs as a socially organized people who managed to wage a protracted war against the Spanish, despite inferior weaponry, suggests a people with foresight and a concern for their future. However, Rousseau's need is not for a historicized Carib, but for an imaginative noble savage who can provide his narrative with a prehistorical, pseudo-man. Such a character, though having no basis in historical fact, or perhaps precisely because it has no basis in historical fact, permits Rousseau's narrative to detail the coming into being and the civil progression of European man by contrasting him with an imaginative, non-European savage. Rousseau's noble savage is an ontological device; it is a device that participates in conventional assumptions about progressiveness and backwardness, civility and savagery. It is an ontological construction that would function as an important element in the discourse of blackness.

Of course Rousseau is not alone in his reliance on a figment of the European imagination to chart the historical progression of European personhood, but it is not my purpose here to either indict Rousseau or provide a list of European and other thinkers who employ a similar strategy. I want to illustrate the way in which such assumptions and narrative creations constituted a convention, a body of knowledge, which would authorize and legitimate particular readings of so-called persons of color, both in the world and in the text.

Having traveled through time from Thomas Ortiz's sixteenth-century utterances before the Council of the Indies, to Jean-Jacques Rousseau's eighteenth-century descriptions of the Carib, let us listen to J. A. Hobson's early twentieth-century argument in his work, *Imperialism*. Hobson states: "Assuming that the arts of progress, or some of them, are communicable, a fact which is hardly disputable, there can be no inherent natural right in a people to refuse that measure of compulsory education which shall raise it from childhood to manhood in the order of nationalities."[12] In addition, he states: "Now the ease with which human life can be maintained in the tropics breeds indolence and torpor of character. The inhabitants of these countries are not progressive people; they neither develop the arts of industry at any satisfactory pace, nor do they evolve new wants or desires, the satisfaction of which might force them to labour."[13] Hobson, writing in 1902, sounds uncannily like Thomas Ortiz addressing the Council of the Indies in 1525: "They [the Taino] exercise none of the humane arts or industries . . . [they] refuse to improve in anything." And how like Rousseau's "the people of the North are more industrious than those of the South" is Hobson's, "Now the ease with which human life can be maintained in the tropics breeds indolence and torpor of character." Across the centuries, we witness the progression of "knowledge" about the non-European, the imaginatively created, though historically false, noble savage. We observe the pervasiveness of a set of assumptions, predominantly about nonwhite peoples, functioning as "knowledge," not only among literary historians and critics, recalling Toni Morrison's observation, but also among numerous philosophers and social scientists such as Rousseau, Kant, Hegel, and Hobson. Thus, assumptions such as those we have been considering, conventionally accepted across historical periods and gaining the force of "knowledge," speak authoritatively across disciplines and even in the face of experience that would contradict such "knowledge."

When English literary critic Louis James edited *The Islands In Between: Essays on West Indian Literature*, a collection of essays on the burgeoning literature of that area of the Americas, published in 1968, he was able to state without any intended malice: "[I]n the Caribbean the satisfied senses do not need the movement into the intellectual plane of beauty in the same way that they do in less temperate climes."[14] Here is the echo of Hobson's conflation of tropical climate with indolence and torpor of character; here is the echo of Rousseau's generalization that "the peoples of the North are more industrious than those of the South because they can less afford not to be." James was able to arrive at this conclusion as a disinterested literary critic, despite having sojourned in the Anglophone Caribbean for a lengthy period, and despite having witnessed evidence to the contrary, because he subscribed to a set of assumptions which participate in the "knowledge" of the other, the different, the "not-me."

This body of knowledge about the other, about the noble or not so noble savage, provides us with a kind of shorthand for representing various ways of being in the world. It allows us to foreclose certain readings, to read in the dark, in a manner of speaking, because this shorthand of representation tends to silence oppositional ways of seeing and being in the world. It tends to silence oppositional ways of seeing and being in the text.

Consider this scenario, for example, which Henry Louis Gates Jr. brings to our attention in his introduction to *"Race," Writing, and Difference*. Commenting on Immanuel Kant's conflation of intelligence and race in *Observations on the Feeling of the Beautiful and Sublime*, Gates cites Kant's interpretation of an exchange between a white priest and a black carpenter in the Francophone Caribbean: "Father Labat reports that a Negro carpenter, whom he reproached for haughty treatment toward his wives, answered: 'You whites are indeed fools, for first you make great concessions to your wives, and afterward you complain when they drive you mad.' And it might be that there were something in this which perhaps deserved to be considered; but in short, this fellow was quite black from head to foot, a clear proof that what he said was stupid."[15] Blackness functions here as a sign of closure in Kant's thinking. The black body erases any possibility that utterances that emanate from it might be intelligible and consequential, and so Kant's musings on what would ordinarily be construed as a dialogue, become instead a monologic discourse on otherness and the incapacity of that otherness to represent itself.

This naturalized knowledge of "blackness," by which I mean all that is not readily comprehended as existing within the domain of white experience, is the discursive canvas upon which "whiteness" comes into view. Perhaps this is part of the reason that conservative analyses of canonical American literature maintain the idea that this literature is, recalling Morrison's skepticism, "free of, uninformed, and unshaped by the four-hundred-year-old presence of, first, Africans and then African Americans in the United States.[16] To focus on the canvas of "blackness," to de-naturalize it would be to simultaneously denaturalize "whiteness" as a historical construct, consequently bringing its association with sociopolitical and economic privileges under greater scrutiny. Even more unsettling perhaps, is that such a critical practice, brought into widespread use would disturb the ontological foundations of "whiteness" and profoundly challenge us to revolutionize our comprehension of concepts like "humanity," "freedom," and "democracy." Toni Morrison comments on the function of the discourse of blackness in American letters:

The ways in which artists—and the society that bred them—transferred internal conflicts to a "blank darkness," to conveniently bound and violently silenced black bodies, is a major theme in American literature. The rights of man, for example, an organizing principle upon which the nation was founded, was inevitably yoked to Africanism. Its history, its origin is permanently allied with another seductive concept: the hierarchy of race. As the sociologist Orlando Patterson has noted, we should not be surprised that the Enlightenment could accommodate slavery; we should be surprised if it had not. The concept of freedom did not emerge in a vacuum. Nothing highlighted freedom—if it did not in fact create it—like slavery.[17]

This idea, which Orlando Patterson also examines in *Freedom in the Making of Western Culture*, is quite interesting. Would the reification of freedom, the almost tangible representation of this abstract concept on the American landscape, would it have been as readily available for reification without the actual presence of the "unfree" on the landscape of the Americas? Perhaps this consideration might be used, for example, to reinvigorate what some critics have construed as the flawed ending in Twain's *Adventures of Huckleberry Finn*.

Readers will recall that at the conclusion of the narrative, Jim has been granted his freedom, but Tom Sawyer is interested in indulging an elaborate scheme in which, with Huck's help, he will imprison and then liberate the already legally free Jim. Huck is not particularly impressed by Tom's scheme, and he wonders what value there is in freeing someone who is already free. However, given the interdependence, as Orlando Patterson suggests, between the reification of freedom and the enslavement of Africans in the Americas, Tom Sawyer's dilemma, revealed by his protracted "liberation" of the already free Jim, is that his own concept of himself as a free being is threatened by the possibility of a society where none are enslaved. How is he to delineate his freedom and his humanity if there is no longer a readily available "other" against which his self-knowledge can be drawn in stark relief? His strategy seems to suggest that he is reluctant to imagine selfhood beyond the master/slave, whiteness/blackness paradigm. In the concluding chapter of the narrative, Huck provides the reader with Tom's sense of an ending:

The first time I catched Tom private I asked him what was his idea, time of the evasion?—what it was he'd planned to do if the evasion worked all right and he managed to set a nigger free that was already free before? And he said, what he had planned in his head from the start, if we got Jim out all safe, was for us to run him down the river on the raft, and have adventures plumb to the mouth of the river, and then tell him about his being free, and take him back up home on a steamboat, in style, and pay him for his lost time, and write word ahead and get out all the niggers around, and have them waltz him into town with a torchlight procession and a brass band, and then he would be a hero, and so would we. But I reckoned it was about as well the way it was.[18]

Tom's resultant heroism, had his plan succeeded fully, would have been a consequence of Jim's being kept in the dark about his own freedom and right to self-determination. It would thus have been the result of Tom's maintenance of the power to enslave Jim or to set him free. This situation, at this point in the narrative, reveals a great deal about Tom's ontological crisis, a crisis consequent on emancipation's potential to uncouple freedom from whiteness. Indeed, even Huck himself, who has become much more self-conscious than Tom as a consequence of his own adventures with Jim on the raft, and his experiences of the inhumanity to be discovered among the civilized folk on the shores of the great river, can only conceive of Jim's humanity and freedom by informing the reader that, "I knowed he was white inside."

The difficulty involved in uncoupling whiteness and freedom is further complicated when one considers the manner in which whiteness has also helped to obfuscate class relations in the American context. The coupling of whiteness and freedom on the American landscape would appear to be somewhat comparable to the rise and reification of "citizenship" in sixth-century Athenian culture. According to Orlando Patterson, the increasing slave population in sixth-century Greece exacerbated the nature of envy and competition among the mass of Greek farmers who did not understand themselves to be benefiting from the wealth created by the increasing slave populations:

What impressed the average Greek male about slavery was not the plight of the slave but the power and honor enhancement of the master. In the zero-sum approach to life which typified these men, rich and poor alike, the recognition of the master's gain would immediately have induced a sense of outrage about what was being lost to those who were not benefiting from the large-scale introduction of slavery . . . what was being lost, or rather being threatened, was the integrity of the homeland. The slave's . . . alienness was emphasized because it was precisely on this basis that the class of large-scale masters was most vulnerable . . . the slave's alienness enhanced the value of the freeman's nativeness. And the master class, in turn, paid for its desecration of the community with the intrusion of slaves and other foreigners by making a special value of what it shared with all who were nei-

ther slaves nor aliens. Citizenship, then had its crucible in the contradis-
tinction with the non-native, the most extreme case of which was the slave.[19]

Where citizenship served to blur class distinction and placate the economically disenfranchised in sixth-century Greece, whiteness would
arguably serve a similar purpose in the so-called New World. Pap, in
Huckleberry Finn, is keenly aware of the privileges of whiteness, and as
a consequence, he rails against what he construes as the erosion of such
privilege:

> There was a free nigger there from Ohio—a mulatter, most as white as a
> white man . . . and there ain't a man in that town that's got as fine clothes as
> what he had; and he had a gold watch and chain, and a silver-headed cane
> . . . They said he was a p'fessor in a college, and could talk all kinds of lan-
> guages and knowed everything. And that ain't the wust. They said he could
> vote when he was at home. Well let me out. Thinks I, what is the country
> a'coming to? It was 'lection day, and I was just about to go and vote myself
> if I warn't too drunk to get there; but when they told me there was a state
> in this country where they'd let that nigger vote, I drawed out. I says I'll
> never vote ag'in.[20]

Huck's alcoholic father regards his whiteness as possessing greater
value than the mulatto professor's education and wealth. If the professor is able to vote, it means that, in addition to his superior class status,
he also shares the privileges of citizenship with Pap. If this situation
becomes normative, then Pap will have no readily available access to
status and privilege. His crisis is rooted in racism, but it is fundamentally an ontological crisis. If we relinquish racism's conventional
assumptions, if we truly uncouple the historical linkages in the Americas, between whiteness and freedom, between whiteness and citizenship, what new ontological ground will we cultivate? Current debates
and analyses around multiculturalism would seem to offer the possibility of new identity configurations, but more often than not, we are presented with old wine in new wineskins.

It is still often true that multiculturalism functions as a euphemism
for all that is not stereotypically associated with white experience, with
"whiteness." It would seem that a rigorous comprehension of multiculturalism renders it as at least as old as that fateful fifteenth-century
meeting of Old World and "New World" cultures, but, as we are aware,
that meeting did not speak of multiculturalism in the sense of mutual
cultural interchange or acculturation. That five-hundred-year-old
encounter spoke in decidedly binarist terms, of conqueror and con-

quered, human and noble, as well as ignoble savage, master and slave, and so on. Even in its present configuration, multiculturalism still often speaks in binarist terms, of "First" World and "Third," of "World" music and, I imagine, just ordinary or normal music, of ordinary, normative people and then of "people of color." I certainly am not being frivolous here and I recognize that one needs to name differences and distinctions, perhaps especially where there are socioeconomic and political consequences regarding those distinctions. Nevertheless, it is equally important to recognize that changes at the level of signifiers do not necessarily speak of fundamental or even incremental changes in the hegemonic status quo. At one level of understanding, we all know that the phrase "people of color" really means everybody except white folk. A multiplicity of racial and ethnic groupings gets thrown together in that catchall phrase, even as whiteness stands outside it all. As such, the gathering of all nonwhiteness together, despite significant cultural and other relevant differences among such groupings, stands distinct from, if not opposed to whiteness. Whiteness operates as a sort of normative, hermeneutic mode, somewhat like the omniscient narrator in a text. It exists outside analysis, scrutiny and interrogation while representing to the readers of race, all those other "raced," and thus deviant, characters in the text.

The practices of analysis, scrutiny, and interrogation are reserved for all those myriad groups collectively referred to as "people of color," not for the omniscient narrative voice. Indeed, even the general comprehension of the term "multicultural" has at its back, the echo of the idea of the mono-cultural, the culturally pure. Perhaps we speak less these days of the idea of cultural assimilation, but arguably, the popular understanding of the term "multicultural" with its implied opposite, "monocultural" has allowed the idea of assimilation and the notion of cultural and racial purity to remain intact. "Monocultural," not in the strict sense of only one, pure cultural strain, but as a construction of cultural pedigree, may not be exotic and chic, but it bespeaks the idea of purity.

Language and discourse are quite adept at forging and forcing distinctions in order to construct and salvage notions of purity, even in the face of obvious challenges to such notions. Consider, for example, the discursive separation of race, that is to say, the foreclosure on multiculturalism when it began to threaten notions of racial purity in the form of miscegenation on Caribbean slave plantations. In *Cambridge*, one of Caryl Phillips's narrators recalls that: "The offspring of a white man and a black woman is a mulatto; the mulatto and the black produce a sambo; from the mulatto and white comes the quadroon; from the quadroon and the white the mustee; the child of a mustee by a white man is called a musteefino."[21] But this exercise was not merely a matter of linguistic play, for we discover that, "the children of a musteefino are free by law, and rank as white persons to all intents and purposes."[22] Thus, multiculturalism, in the form of miscegenation on the Caribbean slave plantation, did not weaken the notion of racial purity and the privileges of whiteness, but rather served to reinforce such a notion and its attendant privileges. Indeed, so steadfast were such constructions of purity, that the idea of cultural impurity, even where racial purity was assured, was frequently associated with disease and mental instability. Such conventional assumptions would be taken up, whether self-consciously or inadvertently, by literary texts of the period. One such text is Charlotte Brontë's *Jane Eyre*.

Edward Rochester feels driven to commit bigamy, so intent is he upon marrying Jane Eyre, because his tragic first marriage to a Jamaican Creole woman has ended in her insanity and his utter misery. A solicitor, Mr. Biggs, who speaks up at the marriage ceremony on behalf of Rochester's brother-in law, Richard Mason, provides the details of his earlier marriage. "I affirm and can prove that on the 20th of October, A.D.,—(a date of fifteen years back) Edward Fairfax Rochester, of Thornfield Hall, in the county of——and of Fearndean manor, in—— shire, England, was married to my sister, Bertha Antoinetta Mason, daughter of Jonas Mason, merchant, and Antoinetta his wife, a Creole— at —— church, Spanish Town, Jamaica."[23] The narrative provides details, through Mr. Biggs, of the marriage that took place in Spanish Town (an actual place) in Jamaica, and indicates that the bride's mother is Creole, that is to say, a person of European descent born in the Caribbean. Interestingly, when on one occasion, Jane Eyre glimpses the mad Bertha who has inadvertently awakened her, she tells Rochester with alarm that the figure resembled none of the personalities she had come to know in Rochester's home. Jane says: "Fearful and ghastly to me—oh, sir, I never saw a face like it! It was a discolored face—it was a savage face. I wish I could forget the roll of the red eyes and the fearful blackened inflation of the lineaments!"[24] She then indicates that the figure reminded her, "of the foul German specter—the Vampire."[25] But Rochester's description of his predicament is even more revealing in the context of our prevailing discussion. He states:

> Bertha Mason is mad; and she came of a mad family; idiots and maniacs through three generations! Her mother, the Creole, was both a mad woman

and a drunkard! as I found out after I had wed the daughter . . . Bertha like a dutiful child, copied her parents in both points . . . I invite you all to come up to the house and visit Mrs. Poole's patient, and *my wife!* You shall see what sort of being I was cheated into espousing, and judge whether or not I had a right to break the compact, and seek sympathy with something at least human.[26]

Bertha is not only an insane drunkard, but she is not quite human. Perhaps it is this absolute "otherness," her characterization as nonhuman in Brontë's novel, which allows the reader to retrospectively excuse Rochester's intended bigamy. Bertha's cultural impurity as a white Creole is understood to predispose her to insanity and drunkenness, but the real tragedy is that such "multiculturalism" also makes her less than human. She is a sort of inverse of the slave Jim in the *Adventures of Huckleberry Finn*. Jim's inner whiteness, i.e., his cultural assimilation to the ways of white folk, mediates his blackness so that Huck can begin to think of him as human. On the other hand, Bertha's racial whiteness is betrayed by her cultural exposure to blackness in her Caribbean setting, and so her English husband cannot envision her humanity.

Insanity or some other form of psychological crisis is frequently used as a fictional device, to narrate cultural antagonisms of this sort and to represent the encounter between whiteness and blackness, self and other. If we shift regard from the literally unfree, the slave, to the metaphorically unfree, those individuals of African descent who, as Bob Marley reminds us in "Redemption Song," need to emancipate themselves from mental slavery, we can observe an important connection between W. E. B. Du Bois's critical observations in *The Souls of Black Folk*, and Toni Morrison's critique in *Playing in the Dark: Whiteness and the Literary Imagination*. The text I want to employ, briefly, to demonstrate this link is Zora Neale Hurston's *Their Eyes Were Watching God*. Readers will recall that in Hurston's novel, Jody Starks sees himself through the eyes of white folk. For all his material and political success as Mayor of Eatonville, Jody models himself on the image of a hierarchical, white manhood. Thus, when he first enters Eatonville with Janie at his side, and learns that the town has no mayor, he says to Lee Coker, "Ain't got no Mayor! Well, who tells y'all what to do?"[27] In Jody's view, someone must be master for there to be social order. His hierarchical self-concept is not only grounded in gender difference, but even more importantly for him, it is rooted in racial difference. This idea of Jody imagining himself through the eyes of whiteness is reinforced in the narrative when he purchases Matt Bonner's decrepit mule in order to set it free. Janie remarks: "Freein' dat mule makes uh mighty big man outa you. Something like George Washington and Lincoln. Abraham Lincoln, he had de whole United States tuh rule so he freed de Negroes. You got uh town so you freed uh mule. You have tuh have power tuh free things and dat makes you lak uh king uh something."[28] Of course, entrapment, confinement, and enslavement precede emancipation, so that if there were no confinement in the first place, there would be no need for emancipation, and the Jody Starks of the world would have to find alternative ontological paths in order to know themselves as free men.

In *The Souls of Black Folk*, Du Bois presents us with his sense of the African American's psychological and ontological conundrum. In his oft quoted observation, Du Bois states:

> After the Egyptian and the Indian, the Greek and Roman, the Teuton and Mongolian, the Negro is a sort of seventh son, born with a veil, and gifted with second-sight in this American world,—a world which yields him no true self-consciousness, but only lets him see himself through the revelation of the other world. It is a peculiar sensation, this double-consciousness, this sense of always looking at one's self through the eyes of others, of measuring one's soul by the tape of a world that looks on in amused contempt and pity. One ever feels his two-ness-an American, a Negro; two thoughts, two unreconciled strivings; two warring ideals in one dark body, whose dogged strength alone keeps it from being torn asunder.[29]

In this regard, Toni Morrison's analyses in *Playing in the Dark* expand upon Du Bois's meditation in *Souls* to suggest that in the world of critical exegesis of canonical American literature, there can be no true literary self-consciousness in American letters as long as such critical analyses continue to believe that canonical American literature is uninformed and unshaped by the presence of, first, Africans and then African Americans in the United States. Perhaps what *Their Eyes Were Watching God* succeeds in doing, in a kind of intertextual way, following on Du Bois's *Souls*, and preceding Morrison's *Playing in the Dark* is that it reveals, through a character like Jody Starks, the tragedy of a schizophrenic, double consciousness, endured for too long. Simultaneously, it offers, through its development of Janie, and Tea Cake, characters that eschew the gaze of whiteness for a comprehension of self that is rooted in black folk culture.

Let us now consider another fictional example of ontological crisis, on this occasion, represented as a type of modernist angst in Ralph Ellison's narrator/protagonist in *Invisible Man*. He stops short of killing a white man who had insulted him, and he informs the reader that he spared the man's life when it became clear that the man had not actually *seen* him. As the narrative continues, it is clear that the reader is being challenged to see this violent encounter not only in physical terms, but in ontological terms as well: "Something in this man's thick head had sprung out and beaten him within an inch of his life . . . Would he have awakened at the point of death? Would Death himself have freed him for wakeful living?"[30] The assault that is recounted is as much about an ontological crisis, which has the capacity to rend this white man asunder, as it is an account by a black man who almost slit a white man's throat. Thus, the concern voiced by Toni Morrison at the beginning of this analysis is not only a literary concern or a disciplinary concern, but is indeed a concern with the nature and fabric of "Americanness." One might even extend this idea to say that it is a concern with the nature and fabric of our existence in the Americas.

Huck Finn's full humaneness is born of the recognition of Jim's humanity. The peculiarities of Twain's explorations in his text are particularly American, but the themes, the historical and ontological contexts are of the Americas. This "of the Americas" quality is a significant part of what a work such as Twain's shares with fiction by writers as diverse as James Baldwin, Zora Neale Hurston, Ralph Ellison, Paule Marshall, Claude McKay, Toni Morrison, Jean Rhys, George Lamming, Wilson Harris, Michelle Cliff, Caryl Phillips, Erna Brodber, and others. In such texts, we observe the imaginative effort to explore and expand intra-cultural and intercultural frontiers, to reestablish, if you will, the ground upon which Columbus and Guacanagaree met over five hundred years ago, so that they may meet anew, through our contemporary moment, as equals.

NOTES

1. Keith Strudler, commentary, National Public Radio broadcast, February 25, 2006.

2. Toni Morrison, *Playing in the Dark: Whiteness and the Literary Imagination* (New York: Vintage Books, 1993), 4–5.

3. Christopher Columbus, *The Journal of Christopher Columbus*, trans. Cecil Jane. (New York: Clarkson Potter, 1960), 27–28.

4. Ibid., 28.

5. Lewis Hanke, *All Mankind is One: A Study of the Disputation between Bartolome de Las Casas and Juan Gines de Sepulveda in 1550 on the Intellectual and Religious Capacity of the American Indians* (DeKalb: Northern Illinois University Press, 1974) 11–12.

6. Ibid., 43.

7. Jean-Jacques Rousseau, *Discourse on the Origin of Inequality Among Men*, trans. Franklin Philip, ed. Patrick Coleman. (Oxford; New York: Oxford University Press, 1994), 108.

8. Ibid., 116–17.

9. Ibid., 117.

10. Louis Allaire "The Caribs of the Lesser Antilles," in *The Indigenous People of the Caribbean*, ed. Samuel Wilson (Gainesville: University of Florida Press, 1997), 180.

11. Ibid., 182.

12. John Atkinson Hobson, *Imperialism* (London: Allen & Unwin, 1938), 229.

13. Ibid., 227.

14. Louis James, ed. *The Islands in Between: Essays on West Indian Literature* (London: Oxford University Press, 1968), 14.

15. Henry Louis Gates Jr., ed. *"Race," Writing, and Difference* (Chicago: University of Chicago Press, 1986), 10–11.

16. Morrison, *Playing in the Dark*, 4–5.

17. Ibid., 38.

18. Mark Twain, *Adventures of Huckleberry Finn*, foreword by Shelley Fisher Fishkin (New York: Oxford University Press, 1996), 375.

19. Orlando Patterson, *Freedom in the Making of Western Culture: Vol. I* (New York: Basic Books, 1991), 78.

20. Twain, *Adventures of Huckleberry Finn*, 50.

21. Caryl Phillips, *Cambridge: A Novel* (New York: Knopf, 1992), 53.

22. Ibid.

23. Charlotte Brontë, *Jane Eyre* (New York: Doubleday, 1997), 258.

24. Ibid., 252.

25. Ibid.

26. Ibid., 260.

27. Zora Neale Hurston, *Their Eyes Were Watching God* (New York: HarperCollins, 1990), 35.

28. Ibid., 58.

29. W. E. B. Du Bois, *The Souls of Black Folk* (New York: Barnes & Noble Classics, 2003), 10–11.

30. Ralph Ellison, *Invisible Man* (New York: Random House, 1982), 4–5.

Constructing Black Masculinity Through the Fiction of Gloria Naylor

Linden Lewis

> I believe in the Devil and his angels, who wantonly work to narrow the opportunity of struggling human beings, especially if they be black; who spit in the face of the fallen, strike them that cannot strike again, believe the worst and work to prove it, hating the image which their Maker stamped on a brother's soul.
>
> —W. E. B. Du Bois, *Darkwater: Voices From Within the Veil*

WHAT DOES IT MEAN TO CONSTRUCT A NOTION OF BLACK MAN-hood? Is there something peculiar about manhood lived inside a dark body that requires any special attention? Are there cultural universals that equally apply to black, white, Latino, and Asian masculinity? It is important to wrestle with these questions if one is to find a particular terrain on which to map a peculiar racialized male experience. It would be useful therefore to begin to conceptualize what one might mean by constructing a notion of manhood, and then seeing what might be involved in the specificity of black manhood within the context of the United States.

Masculinity is a set of social practices of men in society that revolves around ideas of appropriate gender roles, ways of behaving, ways of experiencing and navigating one's way through a world that demands conformity of individuals through rewards, and punishes expressions of difference. Clearly, this is learned behavior. Masculinity is the practice of an awakening consciousness of one's self as a man. It is a conscious-ness of an identity that is forged in relation, and in opposition, to that of femininity. It means therefore, that masculinity has much to do with men seeking the approval of women but more importantly, seeking the honor, respect, and recognition of other men. At a certain level, mas-culinity, like many other social practices, tells us more about aspects of culture as constraint rather than the freedom we imagine it to be. We need to bear in mind, however, that masculinity is not a fixed quality; it is dynamic one. Neither is it homogeneous or monolithic. It is then, perhaps, as messy a concept as is race, as suggested by Wahneema Lubiano in her keynote address at the opening of the conference from which this book emerges.[1]

Black masculinity in the historical context of the United States must therefore come to terms with the legacy of enslavement, Jim Crow segregation, and the daily visitation of slights, which meld into a perceived pathology against which all black men, bourgeois or proletarian, must struggle continuously. This is the reality of what Fanon called the fact of blackness—the existential reality of understanding oneself as an object in the eyes of a white majority culture. As Fanon notes: "As long as the black man is among his own, he will have no occasion, except in minor internal conflicts, to experience his being through others."[2] Attempting to address the experiences of black men in the United States cannot ignore the myriad ways in which race is inscribed on the black body as a text.

Many African American intellectuals and writers have addressed this historical context in their work, both women and men. Ida B. Wells, Gayl Jones, Zora Neale Hurston, Ralph Ellison, James Baldwin, and Ernest Gaines are among the many to do so. One of the best examples of assessing black masculinity from a literary perspective can be seen in the work of Richard Wright, beginning with *Uncle Tom's Children* and eloquently addressed in *Native Son*, *Black Boy*, and so many of his other books and essays. No one tells the story of the plight and travails of the African American male quite like Richard Wright. Most of his oeuvre is about telling and retelling this story of the construction of masculinity in the context of the United States. In recent years, there has been the emergence of a popular kind of discourse on masculinity that can be seen in texts such as Alice Walker's *The Color Purple* and Terry McMillan's *Waiting to Exhale* and *How Stella Got Her Groove Back*. For the most part, in these works, masculinity is positioned as the object against which femininity reacts. The characterization of black masculinity is sometimes accurate, but rarely represented as nuanced and complex, and frequently caricatured.

It is at this juncture then, that we must begin to look at the representation of African American masculinity in *The Men of Brewster Place* by Gloria Naylor. In 1982 Gloria Naylor came to national prominence with the highly acclaimed novel *The Women of Brewster Place*. It went on to win the National Book Award and was brought to the attention of many millions more through the television miniseries produced by

Oprah Winfrey and starring the talk-show hostess herself in the lead role of Mattie Michael. Brewster Place is a sealed-off community, the product of corrupt deals between an alderman and a director of a real estate company. It is originally built for people of Mediterranean or at least of Southern European origin. As people of African American descent moved into the neighborhood, the people of Mediterranean origin gradually left the area. In an Internet chat room sponsored by Barnes & Noble, Naylor said, "Brewster Place is not a real street. I put it nowhere so it could be everywhere." *The Women of Brewster Place* is a gripping tale of the struggles, the failures, the kinship, and the sister-hood of seven very powerfully believable women. The reader is made to feel their pathos, to empathize with them, and to yearn for their amelioration.

What was problematic, however, for *The Women of Brewster Place* was its depiction of African American men. "When I was writing *The Women of Brewster Place* I had not developed these male characters beyond the roles of antagonists for the women who were my central concern. At that time the men were used as dramatic devices to bring conflict, of some sort, into the lives of the women."[3] All but two of the main male characters in the novel were deeply flawed men, largely undeserving of the reader's sympathy. The character that comes clos-est to geniality is Ben, the handyman of Brewster Place, who is consol-ing to Lorraine, one of the lesbian lovers, marginalized by the men and women of the area. Determined to avenge her gang rape by some street thugs from the neighborhood, in a fit of desperation Lorraine ironi-cally kills Ben—the first man she encounters after the rape. However, one has to get past the veneer of Ben, the affable neighborhood drunk, in order to understand him as an individual, and few in Brewster Place have the luxury of time to invest in excavating his soul.

There is Abshu Ben Jamal, the boyfriend of the black, middle-class, liberal Kiswana Browne, who hopes to understand her purpose in life, experientially, by living among the common folk of Brewster Place. In *The Women of Brewster Place*, Abshu is a character on the edge of good-ness. We get a sense that he is well meaning, but little beyond the fact that he is a man with an obvious foot fetish. One senses that this is a Renaissance man in this community of misogynists and sexists. He pro-motes community arts. Though we are inclined to believe that this is a sensitive young black man, we get no sense of his commitment to the relationship with Kiswana, no sense of his support of her efforts at community organizing, even though presumably this is one of his inter-ests, and finally, we get no sense of his condemnation of the treatment of women in his neighborhood, even though he is obviously a role model for some of the young men in the area.

Given this background, Naylor was criticized for the representation of African American masculinity in *The Women of Brewster Place*. Sixteen years later, Naylor finally responds to her critics with the publication of *The Men of Brewster Place*. What is useful to bear in mind is that Naylor revisits Brewster Place in light of both the death of her father and the occasion of the Million Man March, held in Washington, D.C., in 1995. She notes in an Internet extract, "Like many in this country I was profoundly moved by the Million Man March and the images of all those black men calling themselves to task, promising to return home and be better citizens by concentrating on being better fathers and brothers. The march provided an alternative to the popular media image of the troubled black man."[4] "I wrote *The Men of Brewster Place* as a testament to the hidden majority, men like my father who worked hard all of their lives, who struggled to keep their homes together against incredible odds and who remained even after their deaths unsung, unknown."[5] We know very little about Naylor's father. What we were more aware of, however, were the many controversies that swirled around the staging and focus of the Million Man March, its creative impulse for reflection on black men, their behavior and their gendered identities. The stated points of focus of the march were all fraught with concern and unease from the outset.

Some women and progressive men were concerned that the march excluded women. Writing in the *New York Times*, Donna Franklin argued that the creation of a new black patriarchy was the last thing that black women needed. "Black men are not the only ones facing troubled times."[6] Franklin argued that given the historical record of sacrifice of African American women for family and the men in their lives, it was difficult not to interpret the exclusion of women from the Million Man March, in concert with the subordinate role of women in the Nation of Islam, "as an effort to rekindle black men's nostalgic desire to gain control over family life, a sphere many have abandoned."[7]

Some viewed the march in more ideological terms. Adolph Reed attacked the messenger of the march, Louis Farrakhan himself: "Farrakhan's conventionally black nationalist 'do-for-self, can't-look-to-government, develop-our-own-communities' line meshes perfectly with the bipartisan right-wing consensus about social policy and civil rights enforcement."[8] Reed reserved his harshest criticism for Farrakhan's leadership and vision for the black community: "His vision for black Americans is authoritarian, theocratic, homophobic, and, like nationalisms everywhere, saturated in patriarchal ideology."[9] For Reed then, the march reflected much of the black procapitalist and conservative message that had long been the philosophy of the Nation of Islam. Reed and Franklin's criticisms of the march were typical of the type of reservations some had about the event, and though the gathering garnered a lot of support ultimately, even praise for Minister Farrakhan himself, a number of lingering concerns persisted. One of those concerns revolved around the issue of atonement.

The concept of atonement was pivotal to the staging, purpose, and legacy of the Million Man March. As problematic as this idea was, it finds broad support in much of the sentiments of *The Men of Brewster Place*. So that there is little surprise when one sees in this novel a special effort being made by Naylor to have her characters atone for past misogynist sins. Of course not all of the seven main characters achieve redemption, and one in particular, C.C. Baker, remains unrepentant and seemingly incapable of rehabilitation.

There are seven major characters in this novel. This chapter seeks to look very closely at four of these characters: Ben, Basil, Eugene, and C.C. Baker, and to offer some observations about the cultural site of the Barbershop.

BEN

Ben is a native of Tennessee. In a moment of sober reflection Ben observes: "one of the things that bothers me the most is that I ain't never been in a situation where anybody ever call me sir."[10] Given the nature of Southern culture of the time, a black man would never earn the kind of respect that would confer the title "sir" on him. Such an honorific presupposes a level of equality that was not forthcoming in the era of Ben's time. Moreover, the desire to have the title "sir" directed toward a black man indexes a yearning for full recognition as man, in the eyes of other men and women. It is no coincidence, for example, that as late as 1968, the Memphis sanitation workers, who were striking against unfair and unsafe conditions of employment, carried signs indicating "I AM A MAN." Their protest represented simultaneously an industrial action and a demand for human dignity. Ben's remarks were therefore understandable in a context in which simple gestures of civility were denied black men and where the adult black man suffered the indignity of being referred to as "boy."

We get a glimpse also of the conditions of labor in a Jim Crow setting, where Ben works cleaning the spittoons at a local hotel. He recalls: "It made some of 'em feel good as I was there bending over to dump the spittoons to pretend they didn't see me as they let go with a wad of tobacco."[11] Ben's recollection resonates with the sense of racial injury alluded to in Du Bois's epigraph cited at the beginning of this chapter. Naylor never quite spells out the ways in which these assaults on the black man affect the black psyche and destabilize his notions of masculinity. These matters of race occupy Ben's attention but seem to be restricted to his experiences in the South, but never quite enter his consciousness during his sojourn in Brewster Place. He muses: "What was there about white folks that made them feel comfortable when a Negro smiled?" He continues: "It seemed they worried about us being angry; maybe because they felt they would be if they were in our place"[12] Ben perhaps understands the extent to which a black man smiling is comforting to whites. There is some assurance in this facial gesture, that the black man is not angry. The smile therefore becomes a disarming sign; it assures whites that the black man need not be considered a phobogenic object, a stimulus to fear and anxiety.[13] When all is said and done, the black man's smile is nothing more than Paul Laurence Dunbar's mask and W. E. B. Du Bois's veil rolled into one signifier.

Unfortunately, Ben seems to suspend this kind of observation when it comes to the environment of Brewster Place. Since Brewster Place does not fall outside of the social reality that is America, one wonders why Naylor holds off of some more penetrating analysis of this type in the novel. Instead, Ben turns out to be an acceptable and unthreatening "Negro" who becomes the first to move into the neighborhood of Mediterranean people of Brewster Place. Ben is mindful, however, of being prudent about how he is perceived: "You see, thinking the things I really felt instead of saying them meant I was a nice colored man."[14] He consoles himself therefore with the aphorism that "We all live inside."

Ben's literary usefulness is to be found in his inventory of the comings and goings of Brewster Place. He is very observant and so is brought back into service in *The Men of Brewster Place* for his ability to weave the thread of narrative around the lives of these men of his neighborhood, providing us with understanding for some of their behavior. Moreover, he is prescient when it comes to the character of men: "I don't know fancy words, but I do know men. And the ones here, proud most of 'em, pitiful some—but hard working, all of 'em. If they was working at a job or just working at despair."[15]

For all of his wisdom and insights, Ben lacks the courage to stand up to the insults and put-downs of his wife Elvira. He considers the possibility of killing her but decides against it because of the "grain of truth in her words."[16] Elvira eventually does him what he describes as a favor, by running off with another man. There is notably and characteristically no anger or emotional outrage here. Ben simply accepts his wife's abandonment. It is almost as though Ben were relieved of a particular burden of masculinity with this act of betrayal from his wife. He demonstrates a similar lack of fortitude with respect to his dealings with the white man who is sexually abusing his handicapped daughter. Instead, he finds comfort in the bottle: "I discover that if I sit up drinking all night Friday, I can stand on the porch Saturday morning and smile at the man who whistles as he drops my lame daughter home. And I can look into her beaten eyes and convince myself that she has lied."[17] In contrast to Ben's resignation, W. E. B. Du Bois was outraged by such abuse of black women.

> I shall forgive the white South much in the final judgment day. I shall forgive its slavery, for slavery is a world-old habit; I shall forgive its fighting for a well-lost cause, and for remembering that struggle with tender tears; I shall forgive its so-called "pride of race," the passion of its hot blood, and even its dear, old, laughable strutting and posing; but one thing I shall never forgive, neither in this world nor the world to come; its wanton and continued and persistent insulting of the black womanhood which it sought and seeks to prostitute to its lust.[18]

Naylor provides no explanation at this juncture for Ben's response, which appears quite accommodating, as opposed to confrontational or marked by outrage. Unlike Richard Wright then, Naylor proposes a different type of masculinity. The question becomes, what are the implications of this type of black masculinity? Is it deliberately more sensitive or does such a response open itself to accusations of naiveté or the politics of accommodation and avoidance? In the end therefore, Ben settles for the nihilism of self-destruction.

Ben may be a beaten man, but he is mindful of the limitations of his options at one level: "I inherit more than my share of the pain riding on the question, what does it mean to be a man? Even now at sixty-eight I'm still wondering. If I had killed Clyde Haggard, the law kills me. If I had killed Elvira, the law puts me in jail for life. If I killed myself, there was no one but an understanding God to face. So I settle on killing myself—slowly with booze—and on God understanding that I'm fighting for my manhood."[19]

What is missing here, if not entirely in the text, is a deeper understanding of what Fanon calls the fact of blackness—the ontology of
blackness. It is not just Ben's manhood that is involved here but also a
fight for his dignity and respect as a black man in America. It is a coming to terms with what Fanon says is the existential reality of a black
man who is confronted by a world that challenges his claims to manhood and personhood. He notes for example: "A man was expected to
behave like a man. I was expected to behave like a black man or at least
like a nigger."[20] This existential reality leads Fanon to conclude: "My
blackness was there, dark and unarguable. And it tormented me, pursued men, disturbed me, angered me."[21] This profound ontological
blackness is not really addressed in any significant way in any of the
other characters in the novel and therefore represents a weakness of the
text. In another of Naylor's characters, Basil, the ontological questions
are posed differently. Basil seeks redemption through surrogate father-
hood, the purpose of which seems to be to induce a different type of
masculinity, while exorcising the betrayal of his mother's trust.

BASIL

Basil is the prodigal son of Butch Fuller and Mattie, two characters
from *The Women of Brewster Place*. Mattie clings to Basil as a form of
compensation for all that went wrong in her relationship with his father
Butch. Mattie projects all her fears, frustrations, and hopes on Basil.
She invests emotionally and financially in her only child. Basil, however, never seems deserving of or sensitive to his mother's sacrifices. In
time he is charged with manslaughter for killing a man and wounding
an officer in a fight over a woman at a club. At our last encounter with
Basil in *The Women of Brewster Place*, Basil jumps bail, causing his
mother to lose her hard-earned house, which results in her having to
end up in despair in a neighborhood like Brewster Place. Basil has a lot
of time to reflect on his actions, and predictably he becomes contrite,
vowing to be a better person. There is clearly a resonance here with the
main theme of the Million Man March. Atonement and owning up to
one's past misdeeds are central to this cosmology. It is worth noting that
atonement is never a central issue in *The Women of Brewster Place*, not
even for as capricious a character as Etta Mae Johnson. In effect, the
characters of *The Men of Brewster Place* are men who are starting from
a place that requires correction, redemption, and forgiveness. Masculinity therefore becomes a journey that requires transcendence—this

is a problematic space from which to begin to understand male behavior or to bring some clarity to it.

While Basil goes about working on himself, there is an interesting process of rehabilitation that is taking place in the character of his father Butch. In *The Women of Brewster Place*, Butch was a mostly unsavory character whom Mattie's father once described as "a no-count ditch hound, and no decent woman would be seen talking to him."[22] However, in *The Men of Brewster Place* we learn that though Butch suspected that Mattie's child might be his, she never revealed this fact to him. In *The Women of Brewster Place*, the reader is left with the impression that Butch is simply irresponsible and leaves as soon as he finds out about Mattie's pregnancy. There is ambivalence on Butch's part, we later learn, because of a low sperm count that doctors had informed him about. However, in *The Men of Brewster Place*, the reader learns that Butch tries to do the right thing by seeking to marry Mattie, but her father, retaining earlier prejudices about him, essentially blocks all efforts in this regard. Atonement gives way to frustration. Butch is not a very savory character, but he is not as crude as we had come to believe in *The Women of Brewster Place*.

It is certainly not clear why Butch's character is rehabilitated in this way. There was nothing in *The Women of Brewster Place* to merit this remake; thus, one is left to speculate about Naylor's intent here. If Butch's makeover is hard to fathom, Basil's redemption is even more puzzling. Resolved to make a difference in the world as atonement for his betrayal of his mother's trust, Basil convinces Keisha to marry him. This move is intriguing if only because Basil tells us: "It was clear to both of us that I wasn't marrying Keisha, I was marrying her boys."[23] In a context where it is sometimes difficult to get some black men to take ownership of their parental responsibilities, we have in Basil a man who does not merely claim responsibility for two kids who are not his own, but marries their mother—a woman with whom there is no serious relationship—so that he might legally adopt them. This position is indeed a hard one to sell, and it would be difficult to fathom whether or not Naylor is able to convince anyone of the sincerity of the effort. One is left to wonder if Basil is a truly believable character or if he is an ideal that Naylor constructs in order to counterpose him to existing representations of masculinity.

It is counterintuitive to believe Basil as a character not merely because of his actions described above, but also because of Keisha's other qualities. Basil acknowledges that Keisha was using his money to buy gifts for other men.[24] He also notes: "It was not a marriage involving love between us; and so I never questioned the nights she spent out."[25] Keisha got to the point that she started bringing men to the home she shared with Basil. At this point Basil admonishes her, not on his own behalf but in the interest of shielding the boys from such corruption. " 'I will kill you,' I said softly, 'if you bring scum into my home around these boys again.'"[26] Basil's devotion to saving these two boys supposedly springs from his own guilt over the way he treated his mother's kindness. This is perhaps a noble gesture, but his altruism seems much too contrived in this regard.

Presumably, Keisha—his wife/nemesis—alerted the police to his whereabouts when Basil was still a fugitive from the law. The detectives turn up at his job, but somehow he manages to get them to accede to his request to go home first to see his sons one last time. This is a highly unlikely story. In an era of well-publicized cases of police brutality in New York City, Los Angeles, and Cleveland, this action on the part of the police stretches the imagination of the reader to breaking point. Beyond this unusual circumstance, however, one of his sons asks Basil: "Can't you stay for my birthday and then go away?"[27] At this point Basil makes a halfhearted appeal to the detectives for clemency, which is denied, but he notes: "They were seasoned cops, those detectives. Tough and street-smart. But neither of them had dry eyes when they shook their heads, no."[28] This entire episode at minimum lacks credibility and seems profoundly at variance with the existential reality of black male encounters with the police. The reader reaches some closure with the character of Basil, who goes off to serve his jail sentence for manslaughter. He returns after six years to find that all his efforts at making life a better place, and his attempts to rescue the boys from the streets, have been whittled away by the overwhelming oppression of poverty in black life. The task of saving these young boys was Sisyphean to begin with. The contradictions were evident from the outset. Basil's efforts represented an attempt at social engineering in a context in which he had not solved his own moral dilemma of jumping bail for manslaughter, but envisioned passing on ennobling values to two adopted sons. More importantly, however, his ultimate failure to save these boys had to do with the decidedly individualist approach to a profoundly structural problem. Basil's intervention points to the limitations of the use of such an approach to saving these young boys from the capriciousness of a system that racializes, criminalizes, and marginalizes them, severely constraining their options. If Basil's efforts are limited, Eugene, another main character in the novel, not only feels as though his options are constrained but finds himself in a lifelong struggle over the issue of his sexual identity. In the end, Eugene is also in search of redemption for past misdeeds.

EUGENE

The character of Eugene is introduced in *The Women of Brewster Place* as the boyfriend of Luciella Louise Turner (Ciel). At that time his irresponsibility rivaled that of Butch Fuller's. He refuses to go to his daughter's funeral because "the way Ciel's friends look at me and all—like I was filth or something."[29] The last the reader sees of Eugene, he is making a unilateral decision to leave his family to go away, because he could not face up to his responsibilities as a father. In *The Men of Brewster Place*, Eugene renders an explanation for his hasty departure and his estrangement from his wife, Ciel.

In *The Men of Brewster Place*, it turns out that Eugene is a "down low brother."[30] Eugene has been struggling all along to make sense of his sexual identity. This struggle is the main cause of his constant conflicts with wife Ciel, whom he genuinely loves, at least initially. Eugene tells Ciel about his first encounter with Bruce, a man whom he describes as "everything I believe a black man should be: big, dark, and mean.".[31] Bruce, despite his gay machismo, seems rather sensitive and discerning of the struggle that Eugene is waging with his sexuality. He facilitates Eugene's transition to "the life." Unlike Bruce, who seems comfortable with his homosexuality, Eugene is concerned with social opprobrium, especially the contempt that he anticipates would come from Ciel upon discovery of his true sexual orientation. He ruminates: "After that first night at the Bull & Roses, when I opened up that part of myself I'd been running from most of my life, I saw our marriage as a trap. You and I both caught in the web of my denial; in a two-year-old marriage with no easy out. Somebody was going to bleed from this. And at first, it was only me."[32] Eugene remembers that the first night he went home with another man from the bar he felt "complete," until pangs of conscience about his marriage attacked him. It was soon after this sexual awakening for him that Chino, the Latino S&M drag queen from the Bull & Roses, admonishes him to make a break with Ciel. "If you don't make a clean break, you're going to start hating her one day."[33] This eventuality haunts Eugene until he actually decides to make the break, using the pretense that he was going in pursuit of a job on the docks of Maine, and then Newport, because he could not remember which destination he had lied about to Ciel. In the argument that ensues between the couple, they both forget to supervise their daughter Serena, who is playing in the living room, and who ends up sticking a fork into a socket that electrocutes her. Eugene begins to feel tremendous guilt over this unfortunate incident and finds it difficult to shake off. "You don't wait for pain like this to go away because it only gets worse with time. I had either to ignore it—ignore that overnight my hair was turning gray— or replace it with something else. Could there be a greater pain than this? I didn't know but I was going to try and find out."[34] It is at this point that Eugene seeks the assistance of Chino, the S&M specialist from the Bull & Roses bar, who is skilled in the art of inflicting pain on others. Eugene notes, "I wasn't going to him for sex, I was looking as hard as I could for redemption."[35] Redemption, that organizing principle of the Million Man March, once again enters the narrative, though rather ironically in relation to homosexual desire. We will return to this issue below. Eugene's desire to replace the pain of loss of his daughter by some other suffering that would ease his conscience, extends even beyond Chino's customary repertoire of punishment. Indeed, so far had he exceeded the threshold of punishment that Chino implored him to abandon the exercise, but Eugene refused. "He whipped me until his arms grew tired, specks of blood covering everything but the tiled ceiling."[36]

> "Enough, Sweet Water?"
> "No."
> "Please . . ."
> "No."
> So he kept on trying to stomach the work that was replacing my pain.
> Little by little replacing it.
> "Chino . . ."
> "Surely it is enough, Sweet Water."
> "No, I said through a throat that was like sandpaper. I'll tell you when to stop . . . I'll tell you when to stop . . ."[37]

Eugene's method of seeking atonement and redemption is particularly problematic in this regard. Here is a black man who voluntarily submits to a form of punishment historically associated with egregious acts of racism, cruelty, and brutality inflicted on the backs of slaves— his forebears.[38] Such punishment as Eugene was now seeking was never meant to be redemptive but rather represented an exercise in humiliation, emasculation, and dehumanization. As David Theo Goldberg points out, the body is central to ordinary experiences and comes to symbolize society at some level.[39] Given the historical memory of racist abuse of the black body, could Naylor have envisioned an alternative method for Eugene to exorcise his demon of neglect, other than to impose this punishment on his own body? In addition, given the racial discourse of the body in the context of the United States, it becomes even more problematic to understand the necessity of involving two minority men—one Latino and the other African American—in this transformation of the body from a site of memory and identity to one of contrition. There is therefore a certain ambivalence of the use of the body here, which is compounded by the problematic involvement of subordinated masculinity in the process of transfiguration. More-over, Naylor's choice of a homosexual character here is somewhat anomalous.

First, there is nothing about the character of Eugene in *The Women of Brewster Place* that even hinted of homosexual desire. Indeed, one is tempted to believe that Eugene is simply irresponsible and not really a person wrestling with issues of sexual identity. Second, given the con-troversy which swirled around what many perceived as the exclusion of homosexuals from the Million Man March, it is strange that Nay-lor would not simply include this characterological dimension but would use the word redemption to describe a desire of Eugene in such a context.

The Nation of Islam, the main organizer of the Million Man March, like most other religious organizations in this country, is very strongly opposed to the practice of homosexuality. Though the call was made to unify black men, and to bring them together in one common cause, it was unmistakably a call to heterosexual men who had already estab-lished or were in the process of establishing traditional nuclear fami-lies. It was in effect a call to underscore the value of patriarchal het-erosexuality. Given the heavy emphasis on traditional roles for men in the family, the organizers did not go out of their way to counter any allegations of exclusion of gay men. Given the record of the Nation on these matters,[40] gay black men were given no real indication of wel-come at this event. The decision of the Black Gay and Lesbian Lead-ership Forum to participate in the march was more an act of subversion of the prevailing heterosexual ethos of the occasion, rather than a ges-ture of solidarity with the organizing principles of the event. In fact, though the then executive director of the forum, Keith Boykin, was later invited to speak at the march, he was one of the speakers who was cut from the lineup of presenters on the day of the march. The question this omission raises then, is if the invitation were a genuine one, or one intended to silence the criticism of the opposition to gay participation in the Million Man March.

The Millions More Movement, the recent ten-year anniversary of the March, solicited and succeeded in including many women in the lineup of speakers. The movement even managed to get Julianne Malveaux, a fierce critic of the original Million Man March, to cohost the proceedings. However, the gay voice was again absent from the platform of speakers. Gay and lesbian leaders protested the movement, accusing organizers of "reneging on a pledge to allow a national gay leader to address the crowd"[41] Once again Keith Boykin, president of the National Black Justice Coalition, who was led to believe that he was going to have an opportunity to speak at the Millions More Movement, was not afforded such an opportunity. This action once again served to generate conflict and disrupt the rhetoric of unity in the African American community at a time that it can ill afford such schisms.

To reinvent Eugene as homosexual in *The Men of Brewster Place* is to inject an element of disputation into the novel. For Eugene as a gay man, the issue of atonement, as articulated by the Million Man March, would only be possible in the context of a renunciation of his homosexual lifestyle. The prevailing religious sentiments would dictate "forgiveness for the sinner" but not the "sin." In other words, Eugene's contrition and redemption, coming largely at the end of Chino's leather whip, is at odds with a novel purportedly inspired, at least partially, by the staging of the Million Man March. This was after all, a march that discouraged, if not outright excluded, any expression of the homosexual masculine presence. In the final analysis, however, even if one were to empathize with Eugene's journey to clarity of his sexual identity, one is still left to ponder his response to the death of his daughter, his relationship to his wife, and exactly how his sexual orientation illuminates who he is as a person, and what it means to be a man. For Eugene, therefore, masculinity is still very much a phenomenon under construction.

While Eugene is working out his sexual and gendered identity however, C. C. Baker is unapologetically hypermasculine. He inhabits a space at the opposite end of the masculine continuum from Eugene. Indeed, people of Eugene's sexual orientation would not be welcome by C.C.'s crew. His attitude to alternative sexualities is pivotal to understanding his reasons for deploying force in order to reproduce sexual conformity.

C.C. BAKER

Naylor reintroduces the character of C.C. Baker to the reader in *The Men of Brewster Place*. C.C. is an unsavory character, the original bad boy, living the "authentic" thug life in the epitome of a thug culture in and around the streets of Brewster Place. C.C. was often inseparable from his hoodlum "posse" of friends who looked up to him as their leader. The reader's first significant encounter with C.C. in *The Women of Brewster Place* occurs when he has a chance meeting with Lorraine, who along with Theresa, her lover, dared to be somewhat open about her lesbianism in the heterosexually hegemonic milieu of Brewster Place. At the time, Lorraine was in conversation with Kiswana when C.C. and his "boys" approached the two. C.C.'s understanding of his own masculinity and the sexual currency of the streets did not provide him with any room to tolerate an alternative sexual orientation, so he was particularly disturbed by the presence of Lorraine. Unpleasant remarks are exchanged between Kiswana and C.C., but it is Lorraine who remains the focus of his attention and the object of his parting remark after a telling verbal attack on his masculinity by Kiswana. When Lorraine smiled in response to the quick wit and sharp barb of Kiswana, C.C. remarks: "Ya laughing at me, huh, freak?"[42] and later threatens: "I'm gonna remember this, Butch."[43] Though Kiswana's repartee wounds him, it is Lorraine's sexual persona that continues to anger him.

Following the above encounter, C.C. and his posse confront Lorraine on that ill-fated return journey from the party she had insisted on attending alone. "You ain't got nothing to say now, huh? Thought you was real funny laughing at me in the streets today? Let's see if you gonna laugh now, dyke?"[44] C.C. clearly enjoys the power and the admiration that this occasion confers on him while his posse observes gleefully. "I'm gonna show you somethin' I bet you never seen before."[45] His misogyny and homophobia boil over into the brutal gang rape and sodomy of Lorraine he and his friends enact with reckless abandon. " 'Hey, C.C., what if she remembers that it was us?' 'Man, how she gonna prove it? Your dick ain't got no fingerprints.' They laughed and stepped over her and ran out of the alley."[46] Disdain, emboldened by ignorance, characterizes the atrocity that they had meted out to a woman, whose only crime was a refusal to embrace male desire; so it became necessary to move beyond verbal abuse and through brute force, show her not just what she was "missing" but what they had considered a precondition of acceptable membership of the Brewster Place community.

It is perhaps worth noting, however, that C.C.'s homophobia notwithstanding, given his pointed remark to Kiswana in the earlier mentioned encounter: "Why don't ya come over here and I'll show ya what a real man can do";[47] it is reasonable to speculate that given the level of his misogyny, any woman refusing his advances, appearing unattainable, or otherwise threatening his sense of gendered identity, could have ended up suffering the fate of Lorraine. The homophobia in this context may simply have functioned as a convenient catalyst for venting his anger, alienation, and vitriol at himself and the society that has made him what he is. C. C. knew of no other way to direct his anger or his energy; he had never learned how to do so.

In *The Men of Brewster Place*, C. C. returns, but unlike the other men of the earlier novel he remains defiant; there is no hint of remorse for the heinous crime committed against Lorraine. He is a defeated soul, totally alienated, with no sense of community affiliation save the culture of the streets, which of course is gritty, nihilistic, and incapable of offering any real solace from a heartless world. "You see me sitting here—this is my fucking family. I owe nobody nothing."[48] C.C. lives by the credo of the streets: "There is no conscience in the streets. And there is only one golden rule: Do unto others, hard, fast, and thorough so the fuckers think twice before doing it back to you."[49]

In *The Men of Brewster Place*, C.C. Baker reaches an inevitable end. The reader encounters him under interrogation by the police for the murder of his half brother, Hakim. Royal, the drug don of the area, deliberately uses C. C. to eliminate a drug-pushing disciple of his archrival in the narcotics business, Tito. Eliminating Hakim is a supreme test of loyalty for C.C., but Royal also sends a very strong message to his rival Tito that nothing is out of bounds and no one untouchable. The drug trade is so ruthless and the stakes are so high that one brother does not hesitate to kill the other, perhaps to avoid suffering the same fate. C.C. stands and awaits his brother. He is concealing a .45 Magnum and he ruminates upon his intended action thusly: "The fucker deserves it. Nobody messes with Royal—he's The Man. And Hakim is just another punk that needs to be taught a lesson."[50] Hakim approaches C.C. and "For the first time in his life, C.C. begins to pray. Please, God, let me do this right. Give me a chance—for once—to be a real winner."[51] C. C. shoots his brother, throws the gun away as instructed and runs off. "C.C. runs and runs until he's crying from the cold wind whipping his face as he thanks God for giving him the courage to do it. The courage to be a man."[52] This supplication, though clearly misguided, represents the first opportunity for the reader to begin to understand some of the inner turmoil that C. C. as a young black man is experiencing. The act of shooting his brother undermines any possibility for pathos from the reader, however.

It would have been useful if Naylor had provided the reader with a clearer sense of the kind of social, cultural, and political forces that acted upon C. C.'s environment to cause him to be the person he became, and how others in similar circumstances had chosen different exit strategies or at least explored alternatives to the life of crime, hedonism, and despair that C. C. seemed to have embraced. It would also have been useful if Naylor had given us some sense if C. C. at any time had envisioned a life that was different from the one he was currently living, or whether he had imagined a future for himself with different possibilities. In other words, did C. C. simply accept his lot in life or was there some form of personal interrogation of his material existence? Could it be that in desiring to obtain the courage to be a man, C. C. was in fact, yearning for a better life, where these issues are, indeed, dealt with differently? In other words, could Naylor have provided us with a more nuanced character in C. C., or was it safer to stick with the unmitigated hoodlum that she reintroduces in *The Men of Brewster Place?* There is therefore no effort in the novel to engage C. C.'s consciousness as a human being. C. C. is not Richard Wright's Bigger Thomas, nor is he Earnest Gaines's Jefferson—both characters with whom the reader can empathize. It is difficult to feel any sympathy for this character, and so C. C. is left very stereotypically and conservatively to wallow in the despair of a pointless existence. Alas, the one character desperately in need of atonement in *The Men of Brewster Place* is never truly afforded such an option. In the end therefore, C. C. remains untransformed and condemned to exemplify the most undesirable characteristics of black masculinity in America.

The Barbershop

Finally, there is the barbershop, an essentially male-gendered space. As Harris-Lacewell and Mills assure us, men go to the barbershop for much more than a haircut. They go because "they have a story to stretch, a fact to check, or an idea to flesh out."[53] Harris-Lacewell and Mills also point to the important fact that "From slavery to freedom, barbers and hairstylists have constituted the overwhelming majority of

entrepreneurs in the African American community."[54] "The Black barbershop . . . is an environment that can bolster egos and be supportive
as well as a place where phony men can be destroyed or at least highly
shamed, from participation in verbal contests and other contests of
skill. It is a retreat, a haven, an escape from nagging wives and the cares
of the world. It is a place where men can be men."[55] Ben tells us that
by closing time the men in the barbershop solve all the problems of the
world. So what are some of these pressing issues of the day that are so
passionately discussed? "The issues they solve boil down to three subjects: white men, black men, and women. The white man carries all the
guilt for messing up the world; the black man gets all the blame; and
women are just a downright confusing issue that a hundred barbershop
politicians wouldn't be able to solve."[56]

Ben describes the barbershop as a place of several sad stories. "It was
a site of the black man's blues.[57] "And like they say, the blues ain't nothing but a good man crying for help."[58]

It seems appropriate to end this novel with some observations of an
African American barbershop, where men spend lots of time, renew
friendships, maintain old ones, and catch up on what is going on in the
community. However, we never get a sense in *The Men of Brewster Place*
of the pivotal role of humor, banter, and witty repartee that is at the
heart of the ambience of the barbershop. If we were to compare Naylor's barbershop to Ice Cube's *Barbershop* movie, the former seems even
more distant from reality. There is for example a poignant moment in
the film in which Calvin Palmer, Ice Cube's character, tells Eddie, one
of the senior barbers (played by Cedric the Entertainer), of his initial
sale of the business. Eddie then implores him to save the shop, not to
sell it. He muses: "This is the barbershop. The place where a black man
mean something. Corner store neighborhood. Our own Country Club.
I mean . . . can't you see that?"[59] Eddie also conveys to Calvin a sense
of the psychosocial benefit of good grooming when he asserts: "A haircut could change how a man felt on the inside."[60] For black men in the
barbershop, all they are left with is this sense of style and the presentation of self in public. In attempting to focus on black masculinity, it
would have been useful for Naylor to explore the community catharsis
of the barbershop in the black neighborhood.

Moreover, in the barbershop in *The Men of Brewster Place* there is no
mention of national sports of any kind, which is highly unusual in such
a male space. It is in the barbershop that childhood/young adulthood
athletic skills are rekindled; armchair quarterbacks see all the plays way

down the field; and basketball nets are so wide, it is amazing how easily professional players fail to make the appropriate shots when they all seem so elementary from the space of the barbershop. In the barbershop the amateur is king. This is a place where masculinity is measured by the yarn, and "trash talking" is the currency of masculine discourse. The barbershop is not a place for modesty, especially not on a weekend when the congregation of men in this space represents an explosion of testosterone and braggadocio. Finally, although there is a generalized acknowledgment of the political in Naylor's barbershop, there is no discourse on politics at this site, which again is highly unusual for a barbershop. The reader is left wanting more description, more folklore about this space, more narrative to flesh out such an important site not only in the African American community in general but more so in a volume that purports to deal seriously with men's matters.

CONCLUSION

The Men of Brewster Place reveals a cast of male characters, all of whom are flawed, few of whom are decent, and none of whom is particularly likable. The novel reads more like a series of biographies about men than a systematic accounting of the lives these men lead. Unlike *The Women of Brewster Place*, the lives of these men never seem to intersect in any way, except perhaps for Basil, who actually goes in search of his father, Butch.

As suggested earlier, the theme of atonement presupposes a position of culpability which one must endeavor to overcome. It was a theme that was problematic for the Million Man March as it was for Gloria Naylor in this novel. For black men in America, atonement presents one additional hurdle to negotiate. Pointing out this problem does not mean that black men are entirely blameless and innocent of all accusations leveled at them. However, rather than starting from a point of pathology, it might have been more fruitful to try to understand their lived experiences, the better to come to terms with why they make the choices they do, and why they lead the lives that they do. More importantly, an exploration of their material conditions of existence would help us to understand if indeed they passively accept the hand that life has dealt them, or whether they seek transformation but constantly lack the means by which to achieve it. In other words, the subject of masculinity explored in this novel cries out for a fresh and alternative genealogy that is more appropriate to black men's lives at the close of twentieth-century America, the period in which this novel is set.

Finally, these men demonstrate little anger at the system in which they live out their existences. Their lived experiences seem to exhaust themselves within the confines of Brewster Place. They seem generally unconcerned with the political economy of their environment, and offer very little reflection on the society in which they live. Both issues of rage and race are essentially muted in this novel. The reader yearns for complexity of character and the nuancing of masculinity in these closing decades of the twentieth century, but Naylor provides no comfort for the perspicacious. None of the characters in *The Men of Brewster Place* can claim any comfort in Martin Delany's declaration of thanks to God for being born a black man. Nor is there any particular virtue in the existential reality of poverty for these men. What one is left with for the most part is a chronicle of the most quotidian of issues that affect men in a small community riddled by social dysfunction. Perhaps this is a story worth telling, but one imagines that some readers might desire more depth, more creative unpacking of masculinity, especially in this conjuncture in which gender so powerfully shapes social identity.

NOTES

The author would like to thank Kenyatta Dorey Graves and Tanya Shields for their insightful and challenging comments and suggestions on an earlier draft of this chapter.

1. Wahneema Lubiano, "Race and Theoretical Hubris," 2002.

2. Frantz Fanon, *Black Skin / White Masks,* 109.

3. Gloria Naylor, "*The Women of Brewster Place* and *The Men of Brewster Place,*" teachervision.com.

4. Ibid.

5. Ibid.

6. Donna Franklin, "Black Herstory," October 18, 1995.

7. Ibid.

8. Adolph Reed, "Triumph of the Tuskegee Will," October 31, 1995.

9. Ibid.

10. Naylor, *The Men of Brewster Place,* 11.

11. Ibid., 17.

12. Ibid., 19.

13. See Fanon, *Black Skin/White Masks,* 151.

14. Naylor, *The Men of Brewster Place,* 6.

15. Ibid., 8.

16. Ibid., 26.

17. Ibid.

18. W. E. B. Du Bois, *Darkwater,* 100.

19. Naylor, *The Men of Brewster Place*, 28.

20. Fanon, *Black Skin*, 114.

21. Ibid., 117.

22. Naylor, *The Women of Brewster Place*, 9.

23. Ibid., 59.

24. Ibid.

25. Ibid.

26. Ibid., 60.

27. Ibid., 63.

28. Ibid., 64.

29. Ibid., 90.

30. "Down low" is an African American vernacular expression, which suggests that information should be kept a secret or not disclosed. J. L. King, the author of *On the Down Low: A Journey into the Lives of "Straight" Black Men who Sleep with Men* (2004), popularized this term using it to refer to a subculture of African American men who posed as heterosexual, and who may even have wives or girlfriends, but who have sex with other men on "the down low"—in secret.

31. Naylor, *The Men of Brewster Place*, 72.

32. Ibid., 82–83.

33. Ibid., 86.

34. Ibid., 92.

35. Ibid., 93.

36. Ibid., 94.

37. Ibid.

38. I would like to thank Kenyatta Dorey Graves for drawing this point to my attention.

39. David Theo Goldberg, *Racist Culture*, 54.

40. See Kendall Thomas, " 'Ain't nothin'," 129.

41. Richard Weiss, "Gays Protest Rejection," A16.

42. Naylor, *The Women of Brewster Place*, 162.

43. Ibid., 163.

44. Ibid., 169.

45. Ibid., 170.

46. Ibid., 171.

47. Ibid., 162.

48. Naylor, *The Men of Brewster Place*, 124.

49. Ibid., 125.

50. Ibid., 128.

51. Ibid., 129.

52. Ibid.

53. Melissa Victoria Harris-Lacewell and Quincy T. Mills, "Truth and Soul," 162.

54. Ibid., 164.

55. Ibid., 181.

56. Naylor, *The Men of Brewster Place*, 158.

57. Ibid., 161.

58. Ibid., 162.

59. *Barbershop*, dir. Tim Story, 2002.

60. Ibid.

BIBLIOGRAPHY

Barbershop, dir. Tim Story. A Cube Production. State Street Pictures/Cube Vision Production. Metro-Goldwyn Mayer Pictures, 2002.

Du Bois, W. E. B. *Darkwater: Voices from Within the Veil.* New York: Harcourt, Brace, and Howe, 1920. New York: Dover Publications, Inc. 1999.

Fanon, Frantz. *Black Skin/White Masks.* New York: Grove Press, 1967.

Franklin, Donna. "Black Herstory." *New York Times*, October 18, 1995, A 23.

Gaines, Earnest J. *A Lesson Before Dying.* New York: Vintage Books, 1993.

Goldberg, David Theo. *Racist Culture: Philosophy and the Politics of Meaning.* Oxford: Blackwell Publishers, 1993.

Harris-Lacewell, Melissa Victoria, and Quincy T. Mills. "Truth and Soul: Black Talk in the Barbershop." In *Barbershops, Bibles, and Bet: Everyday Talk and Black Political Thought*, by Melissa Victoria Harris-Lacewell. Princeton, NJ: Princeton University Press, 2004, 162–203.

Lubiano, Wahneema. "Race and Theoretical Hubris: Narrative Utility, Political Discomfort." Keynote address, Color, Hair and Bone—The Persistence of Race into the Twenty-first Century Conference, Bucknell University, September 26–28, 2002.

McMillan, Terry. *How Stella Got Her Groove Back.* New York: Viking Press, 1996.

Naylor, Gloria. *The Women of Brewster Place.* New York: Penguin Books, 1983.

———. *The Men of Brewster Place.* New York: Hyperion, 1998.

———. "*The Women of Brewster Place* and *The Men of Brewster Place.*" Penguin Putnam Inc. Family Education Network, Inc. 2002–2003. http://www.teachervision.com/lesson-plans/lesson-4089.html.

Reed, Adolph. "Triumph of the Tuskegee Will." *Village Voice*, October 31, 1995, 35.

Thomas, Kendall. " 'Ain't nothin' like the real thing': Black Masculinity, Gay Sexuality and the Jargon of Authenticity." In *The House that Race Built*, edited by Wahneema Lubiano. New York: Vintage Books, 1998, 116–35.

Walker, Alice. *The Color Purple.* New York: Washington Square Press, 1982.

Weiss, Eric. "Gays Protest Rejection of Speaker at Gathering." *Washington Post*, October 16, 2005, A16.

Wright, Richard. *Native Son.* England: Penguin Books Ltd., 1972.

Pancakes, Chocolate, and the Trap of Eternal Servitude: A Reading of Race in the United States and Germany

Isabell Cserno

FOR A BRIEF PERIOD OF TIME IN 2002, WHEN ENTERING THE CHOCO-late Museum in Cologne, Germany, each visitor was greeted by an approximately six-foot-tall statue made out of pure chocolate. It was a life-sized version of one of Germany's most popular brand-name icons, the "Sarotti-Mohr."[1] The six-foot-tall chocolate statue made visitors' faces, pleased by the presence of a well-recognizable cultural icon, light up with joy about being welcomed by a cherished and valued figure of German commercial culture. Sarotti is one of Germany's most popular and well-known chocolate brands. Originally founded in 1868 by Hugo Hoffman in Berlin, and after a variety of mergers in the twentieth century, the Sarotti corporation was acquired by the Swiss-French corporation Barry Callebaut in 2002. The popular figure of the Sarotti-Mohr, a black servant in oriental clothing, wearing a red-and-blue turban, a blue jacket, and red-and-gold puffy pants (also called "harem pants"), with golden shoes, traditionally carries a tray on which different kinds of chocolate products are placed. Since 2004, the figure has undergone some changes, which I will refer to later.

Due to its popularity among collectors, any kind of cultural artifact with the Sarotti-Mohr on it has become a valuable item, similar to what Patricia A. Turner calls "contemptible collectibles" such as Aunt Jemima cookie jars or postcards with pickaninnies; in short, material objects that display stereotypical images of black people.[2] In the United States, derogatory images of blacks became a powerful tool to justify black enslavement and, after the Civil War, to deny civil rights to the African American population. Germany, lacking a large population of African descent compared to the United States, utilized negative and stereotypical imagery of blacks to justify colonization, especially in the late nineteenth century, when Germany became a colonizing nation.

69

Standing display for Sarotti Chocolate, wood, ca. post-World War II. (Stollwerck Archiv, courtesy of the Rheinisch Westfälisches Wirtschaftsarchiv, Cologne, Germany.)

Advertising for King's Quick Rising Buckwheat, publication unknown, ca. 1880s. (The Warshaw Collection of Business Americana, courtesy of the Archives Center, National Museum of American History, Smithsonian Institution, Washington, D.C.)

The presence of these belittling depictions of blacks throughout the twentieth century seems also to suggest that they obtained a function beyond the immediate need of either justifying slavery or colonial exploitation in the eighteenth and nineteenth centuries. During the course of the centuries, these objects and visual representations turned into artifacts of everyday life and took on a deeper meaning of defining identity for those who were exposed to them in mundane environments. These objects of material culture in both societies turned into silent witnesses to the way Germany and the United States employ constructions of race to organize social and cultural realities. In both cultures, popular representations of blacks often appear as images of the enslaved or as servants. Visual representations such as the Sarotti-Mohr and Aunt Jemima are signposts at a crossroads of complex identity figurations, encouraging us to think about the complexities of race, class, gender, sexuality, nationality, and intimate cultural desires and fantasies in the Western world.

In this article, I will sketch out some of the underlying cultural meanings in selected material culture artifacts of German and U.S. consumer culture. In combination with discussions on whiteness and national belonging, I will focus on exploring how specific brands have successfully used racialized imagery to promote their products. A critical view on material artifacts and cultural representations can expose ways that one-dimensional and stereotypical portrayals of racial difference have had a remarkable impact on our views on and experiences with various racial and ethnic groups. The repeated usage of ethnic and racialized characters in consumer culture suggests that material objects and visual images are central to our understanding and articulation of racial differences. Comparing U.S. and German products can help to uncover some larger trends in Western conceptions of race and the dissemination of these ideas through visual and material culture.

RACE AND REPRESENTATION

The category of race is at the center of this analysis of material objects in German and U.S. consumer cultures. The persistence of racial and ethnic imagery in consumer culture throughout the nineteenth and twentieth centuries suggests that objects using ethnic and racial themes were important agents in creating everyday meaning of racial difference. Through these commercial objects displaying racialized imagery, racial difference became an ever-present, almost tangible reality of everyday life for many German and U.S. citizens. The cultural artifacts selected for this article indicate that race is not some abstract concept, but something created by human beings for a particular purpose. It becomes part of social structures that change their meanings over the course of time. Cultures in various historical time periods displayed different understandings of how to place people in racial categories and what implications these placements had on people's status in society. The popularity of these artifacts also demonstrates that certain aspects of racial difference have survived historical and cultural changes. The body as the identifying and central marker for race remains constant, which often can lead to ironic and contradictory situations.

The German 1990 movie *Hitlerjunge Salomon* (in the United State *Europa, Europa*) shows the arbitrary nature of theories that attempt to prove racial difference by using physical markers such as the size of one's head.[3] The main character of this movie, Solomon, a German Jewish boy who has lost his entire family, passes as "Aryan" in a school for young men run by Hitler's National Socialist Party, the Hitler Youth. In one particular scene, the teacher demonstrates physical characteristics of Jewish people, according to Nazi standards, on him. Solomon thinks he has finally been identified as an impostor, a Jewish boy posing as Aryan, but it turns out that his teacher is interested in using his body, or more specifically his head, to illustrate Aryan qualities to the class. His teacher analyzes Solomon's facial features in front of his peers and, ironically, gives him the assurance that he possesses all the necessary Aryan features required by Nazi theories of racial identification. This scene questions our ability to chart race on a physical scale, but also illustrates the fact that physical markers play important roles in understanding racial differentiation. If physical appearance is the primary channel to learn and teach about, understand, evaluate, and judge racial differences, cultural representations of highly racialized bodies, such as those of black people,[4] seem to play a significant role in making us understand how the knowledge of race is passed on from generation to generation.

Historical and sociological approaches to critical race theory see race as a social construction that is tied to specific historical and cultural circumstances. Different historical eras, as historical scholarship on U.S. race relations has shown, display many variations on how people differentiate one another based on race.[5] Much of this scholarship advocates that racial differentiation emerged out of the necessity to justify the enslavement of Africans and their descendants on slave plantations in the Americas. In a sense, racial differentiation based on physical traits, mainly skin color, was an invention of modern societies. Thomas F. Gossett, however, suggests that even pre-smodern societies differentiated racial groups based on physical traits: "What is certain is that the tendency to seize upon physical differences as the badge if innate mental and temperamental differences is not limited to modern times. The racism of ancient history, even though it had no science of biology and anthropology behind it, was real, however difficult it may be for us to judge the extent of its power."[6]

Although racial difference is inscribed in laws, governmental structures, economic access, educational opportunities, and many other aspects of social life, determining a person's racial status relies heavily on the visual experience. The physical body is the final frontier for identifying racial belonging. Our primary understanding of race seems to be one of physical difference. The body becomes the primary site of categorizing individuals into one race or the other. "Scientific Racism" in the nineteenth and early twentieth centuries used all sorts of visual material to illustrate racial superiority and inferiority through different phenotypes, sizes of various body parts, and an assortment of charts and maps of human anatomy. Eugenics, as the science of hereditary rules and human evolution, became a popular movement in both the United States and Germany and galvanized much of the popular belief in superior and inferior races.[7] A large variety of publications contained tables and charts that showed racial differences between groups of people and the resulting differences in intellect and ability. The eugenics movement epitomizes the highly visual character of race and our cultural dependence on understanding racial difference through physical attributes and the physical body. Visual and material artifacts that display racial imagery are constant reminders of the physical features that mark racial difference. Nowhere is this corporeality of race clearer than in tangible material culture objects. The physical and visual qualities of race make the critical analysis of representations of popular stereotypes such as mammy or Uncle Tom figurines or little black children carrying chocolate inevitable. Objects of material and visual culture, such as Aunt Jemima and Uncle Tom salt and pepper shakers or a Sarotti-Mohr doll or an ashtray in the shape of a black person's head, are important historical and contemporary witnesses of race relations and as valuable as text-based documents for historical and sociological research on race relations.

Most of the historical motifs depicting people of African descent were created by Europeans or their descendants. The purpose of these representations was not to give its viewers an understanding of the living circumstances and cultural realities of those depicted, but to support the cultural and political agenda of white cultural superiority that ruled the minds of the artifacts' creators. Since these images originated in the psyche of whites on both sides of the Atlantic, they became messengers about the ways white people imagine the world in which they live. According to Pieterse in *White on Black*, "[we need to ask] who are the producers, and consumers of these images, and only then to question who are the objects or representations. The key that unlocks these images is what whites have made of blacks and why."[8] For the most part, Pieterse is quite right. In his extensive study of black collectibles, he makes a compelling argument to read these objects as reflections of white desires and anxieties. However, even though the objects of these images are not primarily about the agency of those whom they depict, it is necessary to bring a reading of these images back to the discussion in which these images, in a very real way, affect the lives of black people. Many African American artists, for example, have dealt with derogatory imagery of black people in their work.[9] Although these images tell us primarily about white society and cultural imagination, they have also been a physical manifestation of institutional racism, constantly reminding black people about their inferior places as second-class citizens. People of African descent are continuously forced to deal with stereotypes that have been promoted by material objects created by white people. It is crucial to connect a critique of the white mind-set with the reactions by people of African descent to their portrayals to understand the full impact of these collectibles and related objects on our cultures.

The necessity of examining the fantasies and desires of white people about black people lies in the fact that without such an examination, the current power paradigm will never shift to a more inclusive distribution of power over cultural representations: "The question that keeps arising is, what interests of whites are being served by these representations? This refers not merely to measurable economic and political interests but also to relations of a subtler nature in cultural, emotional and psychological spheres, and to the various ways in which these relations figure in the phenomenon of subordination."[10] Pieterse's statement captures a central aspect of the significance of these collectibles and images. Representations of black people in Western cultures mostly remind their viewers of the inferior, subordinate status of those depicted. One trope among many others stands out, especially in advertising imagery for consumer products such as chocolate and coffee: the servant or slave. From Aunt Jemima to the Sarotti-Mohr, blacks in rep-

resentations of Western material culture have been presented dispro-
portionately as servants to whites.

In the United States of the late nineteenth century, black "folk"
icons, as historian Jackson Lears labels Aunt Jemima, Rastus from
Cream of Wheat commercials, and Uncle Ben from Uncle Ben's Rice,
seem to serve the need of cultural reassurance to predominantly white
consumers. Changes in economic market structures, urban landscapes,
and social relationships impacted many U.S. citizens of the late nineteenth and early twentieth centuries. The emergence of these black
commercial characters seemed to soothe the anxieties of a "sense of
separation and loss endemic in a mobile market society" and assisted
consumers in imagining a "renewed connection with the *Gemein-
schaftliche* worlds of extended family, local neighborhood, and organic
community."[11] People of African descent were often limited to the
roles of those who cater to other people's needs; their own needs were
of no immediate importance. Historically, exclusive groups that subscribe to the Western ideology of post industrial capitalism, deeply
rooted in Eurocentric beliefs of open-market ideology and European
or white superiority, have controlled the ways in which different
people are represented. Judging by the survival of some of these icons,
contemporary Western societies still seems to subscribe to similar
beliefs that originated centuries ago and created these tradememarks.
Poignantly, these beliefs of exploitative market structures in capitalism
become most apparent in symbols selling consumer products, such as
Aunt Jemima and the Sarotti-Mohr. In addition to promoting specific
products, these images also carry an ideology based on racial differentiation. Historically, racial differences have organized social and economic roles of blacks and whites. In present times, these roles have
become blurred across racial and ethnic lines along with many of the
historical images, but the survival of particular portrayals also suggests
that the racial baggage of Aunt Jemima and the Sarotti-Mohr is still
cluttering our present cultural landscapes.

SAROTTI-MOHR AND AUNT JEMIMA AS CASE STUDIES

As part of the fiftieth-anniversary celebration of the company in 1918,
Sarotti's new trademark icon, the Sarotti-Mohr, was born. German
Graphic designer Julius Gipkens designed the original "3-Mohren
Motiv" (motif with three moors). The original company's headquarters
in the mid-nineteenth century were located in a street called "Mohren-

Original "Drei-Mohren Motiv" by Julius Gipkens, 1918. (Courtesy of the Scho-koladenmusem Köln GmbH, Cologne, Germany.)

straße" (Moor Street) in the center of Berlin.[12] The company's original location is always quoted as the reason for Gipkens' design of the Sarotti-Mohr.[13] His original sketch as well as his and other designers' illustrations have always outfitted the figure with typical oriental attire and clearly reduced the Sarotti-Mohr to the position of a servant. He is dressed what can best be described as "Turkish fashion," or "à la turque," embodying the close connections of the "Orient" and "Black Africa" in German iconography. One possible reason for this mix might lie in the routes of the slave trade in Western Europe. After the loss of Constantinople in 1452, much of the slave trade to Europe was channeled through the Ottoman Empire. Since the mid-seventeenth century, slaves were brought directly from the west coast on the African continent to Europe. The figure of the moor had been a popular image in German culture and was not always portrayed as a servant. Roughly since the thirteenth century, various German and other European cities featured the head of a black man, in most cases a soldier or king, in their emblems.[14] These images do not clearly identify people of African descent as slaves or servants to Europeans. The redirection of the slave trade in the mid-seventeenth century might serve as a possible explanation with the emergence of blacks as servants in European iconography.

Throughout the eighteenth century, the presence of black servants in Germany and many other parts of Europe is well-documented, both in art and literature. Both men and women of African descent were part of European courts. In many cases, relationships between masters/ mistresses and their slaves resulted in illegitimate children. Well-known examples include Alexander Medici, the illegitimate son of Pope Clement VII and an unknown African woman. White aristocratic women also engaged in intimate relationships with their male servants. One French aristocratic woman who was pregnant with the child of her black slave is known to be referred to by her friend Madame de Sévigné as having indulged in "too much chocolate."[15] The oriental clothing of the Sarotti-Mohr bears a noticeable resemblance to the depiction of black servants in paintings, sculptures, and other art forms. Pieterse suggests that the Sarotti-Mohr, as well as other popular images of black servants with oriental clothing, are connected with the popular image of the eunuch, the castrated black servant/slave who protected the women in the harems of the oriental world.[16] The desexualized component of eunuch-like images makes them safe carriers of sexual fantasies. The idea of sexual desire is removed in images like the Sarotti-Mohr and earlier representations of moors by making them childlike and by linking them iconographically with the castrated eunuch. The narration of forbidden pleasures implicit in a complex image such as that of the black servant "à la turque" serves as a particularly useful tool to advertise for products like chocolate and coffee, products that are associated with leisurely consumption.

In many courtly paintings of the eighteenth and early nineteenth centuries, black servants, often just children, are important features of paintings of aristocrats or the bourgeoisie to establish their status of wealth and cultural superiority. Moors also appear in literature, sculpture, and particularly as porcelain statues and on porcelain artifacts such as sugar bowls and coffee cups.[17] The image of the domesticated black servant served as a counter image to the trope of the black barbaric savage. German historian Peter Martin points out that "many statesmen, writers, artists, and scientists, but also many of the 'common people' [in Germany] used Africans as metaphors to depict their views on state and society."[18] Martin's thorough historical analysis on the role of Africans in German culture claims that Germans, and to a certain part most Europeans, perceived people of African descent either as "black devils" or "noble moors" throughout the last nine centuries. These two images of are not complete opposites, excluding each other, but are complementing images, used to justify and expand white superiority.

Representations of blacks are clearly connected to the experience of European colonialism on the African continent and other parts of the world. Germany's involvement in the colonization of Africa was, compared to that of its neighbors England and France, particularly short and late. Only in the late nineteenth century did Germany colonize parts of the African continent.[19] Unlike the United States, German society did not rely on black enslavement to subsidize its workforce. Plantation slavery did not become a trope for blackness and servitude in Germany. The distinct experiences of both societies are predominantly responsible for the fact that in the United States, the most prominent black icon that has survived until now is the representation of an enslaved woman, whereas the German image is that of a black child servant in non-European gear. The figure of Aunt Jemima is clearly female, although she lacks any sexual feminine identity. She is usually portrayed as a full-figured woman without almost any features that would make her sexually desirable. Similarly, the Sarotti-Moor has no clear sexuality. He is depicted as a child servant whose sexuality does not present a threat to the carefully constructed system of Western power distribution. Ironically, both pictures do not represent a reality. In the United States, white slave owners often engaged in sexual relationships with their black female servants, who had often no other choice than to let their master take advantage of them. Similarly, many of the servants in German courts were engaged in sexual relationships with mistresses and masters, as the earlier examples indicate.

The imagery of black servitude and enslavement reveals to us fantasies, desires, and anxieties about power and control. Representations of black slaves and servants have been translated into archetypical stereotypes that have very little relation to the reality of black life in either Germany or the United States at any point in time. However, despite their disconnection with historical and cultural realities of black experiences, these stereotypes have shaped much of the public discourse around race. In the United States, the economic institution of slavery was steadily set up through the enslavement of black bodies. The image of the "mammy," the black female slave, stripped of her individuality as a woman with a distinct sexual identity, has no identity beyond that of the caretaker for white families. The desexualized, physically large, good-natured, and simple black woman quickly developed into a popular stereotype in mainstream U.S. culture.[20] In the late nineteenth century, the "mammy" was one of many popular characters in minstrel shows such as Zip Coon or Uncle Tom. By the early twentieth century U.S. society, blackface minstrelsy had developed into one of the most popular forms of entertainment for the mainstream white population.[21]

In 1889, Chris Rutt, the original owner of Aunt Jemima pancake flour (long since then sold to the corporation Quaker Oats) was inspired by the performance of a minstrel song that featured the character of Aunt Jemima.[22] The same year marks the first appearance of Aunt Jemima on a box selling pancake mix. Rutt and his partner Underwood failed to promote the trademark of Aunt Jemima in profitable ways and sold it in 1890 to the R. T. Davis Mill & Manufacturing Company. The company's owner, R. T. Davis, finally gave the public Aunt Jemima in flesh and blood; he invented a fictional history of a former slave woman and named her after his trademark. During the World's Columbian Exposition in Chicago in 1893, Davis' company hired a former enslaved woman, Nancy Greene, to "play" Aunt Jemima during the fair. Every day, Greene, in her disguise as Aunt Jemima, prepared pancakes for the fair's visitors and promoted the new products, one of them being Aunt Jemima pancake mix.

Boxes of the pancake flour blends became a huge commercial success, largely because, in M. M. Manring's words, "[Davis] mixed the mammy and the mass market, and the two have been inseparable since."[23] In the 1920s, under the leadership of the J. Walter Thompson Advertising Agency, illustrator and artist N. C. Wyeth was commissioned to create six illustrations with Aunt Jemima. One of these panels portrayed her during the Chicago World's Fair in 1893, preparing the pancake mix in front of a white audience with a head scarf, apron, and a wide smile. Even though the image of Aunt Jemima has changed over the course of U.S. history, from the wide-hipped, oversized woman with a scarf on her head to an older black woman with chemically relaxed hair, still smiling, Aunt Jemima cannot be divorced from history and still remains a black servant to white people. Her image conveys a powerful message of black subordination and inferiority to customers all across America: "[Aunt Jemima's] blackness still reminds white consumers that they are white, and that whiteness is a good thing. Her sex reminds consumers that black women belong in the kitchen. In some respect, Aunt Jemima has not changed at all."[24]

THE RACIALIZED BODY AND WESTERN NORMATIVITY

When focusing on objects of material culture, racialized bodies emerge as important components of Western thought. In both the United States and Germany, collectible items featuring Aunt Jemima or the Sarotti-Mohr enjoy tremendous popularity among collectors. James

Newspaper Advertising for Aunt Jemima Malted Wheat Flakes, publication unknown, ca. 1890s. (The N.W. Ayer Collection, courtesy of the Archives Center, National Museum of American History, Smithsonian Institution, Washington, D.C.)

Clifford evaluates "[the] collecting and display [of gathered artifacts] as crucial processes of Western identity formation."[25] The collecting of artifacts representing indigenous cultures from former European colonies as well as images of racialized others as cultural commodities serve as vehicles to construct white Western identities. Juxtaposed with a racialized other, in this case the black servant or slave, Western identities assumed the position of the normalized subject, which, due to the positioning as the standard, loses its equally racialized status. Hence, race becomes something that relates exclusively to people of color, but which is actually owned by white people. Whiteness becomes "normative" or "normate." According to disability studies scholar Rosemarie

Garland Thomson, the term "normate" "designates the social figure through which people can represent themselves as definitive human beings."[26] In order for the Western subject to be defined as civilized, its juxtaposition, the uncivilized subject, a role most often occupied by people of color, has to be the savage barbaric creature that can become a part of the civilized world only when subjugated to the supervision of white civilization in the constant status of the servant or slave.

During the eighteenth century, at the same time that many artifacts depicting black servants were produced, theoretical models of scientifically cataloging and understanding different world populations became imminent in Western intellectual and political circles: "In the mid-eighteenth century, the politics of population growth and measurement started to emerge. In the context of mercantilist thought, the category of 'population' became an economically important resource which lead to the systematic observation of population movements."[27] Theories of scientific racism such as phrenology or eugenics grew out these systems of categorizing and organizing human beings. The simultaneity of the depiction of blacks in material culture as obedient servants and the emergence of scientific approaches to racial cataloging and differentiating by politicians and leading intellectuals suggests that one reinforced the other. Thus, material culture artifacts distributed a particular idea of blackness, supported by racial pseudoscience, in everyday culture and helped to establish whiteness as the norm.

Fatima El-Tayeb's comprehensive study on the significance of race in late nineteenth- and early twentieth-century Germany also proposes the dependence of normalizing whiteness in national thought to the racialization of black bodies.[28] She proposes that the perception of Northern white Europeans, Aryan or Germanic ("Germanier"), as superior to other population groups represented a profound sentiment in Western European scientific theories of the late nineteenth and early twentieth centuries. The belief in racial difference and hierarchy that attempted to rationalize the extermination of more than six million Jews and the destruction of many more lives throughout the world under Hitler's reign in Germany did not originate out of a vacuum, but was an integral part of the discourse around nation and identity in central Europe.[29] El-Tayeb's work brings to the forefront a part of German history that is overshadowed by its close proximity to the Third Reich: Germany's colonial history. Germany's identification as a colonial power, as El-Tayeb shows, did not end with the dismantling of Germany's colonial empire on the African continent, nor did it start with it. Rather, Germany was ideologically and economically deeply connected and involved in the colonization of the African and Asian continents and played a central role in perpetuating racism as an ideology to justify the exploitation of millions of people.

Actually, the fact that these cultural artifacts, displaying black enslavement as a romantic and overall positive memory of the historical past, enjoy so much popularity in the present questions the linear narrative of race progress that has become so popular in the age of celebrated globalization and multiculturalism. In the past, U.S. monocultural analyses of the connection between the origins of slavery and racism as a social structure have not been overtly attentive to transnational movements and shifts of ideas and ideologies. Looking at Aunt Jemima and the Sarotti-Mohr simultaneously can initiate a deeper insight into the complex web of race relations in both cultures. The numerous images from Europe clearly portray black people in subordinate positions in an absence of a need, unlike the United States, to justify slavery as a basic and immediate system of economic production. Europe, of course, was economically tied to slavery and the transatlantic slave system, but contrary to the United States, did not cultivate a plantation system on the continent. The belief in black inferiority and white superiority seems to be more than a justification for the economic system of slavery in the United States. It also served as a tool for Western, particularly European, cultures to render colonialism into a perfectly acceptable and economically necessary system and established whiteness as the normative Western identity. This links U.S. enslavement of black people to European colonial expansion. It seems that Western cultures, on both sides of the Atlantic, developed similar ideologies of white superiority through certain representations of black people. Rationalizing racism only as a justification for slavery does not explain why these images have survived long after the abolition of black enslavement and gained a new kind of popularity and, more importantly, *why these images are still popular.*

Already in early encounters between Europeans and Africans, the juxtaposition of black versus white paved the way to a ready availability of dichotomous relationships between Europeans and non-Europeans. These early encounters helped to create what Thomas F. Gossett names "race theory," although it lacked the professionally scientific nature of later approaches such as Eugenics. Gossett proposes that until roughly the eighteenth century, racial theories did not influence European views of the world, particularly of those parts that were unknown to them. However, he is adamant about the fact that the influence of racial thinking and differentiating cannot be easily dismissed, even at a time when racial hierarchies were not clearly defined in scientific terms: "Race theory, then, had up until fairly modern times no firm hold on European thought. On the other hand, race theory and race prejudice were by no means unknown at the time when the English colonies came to North America,"[30] It seems to be difficult, if not almost impossible, to find the exact moments when racial prejudice turned from a tool to rationalize economic structures to a cultural ideology. During and after the eighteenth century, however, derogatory racialized images were steadily transformed into everyday commodities. This seems to suggest their central role in disseminating racial differences as elements that structure public and private life in meaningful ways. It seems to support the case that during that time, racial prejudice became a tolerated and indispensable way of life in the Western world.

CHILDISHNESS AND NAÏVETÉ
AS TROPES OF BLACKNESS

Both Aunt Jemima and the Sarotti-Mohr share being portrayed as naïve and simple-minded, almost childlike. There is a long tradition of portraying black racialized bodies as childish in Western cultures that justified black disenfranchisement and supervision. The Sarotti-Mohr especially serves as a constant reminder of the childish quality of blacks and illustrates the residues from colonial fantasies in our contemporary culture. With an awareness for the sensitivities of an international market, Barry Callebaut altered the appearance of the Sarotti-Mohr shortly after the acquisition of Stollwerck and Sarotti chocolate. During the International Candy Fair (Internationale Suesswarenmesse) in Cologne, Germany, in January and February 2004, the company announced its decision to "modernize" the imagery of the Sarotti-Mohr. Stollwerck's marketing director Bernhard Pfaff explained that the icon needed to be "rejuvenated and adjusted." The new icon is a golden figure juggling stars, representing, in Pfaff's words, the Sarotti-Mohr's role as a "magician of the senses."[31] Despite this change, the company still uses moor motifs from the 1960s and earlier. A variety of Sarotti products include one or more black servants in playful situations. On one praline box, for example, several Sarotti-Mohrs row together in a gondola. This image from the late 1950s or early 1960s, a time period with a real renaissance of the Sarotti-Mohr, is part of a praline box series of "nostalgic editions."

Advertising motif for Sarotti chocolate, ca. 1950s. (Courtesy of the Schokoladenmusem Köln GmbH, Cologne, Germany.)

Some of the chocolate bar products also have some nostalgic design on them. Most of these are variations of the original three-Moors-motif (3-Mohren Motiv) by Gipkens after World War I. On each of the images, the Sarotti-Mohrs are involved in activities that relate to the particular chocolate flavor. The cover for Amarena-Cherry chocolate, for example, shows one of the little servants holding a cherry, and another one stirring a large pot of red-and-white cream. It looks as if the three Sarotti-Mohrs are involved in actually creating the product that they are advertising. The long overdue change of the original image in 2004 seems to be a move in the right direction, considering the racial stereotypes attached with the original image. However, the transformation from the black servant to the golden magician of the senses seems incomplete. Even though the trademark itself has shed its blackness for a golden glow, the reproduction of old motifs with the moor continue to perpetuate the image of the black servant. These editions recreate the stereotypes of blacks as childish, playful creatures, as pretty ornaments for a Western mind preoccupied with colonial and exotic fantasies.

Chocolate wrapper for Sarotti chocolate, 2005. (Courtesy of the author's collection.)

The depiction of black people as childish still enjoys a tremendous popularity in many places in Europe. In the Netherlands, the "Swarze Piet" (Black Pete) is a well-known character in popular culture. Pete is the assistant of Saint Nicolas and has evolved into a figure feared by children. According to popular myth, Black Pete will punish those who do not obey the rules.[32] To this day, the Dutch celebration of December 6 employs racist caricatures of black servants as a central component of the festivities surrounding this holiday. Popular children's narratives that feature blacks in very simple narrative plots also reinforce the childlike quality of black people's ability. In Germany, for example, the children's book *10 Kleine Negerlein* (10 Little Negroes) narrates the story of ten little black children who, one after the other, disappear and only at the end of the book are reunited. The book, a "classic" in German children's literature, features elaborate pictures of big-eyed and smiling black female and male characters that illustrate the simple, but catchy phrases of the accompanying text.

The widely distributed and accepted images of the Sarotti-Mohr are of course not the only representations of black people in Germany. In recent years, various ad campaigns have attempted to portray Germany as a multicultural society in which people from different origins live happily together. Different companies have used black men and women as models to sell their products. Since roughly the 1990s, West cigarettes, a popular brand in Germany, has run ad campaigns that have fol-

Wrapping paper for St. Nicolas Day (December 6), 2001, Netherlands. (Courtesy of the author's collection.)

lowed a particular kind of format. In many cases, the company has effectively worked with the element of juxtaposition and shock. In many of their ads, a main character with some scandalous outfit, hairdo, or persona is offered a cigarette by a "normal" person. The "anomalous" or "odd" character ranges from a punk to a female stripper. In both print and film ads, the "normal" individual ends up offering cigarettes to her or his extraordinary counterpart. An ad in 2001 effectively drew on the discourse of racialization and normativity of whiteness in the framework of juxtaposing two oppositional characters. The "deviant" individual is a black woman, dressed in a two-piece red, '70s outfit that exposes her belly. She wears her hair in an Afro and resembles a stereotypical portrayal of black women in 1970s' popular culture, especially in the genre of Blaxploitation movies. Her companion is a white man who offers her a cigarette. This ad clearly inscribes whiteness as the norm and blackness as the deviation. Although the black female character is not portrayed as a servant or slave, the narrative of the image still supports the same message that moors in eighteenth-

Newspaper ad for West Cigarettes, 2002, Germany. (Courtesy of Reemtsma Cigarettenfabrik GmbH, Hamburg, Germany.)

and nineteenth-century culture occupied, namely that of black subordination via the discourse of racialized difference. Despite the clear cultural particularity of the image, the ad conveys a message that equates blackness with aberration from a German and Western identities. Despite their differences, both West and Sarotti ads share and promote the cultural memory of white standard and black otherness.

GERMAN = WHITE?

In the recent years, a lot scholarship in American Studies, History, Literature and other academic fields has addressed the issue of whiteness as a racial category.[33] Anthropologist Uli Linke shows how whiteness is inscribed into the idea of German identity: "German nationality is imagined as a flow of blood, a unity of substance. Thinking about the German nation takes the form of origins, ancestries, and racial lines, which are essentializing images."[34] Linke's usage of the term "unity of substance" is striking and, when read as "whiteness," provides an interesting entry into a discussion of core elements in German identity formation. Her argument goes along with the message of German material and visual culture since the eighteenth century, if not even earlier, that whiteness is the norm for German identity. This whiteness, however, at least visually, is justified by the racialization of blackness via stereotypical representations of blacks. White here means not raced or racialized, despite active participation of whiteness in the structured binary opposition of white and black that lies at the core of Western cultural identity. The images of blacks distributed in German material culture and their wide and often unquestioned acceptance certainly show that Germans have an understanding of racialized differences as signified by skin color. However, race is perceived to be owned by non-white people, serving exclusively as a signifier for difference and subsequently for non-Germaness. Since race is then perceived as a construct that is not applicable to white people and Germaness is perceived to be white only, Germaness becomes unraced, which makes the articulation of nonwhite German identities particularly difficult and painful.

The way German law determines who is a legitimate citizen provides an insight into the core understanding of German identity as connected to a discourse on racial superiority. There are two basic forms of citizenship law that have emerged in Western law discourses. One determines who is a lawful citizen by association with the place of birth, the "soil." In the United States, for example, one is born into a national community, notwithstanding the national background of one's parents. Ancestry or descent has been an alternative in creating national communities. Everybody with any blood-related connection to the nation is a lawful citizen. This means that the location of one's birth is meaningless in determining national allegiance. What matters is to what culture one is related by one's family:

> [The *ius sanguinis*] has no historic point of reference, but it is based on the myth that at one time there was a clearly defined territory inhabited solely by "Germans" and that thus community in some sense still exists today despite the massive migrations and territorial changes which have occurred in the meantime. Ethnic Germans today are defined as the descendants of this mythical community. Individual identity is therefore not based on conscious allegiance to the state into which one was born or has immigrated, but on a feeling of belonging to a group whose origins are shrouded by the mists of prehistoric thought."[35]

This virtually biological understanding of nationality as descending by blood relations, illustrates an almost ahistorical nature of this law. As long as one can prove ancestral lineage, cultural and historical connections are meaningless. The way German law determines who is a legitimate citizen provides an insight into the core understanding of German identity as connected to a discourse on racial superiority

There are two basic forms of citizenship law that have emerged in Western law discourses. One determines who is a lawful citizen by association with the place of birth, the "soil," the other by association with ancestry, the "blood." These differences according to ancestry and location, reveal deep insights into the framework of nation-building projects. According to Benedict Anderson, national communities are "imagined communities." Even more so, Anderson suggests that the advances of print capitalism were fundamental in advancing nation-building projects in the West. The increasing availability of visual imagery to large masses of people is closely connected to the improvements in the print industry. The developments in print technology also had a great impact on the creation and wide distribution of printed ephemera such as trade cards and chromolithographs. Many of these artifacts dispersed racialized imagery among large groups of people.[36] Depending on the determination of citizenship, the imagination of either physical location or ancestral lines as founders for national community forms the core of nation-states. In cultures founded on "ius sanguinis" (law of blood), such as Germany, blood lines and ancestry determine national allegiance and ownership. The normative subject in Germany has traditionally been constructed as white. Ancestral lineages are connected with a specific concept of physical origins and racial purity that seem to suggest an investment in racially coherent lineage. Blackness becomes the necessary trope of otherness to legitimize whiteness as normative: "As long as race is something only applied to non-white peoples, as long as white people are not racially seen and named, they/we function as a human norm. Other people are raced, we are just people."[37] Even in Western cultures with concepts of citizenship based on "ius solis" (law of soil), blackness, signifying exoticism and infantilism, usually determines one's outsider status, in many national communities defined by societal and cultural norms.

The Western concept of race seems to tell us more about the myths and fantasies that a culture is invested in than about the mundane reality of people who are caught in the web of racial signifiers. In German culture, as the representations of blacks demonstrate, race is connected with the myth of a purely Germanic race, superior in physical, emotional, moral, and intellectual capacity to other groups. However, as the historical research suggests, German culture has always been exposed to a multiplicity of cultural influences that have shaped cultural norms, rituals, and behaviors. The geographical location of Germany in the middle of Europe made it very susceptible to various cultural influences, as Linke points out: "The territory that was supposed to form Germany was located in the middle of Europe's center, influenced by a number of cultural developments, by permanent flows of immigration into and away from it."[38] Thus, one function of the representations of black bodies is that of constantly reminding their viewers of an artificial racial unity among nonblacks, which is confirmed every time when one sees such an image. This unity, however, is not real, it is constructed, just like the images of blacks are, as happy and content servants and slaves or as oversexual brutes and seductresses.

"I IMAGINED I MUST BE WHITE, TOO. WHAT ELSE COULD I BE?"

The writings by black Germans thoroughly question this core understanding of Germanness as a unified identity and exclusively white.[39] These texts show that there is a unifying principle in German identity, that of whiteness from which nonwhite Germans are excluded. As Molefi Kete Asante puts it: "Whiteness becomes a legal and social property bestowed upon the population of Germans by their ancestors. In fact, in Germany, one finds a history of racial thinking that rivals the genre in the United States. From the work of the von Humboldts to the apologists for National Socialist Racism to the present skinheads one finds one continuous stream of rhetoric of white supremacy."[40] Similarly to the writings of African Americans, texts by Afro-Germans illustrate that German identity formation is intimately linked with a socially and culturally constructed discourse on racial privilege based on skin color. The written testimonies of black Germans contradict the image of blacks that cultural representations such as the Sarotti-Mohr attempt to create.

In her autobiography *The Invisible Woman*, Ika Hügel-Marshall talks about the constant pressure that living in a white world can create for a black person. Originally published in German in 1998 and translated into English in 2001, the text narrates the life story of its half-African American, half-white German author who was born after World War II. Hügel-Marshall was married to a white German. She thought that this relationship would validate her in the eyes of other white Germans and lead to her acceptance as being German, too: "For a short time, I believed that, due to my marriage with a white man, I would be a full member in society, honored and sometimes even admired. That was not the case."[41] This quote reveals one of the basic tensions for Germans of color, namely the constant need to prove their status as rightfully belonging to the nation. Hügel-Marshall could not conceive of herself as a fully accepted member of German society due to her African American heritage. The autobiographical narratives in the volume *Farbe Bekennen* (*Showing Our Colors*) reiterate the exclusion from German culture experienced by numerous black Germans: "So often I'm asked questions like "Aren't you glad you can stay here?" And it's extremely hard to tell such a person that I'm German and don't belong anywhere else. By virtue of my black skin I am often in the position of explaining and defending myself, and this has been true for as long as I can remember."[42] In Huegel-Marshall's words, being white seems to be the only possible way of existing in Germany: "I imagined that I must be white, too. What else could I be?"[43] For Hügel-Marshall, whiteness seemed to be the only identity location. The "what else could I be" narrates the impossible subject location of black Germans as being black and German at the same time as it is perceived and defined by German ideology. This quote speaks to the centrality of whiteness as a normative standard in German culture in particular and Western cultures in general.

Reactions by African Americans to the stereotypical constructions of black identities, as disseminate by material cultural artifacts and visual imagery, serve as important critiques of how whiteness has been cemented into the core of U.S. identities. According to Kenneth Goings in *Mammy and Uncle Mose*, "[f]or the most part, African-Americans saw the collectibles both as a denial of their history and as a grotesque distortion of their identity."[44] As Goings argument points out, the collectibles reflect the mindset of those who created them and, as can be safely assumed, their motivations to depict black people in denigrating ways and subservient positions. Black people in the U.S. did react to these stereotypes; however, the ways of signifying on them and turning the objects and images into artifacts that actually document the everyday nature of racism in U.S. culture tended to be limited, particularly in terms of reaching a wide public audience.

Black America has carved out numerous places in which it reacts to the white fantasy of Aunt Jemima, Uncle Tom, Sambo, and all those numerous other stereotypes. Folk culture, passed on orally from generation to generation, theater plays, paintings, and of course, literature are just a few sites of active resistance by African Americans against the limited confinement that white culture has placed them in.[45] The role of "mammy" has been captured in the U.S. imagination by Hattie

MacDaniel's portrayal of Mammy (*nomen est omen!*) in the 1939 film of Margaret Mitchell's globally successful novel *Gone With the Wind* and of course the ever-present Aunt Jemima, serving pancakes to the American public since the late nineteenth century. Contrary to the asexual nature of the "mammy," African American female household slaves were more often than not sexually available bodies to their white male owners. Instead of being a motherly figure, black female slaves were often forced to cater to the immediate sexual needs of the white men in and around the households. Actually, the icon of the "mammy" became particularly popular *after* the abolition of slavery, capturing a romanticized notion of the Old South in which, contrary to the post-Civil War era, society's racial boundaries seemed to be clearly defined. Material objects featuring mammy-esque portrayals of black women on day-to-day items gained popularity, particularly at the end of the nineteenth century and well into the twentieth century. Hence, the black female slave became a valued icon at a time when blacks, at least in theory, gained political rights and protection from the state and the union.

In literary texts by black female writers, we see the mammy "talk back" to tell her side of the story. In her novel *The Color Purple*, Alice Walker gives voice to more realistic feelings of black enslaved women who were forced to cater to the need of white families while neglecting their own. In one passage, one of the characters, Sofia, whose punishment for manslaughter was to be the personal servant to the white mayor's household for several years, voices her true feelings about taking care of white children. Sofia took care of the mayor's daughter who, not uncommonly, developed a close relationship with Sofia. This young woman, after being married and giving birth to her first child, a son, visits Sofia to show off her pride and joy and to get Sofia's approval and praise for her child, but Sofia has quite a different response for her: "I love children. But all the colored women that say they love yours is lying. They don't love Reynolds Stanley any more than I do. But if you so badly raise as to ast 'em, what you expect them to say? Some colored people so scared of whitefolks they claim to love the cotton gin."[46] Hence, the archetype of the mammy tells us more about the imagination and desires and even fears of white people who constructed the image and needed it to validate the institutionalized system of black enslavement and, after emancipation, economic, social, and psychological subordination to ensure their economic progress and cultural superiority than about the experiences of the enslaved.

Not surprisingly, black Germans' reactions to these stereotypical images are similar to African American responses. Black Germans reject the limiting representations of blacks in German material culture and protest strongly against the racist messages that these representations send to the German public. Numerous Afro-German activists evaluated images of the Sarotti-Mohr as racist artifacts that illustrate the day-to-day racism they experience in Germany. However, for many white Germans, the Sarotti-Mohr is reduced to a nice motif that has no political meaning and is far removed from racism. People do perceive reality in different ways. The difference in these perceptions, however, speaks to a general ignorance of racism and an unwillingness by its nonblack population to acknowledge racist structures in German society. One black German activist spoke about the fact that he had written a letter to the Sarotti company with complaints about the use of a black figure as the trademark symbol to sell chocolate. The response by the company's public relations office was that the Sarotti-Mohr has no racist intentions. It is merely a symbol that is designed to convey the understanding that the Sarotti chocolate originates in foreign countries.[47]

Of course, with the recent changes of the trademark icon, the constant critique of the Sarotti-Mohr by black Germans and others seemed to finally have been heard. Considering, however, the company's decision to continue some of the racialized imagery as nostalgic editions, one might doubt the motives for this change as one that realizes the cultural and social implications of this change. It seems that the company headquarters, in an effort to make everybody happy, the Sarotti-Mohr lovers as well as potential consumers in non-German, especially U.S. markets, the result is far from being satisfactory. Ultimately, the decision for the altered image was one of capitalist expansion and increase in sales figures. It was not guided by a thorough understanding of the implications in using such an image and, therefore, really does not change anything at all.

CONCLUSION

The historical legacy of images such as Aunt Jemima and the Sarotti-Mohr and their continued existence in our cultures make it difficult if not impossible to perceive nonwhite identities as Western identities, despite the contribution to and involvement of people of African descent to Western cultures. The figure of the Sarotti-Mohr as well as the image of Aunt Jemima travel with a tremendous baggage of the history of African colonization, the transatlantic slave trade, the massive enslavement of Africans and people of African origin in Western cultures, and the exotization of black bodies. In the context of normalized whiteness in many Western cultures, of which the United States and Germany are only two examples, racialized artifacts are important cultural signifiers for the persistence of racism in our cultures. They are reminders of how Western identities rely on the binary construction between white civilization and black savagery in which the only acceptable status for the black woman, man, or child is that of a servant or slave to whites.

These images, as well as narratives by people of color, constantly reaffirm the centrality of whiteness as being necessary to belong to German or U.S. culture. Limited constructions of race and gender identities for servants and the enslaved, created by Western imagination, entrap black bodies in perpetual servitude, even in the twenty-first century. They feed our need for a soothing colonial fantasy that stands at the center of identity configurations in both the US and Germany. At the core of our sophisticated and technologically advanced societies still stands the ever-smiling servant or slave, trapped in the bodily markers of her or his nonwhite skin. Although this ad for Luzianne coffee dates back to the 1920s, many of its essential components affect contemporary arrangements along racialized difference. Luzianne, who

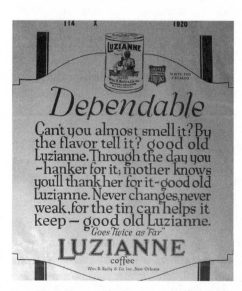 

Proof of a newspaper advertising for Luzianne coffee, 1920. (The N.W. Ayer Collection, courtesy of the Archives Center, National Museum of American History, Smithsonian Institution, Washington, D.C.)

lends her name to the coffee brand, possesses all the typical markers of
a black servant, a "mammy" (the head wrap, a full-sized figure, servant
clothes). Although portrayed in seeming independence, drinking coffee without anybody to serve, the language in the ad still presents her
as "good old Luzianne," which stands for the familiar and treasured
black servant/slave. According to this ad, the coffee, and hence
Luzianne herself, is "dependable" and it "never changes," just like the
image of the subservient black body on the can. "Good old Luzianne"
is more than just the coffee. Like the product, Luzianne herself can be
contained and preserved, if not in the tin can, like the coffee, than in
our racialized imagination.

NOTES

1. In this article, I will continue to use the German term "Mohr" (moor) when
referring to the Sarotti trademark. Roughly translated, Sarotti-Mohr means the "moor
of Sarotti." The German expression for Moor ("Mohr") is still used to describe a black
person.

2. African American collectibles have been and probably will remain popular material objects for collectors of various cultural backgrounds. Turner designates them as
"contemptible collectibles" to draw attention to the fact that these objects contain cultural and social narratives of U.S. race relations. She defines contemptible collectibles
as objects that are witnesses for the existence and perpetuation of racism in U.S. society: "These artifacts can all be identified in terms of what they symbolize—a recog-
nizable racist or, more specifically, an antiblack component rooted in their unswerving
depiction of distasteful characteristics. They represent one of the most deplorable and
least well documented impulses in American consumer history," in Patricia A Turner,
Ceramic Uncles & Celluloid Mammies: Black Images and their Influence on Culture (New
York: Anchor Books, 1994), 11.

3. Agnieszka Holland, *Hitlerjunge Salomon* (*Europa Europa*) Germany, France,
Poland: CCC Filmkunst GmbH, 1990.

4. This is not to suggest that only the bodies of black people are racialized. However, Western cultures have rendered whiteness as the norm, thereby making its equally
racialized status invisible, leaving black bodies as the ones out of the norm, turning
them into, following Foucault's terminology, deviant bodies, in Michel Foucault, *Discipline and Punish: The Birth of the Prison*, 2d ed. (London: Vintage Books, 1995).

5. There are numerous works by historians, in particular U.S. historians, who
account for the historical change of racial theories, providing a comprehensive
overview on how early U.S. society was shaped by various forms of administering slavery and on how whiteness and nonwhiteness was negotiated from the nineteenth to the
twentieth century. See Ira Berlin, *Many Thousands Gone: The First Two Centuries of Slavery in North America* (Cambridge: Harvard University Press, Belknap Press, 1998) and
David Roediger, *The Wages of Whiteness: Race and the Making of the American Working
Class* (London: Verso, 1991).

6. Thomas F. Gossett, *Race: The History of an Idea in America*, new ed. (New York: Oxford University Press, 1997), 3.

7. For further discussion on eugenics in the United States and Germany, see Nancy Ordover, *American Eugenics: Race, Queer Anatomy, and the Science of Nationalism* (Minneapolis: University of Minnesota Press, 2003), Lois A. Cuddy and Claire M. Roche, *Evolution and Eugenics in American Literature and Culture, 1880–1940: Essays on Ideological Conflict and Complicity* (Lewisburg, Pa.: Bucknell University Press, 2003), and Peter Weingart et al., *Rasse, Blut und Gene: Geschichte der Eugenik und Rassenhygiene in Deutschland* (Frankfurt, a.M.: Suhrkamp Verlag, 1992).

8. Jan Nederveen Pieterse, *White on Black: Images of Africa and Blacks in Western Popular Culture* (New Haven: Yale University Press, 1992), 10.

9. Many African American artists have challenged racial stereotypes such as that of the mammy or Uncle Tom. For the most recent and more detailed discussion see Lisa Farrington, *Creating Their Own Image: The History of African-American Women* (Oxford: Oxford University Press, 2004), and Michael D. Harris, *Colored Pictures: Race and Representation* (Chapel Hill: University of North Carolina Press, 2003).

10. Pieterse, *White on Black*, 10.

11. Jackson Lears, *Fables of Abundance: A Cultural History of Advertising in America* (New York: Basic Books, 1994), 384.

12. The Mohrenstraße in Berlin has a moving history. Already by the late seventeenth century, this street existed in the center of Berlin. During Germany's colonial expansion, the street served as a place for parades by African delegates, such as representatives from the Brandenburg colony Grossfriedrichsburg, now a part of Ghana. To this day, the street is called Mohrenstraße and is even the name for one subway station, Ulrich van der Heyden, "Die Mohrenstrasse," in *Kolonialmetropole Berlin: Eine Spurensuche* ed. Ulrich can der Heyden et al. (Berlin: Berlin Edition, 2002), 188–89.

13. In their recent publication on the Sarotti-Mohr, Rita Gudermann and Bernhard Wulff also cite this story as the origin story for the symbol, in Rita Gudermann and Bernhard Wulff, *Der Sarotti-Mohr; Die bewegte Geschichte einer Werbefigur* (Berlin: Links Verlag, 2004).

14. For further discussion, see Mira Alexandra Schnoor and Tobias Schuster, "Der Mohr im Wappen. Wie Afrikaner in bayerische Wappen kamen," *Geschichte quer. Zeitschrift der bayerischen Geschichtswerkstätten* v. 4 (1995): 5–12.

15. Both examples are taken from Weygo Comte Rudt de Collenberg's article on moor servants in eighteenth-century Europe, in which the French Madame de Sévigné is quoted as having said that her friend had eaten too much chocolate ("mange trop de chocolat"), Weygo Comte Rudt de Collenberg, "Haus- und Hofmohren des 18. Jahrhunderts in Europa," in *Gesinde im 18. Jahrhundert*, ed. Gotthardt Fruehsorge et al. (Hamburg: Felix Meiner Verlag, 1995), 278.

16. The imagery of the eunuch is at the crossroads of constructions of both blackness as well as orientalism. The figure of the eunuch captures the double-bind of these two oppressive discourses: "The black servant in these fantasies is essentially the eunuch, the emasculated harem or slave. The black eunuch in an imaginary harem may be the basis for figures such as the Sarotti-Mohr." Pieterse, *White on Black*, 128.

17. Ulla Heise and Beatrix Freifrau von Wolff Metternich edited a volume on coffee and eroticism in the past three centuries. An exhibition of objects and paintings accompanied this publication. In one of the articles in this volume, Wolff Metternich focuses on the image of the "Kaffemohr" (coffee-moor), Beatrix Freifrau von Wolff

Metternich, "Sultan, Sultanin und Kaffemohr," in *Coffeum wirft die Jungfrau um: Kaffee und Erotik in Porzellan und Grafik aus drei Jahrhunderten*, ed. Ulla Heise et al. (Leipzig: Gustav Kiepenheuer Verlag, 1998). For a discussion on moors in literature, see Uta Sadji, "Mohrendiener im deutschen Drama des 18. Jahrhunderts," in *Gesinde im 18. Jahrhundert*, ed. Fruehsorge (1995).

18. Peter Martin, *Schwarze Teufel, Edle Mohren: Afrikaner in Geschichte und Bewusstsein der Deutschen* new ed. (Hamburg: Hamburger Edition, 2001), 10–11.

19. In the recent years, many publications on German colonialism have been published. See the following selection of publications for further discussion: Arne Perras, *Carl Peters and German Imperialism, 1856–1918: A Political Biography* (Oxford: Clarendon Press, 2004); Birthe Kundrus, ed., *Phantasiereiche: Zur Kulturgeschichte des deutschen Kolonialismus* (Frankfurt a.M.: Campus, 2003); Sarah Friedrichsmeyer et al., eds., *The Imperialist Imagination: German Colonialism and Its Legacy* (Ann Arbor: University of Michigan Press, 1998); and W. O. Henderson, *The German Colonial Empire, 1884–1919* (London: F. Cass, 1993).

20. Although depicting an enslaved woman of African descent, the image of the "mammy" did not become popular until after the Civil War and the official ending of black enslavement. For a detailed discussion on the evolution of the stereotype see K. Sue Jewell, *From Mammy to Miss America and Beyond* (London: Routledge, 1993); Alice Walker, "Giving the Party: Aunt Jemima, Mammy, and the Goddess Within," *MS* 4, no. 6 (1994); and Steven C. Dubin, "Symbolic Slavery: Black Representations in Popular Culture," *Social Problem* 34 (April 1987), E. Patrick Johnson, *Appropriating Blackness: Performance and the Politics of Authenticity* (Durham: Duke University Press, 2003).

21. For a detailed discussion on blackface minstrelsy and its relevance in U.S. popular culture, see Eric Lott, *Love and Theft: Blackface Minstrelsy and the American Working Class* (New York: Oxford University Press, 1993) and William J. Mahar, *Behind the Burnt Cork Mask: Early Blackface Minstrelsy and Antebellum American Popular Culture* (Urbana: University of Illinois Press, 1999).

22. In *Slave in a Box*, Manring argues that Rutt's "discovery" of Aunt Jemima is not clearly retraceable. All we know is that Quaker Oats' official company history, published in 1967, states that Rutt visited a minstrel show in 1889, in which he, for the first time, saw the performance of a white actor in blackface and drag as a slave woman called Aunt Jemima. See Arthur Marquette, *Brands, Trademarks, and Good Will: The Story of the Quaker Oats Company* (New York: McGraw and Hill, 1967); and M. M. Manring, *Slave in a Box: The Strange Career of Aunt Jemima* (Charlottesville: University of Virginia Press, 1998).

23. Manring, *Slave in a Box*, 74.

24. Ibid., 178.

25. James Clifford, *The Predicament of Culture: Twentieth Century Ethnography, Literature, and Art* (Cambridge: Harvard University Press, 1988), 220.

26. Rosemarie Garland Thomson, *Extraordinary Bodies: Figuring Physical Disability in American Culture and Literature* (New York: Columbia University Press, 1997), 8.

27. Weingart et al., *Rasse, Blut und Gene*, 17.

28. Fatima El-Tayeb, *Schwarze Deutsche: Der Diskurs um "Rasse" und nationale Identitaet 1890–1933* (Frankfurt a.M.: Campus Verlag, 2001).

29. El-Tayeb argues convincingly that Germany has always been actively involved in colonizing Africa and profiting from it, even though Germans had no direct colonies on the African continent. This active participation has led to the development of racist

theories of exclusion of nonwhite people. This racial consciousness is directly linked with the strong anti-Semitism of Hitler and the Nazi party. The extremist view on the racial purity of the Aryan race, as El-Tayeb states, "was the peak development, and not the final destination of a process, that can be clearly traced back to the turn of the 20th century." Ibid., 202.

30. Gossett, *Race*, 16. The following quote from Gossett's work on race speaks to the fact that even though prior to the development of scientific race theories and explanations of racial inferiority of Africans and other non-European "primitive" peoples, racial bias toward nonwhite people and people with different cultural norms and behaviors was a strong current in European sentiment: "Although in the seventeenth century race theories had not as yet developed and strong scientific or theological rationale, the contact of the English with Indians, and soon afterward with Negroes, in the New World led to the formation of institutions and relationships which were later justified by appeals to race theories." Ibid., 17.

31. Tanja Trenz, "Sarotti-Mohr mit neuem Design," *Lebensmittelzeitung* (February 4, 2004), 56.

32. The history behind the figure of Black Pete is very complex. It is particularly interesting that he seems to reappear in different cultural and historical contexts all over central Europe. For a detailed discussion, see Pieterse, *White on Black*, 163–65.

33. There are too many titles on the topic of whiteness and race to name here, ranging from edited volumes to specific monographs on whiteness in particular geographical and/or historical contexts. The following is a very small sample of works that have had an impact on American Studies starting in the 1990s until today: David Roediger, *The Wages of Whiteness* (1991); Toni Morrison, *Playing in the Dark: Whiteness and the Literary Imagination* (Cambridge: Harvard University Press, 1992); Ruth Frankenberg, *White Women, Race matters: The Social Construction of Whiteness* (Minneapolis: University of Minnesota, 1993); Richard Dyer, *White* (London: Routledge, 1997); and George Lipsitz, *The Possessive Investment in Whiteness: How White People profit from Identity Politics* (Philadelphia: Temple University Press, 1998),

34. Uli Linke, *German Bodies: Race and Representation after Hitler* (New York: Routledge, 1999), 25.

35. Antje Harnisch et al., eds., *Fringe Voices: An Anthology of Minority Writing in the Federal Republic of Germany* (Oxford: Berg, 1998), 11.

36. Anderson, who if often quoted for coining the term "imagined communities" in his book of the same title, also links the evolution of the modern nation-state to the colonial project and suggests the important role of visual and material cultural artifacts for that evolution. In a later chapter on the census, map and museum, Anderson makes some interesting observations on the connection between colonial and nationalist ideologies and their interesting relationships with material and visual culture: "But if one looks beneath colonial ideologies and policies to the grammar in which, from the mid-nineteenth century, they were deployed, the lineage [between colonial and nationalist ideologies] becomes decidedly more clear. For the colonial state did not merely aspire to create, under its control, a human landscape of perfect visibility; the condition of this 'visibility' was that everyone, everything, had (as it were)a serial number. This style of imagining did not come out of thin air, It was the product of the technologies of navigation, astronomy, horology, surveying, photography and print, to say nothing of the deep driving power of capitalism." Benedict Anderson, *Imagined Communities: Reflections on the Origin and Spread of Nationalism*, rev. ed. (London: Verso, 1991), 163, 184–85.

37. Richard Dyer, *White* (London: Routledge, 1997), 1.

38. Linke, *German Bodies*, 134.

39. In 1986, the first publication by black German women was published under the title *Farbe Bekennen*. It was later on translated into English under the title *Showing Our Colors*. Two of the editors, Katharina Oguntoye and May Ayim, published other works in the following years. Oguntoye published her MA thesis under the title *Eine Afro-Deutsche Geschichte* (An Afro-German Story) in 1997, and May Ayim published her first book of poetry in 1996 under the title *Blues in Schwarz-Weiß* (Blues in Black and White). In 1997, after Ayim's untimely death, the Orlanda Frauenverlag published more of her poetry in *Nachtgesang* (Serenades). In the same year, Orlanda also published a collection of essays and talks by Ayim, entitled *Grenzenlos und Unverschämt* (Limitless and Impudent). Hans Massaquoi's autobiography *Destined to Witness*, published in the United States in 1999, has reached mass audiences in both the United States and Germany. And Ika Hügel-Marshall's autobiography, *Daheim Unterwegs* (On the Way at Home) was translated in to English in 2001, three years after its original publication in German. Katharina Oguntoye et al., eds., *Farbe Bekennen: Afro-Deutsche Frauen auf den Spuren ihrer Geschichte* (Berlin: Orlanda Frauenverlag, 1986); Oguntoye et al., eds., *Showing Our Colors: Afro-German Women Speak Out* (Amherst: Massachusetts University Press, 1992); May Ayim, *Blues in Schwarz-Weiß* (Blues in Black and White) (Berlin: Orlanda Frauenverlag, 1995); Ayim, *Grenzenlos und Unverschämt* (Limitless and Impudent) (Berlin: Orlanda Frauenverlag, 1997); Ayim, *Nachtgesang* (Serenades) (Berlin: Orlanda Frauenverlag, 1997); Oguntoye, *Eine Afro-Deutsche Geschichte: Zur Lebenssituation von Afrikanern und Afro-Deutschen in Deutschland von 1884–1950* (An Afro-German Story: On the Living Circumstances of Africans and Afro-Germans in Germany from 1884 to 1950) (Berlin: Hoho Verlag, 1997); Ika Huegel-Marshall, *Daheim Unterwegs: Ein deutsches Leben* (On the Way at Home: A German Life) (Berlin: Orlanda Frauenverlag, 1998); Hans Massaquoi, *Growing Up Black in Nazi Germany* (New York: Morrow, 1999); Huegel-Marshall, *Invisible Woman: Growing Up Black in Germany* (New York: Continuum, 2001).

40. Molefi Kete Asante, "African Germans and the Problems of Cultural Location," in *The African-German Experience: Critical Essays*, ed. Carol Aisha Blackshire-Belay (Westport: Praeger, 1996), 3, 6.

41. Huegel-Marshall, *Invisible Woman*, 77–78.

42. Astrid Berger, " 'Sind Sie nicht froh, dass Sie immer hier bleiben duerfen?'," in Oguntoye et al., eds., *Showing Our Colors*, 118.

43. Huegel-Marshall, *Invisible Woman*, 48.

44. Kenneth W. Goings, *Mammy and Uncle Mose: Black Collectibles and American Stereotyping* (Bloomington: Indiana University Press, 1994), xix.

45. See Lisa Anderson, *Mammies No More: The Changing Image of Black Women on Stage and Screen* (Lanham: Rowman & Littlefield, 1997). Anderson gives numerous examples of black stage writing which critiques the stereotype of the mammy in many different ways. Also, the works by artists Faith Ringgold, Betye Saar, and Joyce Scott, among others, who deconstruct the mammy image in their paintings, sculptures, collages, etc., are examples of how African American artists "talk back" to the limiting images available to them from "mainstream" U.S. culture, see Terry Gips, "Joyce J. Scott's Mammy/Nanny Series," *Feminist Studies* 22, no. 2 (Summer 1996): 310–20; Kate Haug, "Myth and Matriarchy: An Analysis of the Mammy Stereotype," *Dirt and Domesticity: Constructions of the Feminine* (New York: Whitney Museum of Art, 1992); Lisa E.

Farrington, *Creating Their Own Image: The History of African-American Women Artists* (New York: Oxford University Press, 2004).

46. Alice Walker, *The Color Purple* (New York: Washington Square Press, 1982), 233.

47. During the summer of 2002, on a research grant through the David C. Driskell Center for the Study of the African Diaspora at the University of Maryland, College Park, I conducted several interviews with black German activists in Germany as well as with various white Germans whom I have known for several years about the role of race in German culture and particularly about the images of black people in German culture, especially the Sarotti-Mohr. Whereas the black German interviewees were clear about the racism in many of these images, it took most of my white German interviewees some time to understand why images such as the Sarotti-Mohr might be offensive.

German Archaeologists and Anthropologists in the Andes: The Construction of the Andean Image in Germany and the German Identity in the Andes, 1850–1920

Uta Kresse Raina

> Racism, as it developed in Western society was no mere articulation of prejudice, nor was it simply a metaphor for suppression; it was, rather, a full blown system of thought, an ideology like Conservatism, Liberalism or Socialism, with its own peculiar structure and mode of discourse.
>
> —George Mosse

IN THE PAST FEW DECADES, WITH THE DEVELOPMENT AND INFLU-ence of postmodern theories the study of social construction of race has become increasingly popular.[1] In the recent historiography on Latin American "race" has been the subject of many studies, yet the literature deals only marginally with the social construction of race. It generally focuses its analysis on two major racial groups: the *mestizos* in the Andean nations as well as Guatemala and Mexico, and Afro-Latin Americans primarily in the region of the Caribbean and Brazil. In both cases, scholars treat the issues from either a legislative or a cultural perspective. While legislative works aim to explain why these social groups have been excluded by specific racist legislations, the cultural studies on race center on the formation and change of ethnic identities. The main issues investigated are slavery, racial conflicts with dominant socio-economic groups, and the myths of racial democracies.[2]

The literature on the Andes in contrast concentrates on the phenomenon of *mestizaje*. This is surprising since the indigenous people still make up the dominant part of the societies in which *mestizaje* occurs yet studies on indigenous people do not constitute the heart of scholarly research. Instead, *mestizaje* treated in its social, cultural, and racial implications features most prominently.[3] The main questions this literature addresses are what constitutes Indian self-perception as Indian and through which process does mestizaje occur. While the older literature argued that an actual genetic "in-betweenness" between the worlds of the whites and the Indian world had to be necessary, the recent literature understands it as the Indian change in self-perception and the ambition to belong to the white world. The transition takes shape not only internally as the framework of identification changes, but it also manifests itself in obvious behavioral changes and changes in appearance. The typical Indian way of dress and specific Indian behavioral patterns are abolished while the Western dress code and Western behavioral patterns become the norm.

Although "race" has moved more and more into the center of scholarly analyses, it can be argued that due to Latin America's multiracialism (including with the indigenous people, others of European, African, Asian, and American descent) the region could be made even more useful for the development of general studies of race and the social construction of race. Not only throughout Latin America's colonial history, but also continuing during its national period "race" has been a crucial factor in assigning people's social status. During colonial times a strict racial hierarchy dictated people's rank. Even during the national period the categories of race and class were almost overlapping. Racial constructs could be investigated through the prism of each of the social classes and racial groups. The white upper class's image of the Amerindians, Mestizos, Blacks, and Chinese could offer insights into how each socioeconomic group viewed and stereotyped the others and maybe even how social hierarchies were able to persist during the past few centuries. Another related aspect that has been treated only marginally in the literature so far is the formation of racial constructs by immigrants, travelers, or scholars from other parts of the world. Their racial constructions provide us with insights into a perceived world order and allow us to analyze how perceived racial hierarchies mirrored socioeconomic and political hierarchies in the global context.

This analysis picks up on topics that have been treated only marginally in the literature and places German anthropologists in the center of its imperial investigation. It utilizes documents of German anthropologists as a prism to investigate racial constructions of different Peruvian groups in connection with the formation of a German identity from about 1850–1920. Using the context of European imperial-

ism and imperial competition, racism, and the simultaneous development of theories of Aryan racial superiority in Germany, this analysis
argues that the constructed images of the Andean population and those
of the Germans themselves fulfilled multiple functions. Not only did
it help the white upper class to remain in power, but it also allowed
the Germans to establish their racial superiority over the people in the
Andes, thus validating the existing global racial, economic, and social
order that Immanuel Wallerstein and Charles Mills make the center of
their analyses.[4] Ultimately, these racial constructs also served the
domestic political goal of creating a specific German national identity
that would help unite the highly fragmented German territories and
would allow individuals to identify more with their national rather than
with their regional or provincial identities. In this sense, anthropology
and archaeology furthered the construction of a new "German" identity that took shape in strong contrast to "the racial other" that scholars observed and objectified. While many of these other racial groups
that were naturally perceived as beneath the Germanic race were exhibited in shows of curiosities in major German cities, scholars also constructed the new German identity with close ties to ancient high cultures. Thus, anthropology and archaeology not only helped to shape
perceptions of "the other" in Germany, but also constructed a new
national identity. Thus, the investigation of the topic is not only important to confirm the global political order based on racism, but it may
also help to shed some light on the specific German context of the
development of theories of racial superiority in the light of the events
after 1933 when race ideology helped to justify the constructed racial
hierarchy that placed Germans at the top of the global ladder, and
helped to "legitimize" the elimination of specific racial groups.

The case of German anthropologists in Peru is especially interesting
because Peru was never a German colony, yet German interest in the
Andes had a long tradition. Even prior to Alexander von Humboldt's
famous voyage to the New World (1799–1804), many German travelers had made the strenuous trip to South America. In the late seventeenth century, Jesuit missionaries of German origin were sent to Peru,
where they became renowned for their geographic knowledge and for
the accurate maps they left behind.[5] In the late eighteenth century,
German mineralogists were invited into the Viceroyalty as "expert
commission" to analyze the declining colonial mining industry.[6] After
the Andean nations had gained their independence in the early nineteenth century, numerous renowned intellectual German figures began

the long journey over the Atlantic and around Tierra del Fuego to experience the magic of the Peruvian Andes, among them German naturalists (e.g., Eduard Poeppig, F. J. F. Meyen, Karl Schmarda, and Karl Scherzer), writers (e.g., Ida Pfeiffer, Ernst von Bibra, and Friedrich Gerstaecker), painters (e.g., Johann Moritz von Rugendas), sculptors, and geologists (e.g., Wilhelm Reiss and Alphons Stuebel, Alfred Hettner, and Wilhelm Sievers). As academic knowledge of Peru was created in the intellectual and academic circles, this second group of travelers helped to disseminate a more popular image of it in the German society. The magic of Peru began to own its place in scholarly debates, arts, and literature in Germany, and numerous German novels and dramas were set in Peru. German reports and diaries about life in the Andes captured scholarly and popular attention and triggered a strong national interest in the area.

Anthropologists and archaeologists, however, constituted the most influential group of Germans traveling to the Peruvian Andes. In the period from 1850–1920 about fifty German scholars from the disciplines of anthropology and archaeology came to work in Peru. They generated a rich body of literature on the ancient and contemporary Andean people and subsequently transformed Germany in the mid-nineteenth century into the nation with leading academic knowledge of Peru. John Rowe pointed out that "Berlin at that time was probably the most stimulating place in Europe for an aspiring Peruvianist."[7]

The main question that arises is why were the German scholars and intellectuals so concerned with the Andean cultures? What made the long and strenuous journey halfway around the world so attractive or important to them? Why were they so fascinated with the idea or image of Peru? What were the domestic implications as well as the implications for Germany's foreign policy? In terms of power relations, what did the intellectualization of the Andean people achieve?

This analysis uses the document of three German scholars of different ranks: Max Uhle, Heinrich Cunow, and Ernst Middendorf. The selection of scholars indicates the increasing professionalization of knowledge that occurred in the late nineteenth century and the emerging curriculum for the discipline of anthropology. While Ernst Middendorf was not a trained anthropologist, but came to work in the field more or less by accident, the latter two scholars were systematically educated and earned PhD degrees in their fields. Ernst Middendorf was a trained medical doctor by profession, but ended up spending twenty-five years of his life in Peru exploring the indigenous languages and gradually becoming an expert and highly respected scholar.[8] His work investigated the linguistic connections among native groups but focused on linguistic studies of Quechua. He published eight major works (one consisting of six volumes and another consisting of three volumes).

In contrast to Middendorf, Heinrich Cunow was a trained professor of anthropology, ethnographer, and linguist. However, now he seems to be better remembered for his political activity in the German Social Democratic Party (SPD) than for his ethnographic and linguistic works. He served as a representative of Prussia in the German Parliament from 1919–21 and again from 1921–25. His scholarly writings centered on the social dimension of the precolonial Inca societies and he was mostly interested in developing theories about the political and social structure of the ancient Inca civilization. He published two major comparative works on the Inca in which he tried to establish the similarities and differences between the ancient German tribes and the Inca.

Even today Max Uhle is fondly remembered as "the Father of Peruvian Archaeology." He was a highly trained linguist with a specialty in Chinese grammar. However, working closely with Alphons Stuebel (who in conjunction with Wilhelm Reiss had conducted the first systematic excavation in the Andes and rediscovered the pre-Inca burial site in Ancón in 1874) in the Anthropological and Ethnographic Museum in Dresden, Uhle gradually became interested in the ancient Andean civilizations and developed into the most knowledgeable expert of his time. His main achievement for the study of ancient Peruvian civilizations was his dating of the potsherds that served as a guide for all consequent dating methods for that region. His publications that covered issues of linguistic, ethnographic, and archaeological aspects amounted to more than thirty publications including many monographs. He was so recognized that various Universities in the United States and the governments of Chile, Peru, Bolivia, and Ecuador competed over employing him.[9]

The sources of these three German scholars indicate that their scholarly work did not occur in a vacuum, but rather that they stood in interaction with each other and researchers from other German-speaking nations such as Austria and Switzerland.[10] Simultaneously, they were also part of the larger Western intellectual community and exchanged knowledge with British, American, and French scholars.[11] Although an exchange of knowledge existed in this intellectual community, Uhle's correspondence indicates that national division and strong competition (especially his competition with the French archaeologist Bandalier) characterized its climate.[12]

HISTORIOGRAPHY

Today, the discourse about the German anthropologists and archaeologists of Peru, and their findings and implications, is still at the beginning stage. A thorough critical investigation of the sources has not taken place yet, although a number of documents were rediscovered and re-edited in the 1960s, followed by a second wave of interest in the 1990s, when formerly unpublished documents became accessible to the public. So far, the interest has not gone beyond editions and translations of the primary sources.[13]

The few existing works can be divided into two main categories: biographical works and contribution histories. The two existing biographical works are dedicated to the life and work of two most important German scholars for the Andes whose reputation went far beyond their national boundaries: Max Uhle, the so-called father of Peruvian archaeology, and Hans Heinrich Bruenning, the founder of the Northern Peruvian Museum for Ethnography. John Rowe's account of the life and work of Max Uhle, who was unquestionably the most important German archaeologist working in Peru during the period under discussion, is the more systematic yet may be outdated biography. Written in 1954, Rowe relied on Uhle's personal letters and publications to trace the steps in his career and to support his characterization of Uhle, who was extremely passionate about his excavations in Latin America and established collections in Philadelphia, Berkeley, Berlin, Quito, Lima, Santiago, Goeteborg, and São Paulo. As he aged Uhle seemed to lose touch with the intellectual community and to be increasingly removed from reality. He died during World War II, impoverished in exile. Corinna Raddatz's edited collection of articles on Hans Heinrich Bruenning, the most important ethnographer of northern Peru, constitutes the first attempt to save the dedicated German scholar from oblivion. Soon after archivists had cataloged his documents, scholars had forgotten them already and only due to research and interest from the Peruvian side in 1976, did the valuable sources come back to light and finally get published (unfortunately only in fragments) in 1990.[14]

Two general works that exist may classify more as "contribution histories" mention briefly some of the numerous German scholars. Among those, Estuardo Nuñez's general history of travelers to Peru ranks higher because it lists and briefly describes the contributions of German scholars alongside their British, French, and American counterparts and provides a context in which the anthropological and archaeological journeys were undertaken. Gerdt Kutscher's history of

Berlin as center of American studies deals exclusively with German scholars, yet covers German endeavors in both American continents and thus is hardly able to give any detail. The third work that belongs in this category is Doig Frederico Kauffmann's brief chronological study of the contributions that only the best-known German scholars made to the main body of Western knowledge about the Andean cultures. Yet this study also qualifies as traditional contribution history and does not analyze the findings of the German scholars in a critical manner.[15] While a critical evaluation of the findings by German scholars is absent from the literature until today, some scholars have used the information given in their publications, private travel accounts, or letters to confirm sociopolitical or economic events in the Andes.[16]

It is argued here that German anthropological and archaeological endeavors in Peru were much more important than the small body of existing literature suggests. In order to evaluate the issue in an appropriate manner, the framework of European imperial competition and the existing literature on the dichotomy of "anthropology and imperialism" have to be incorporated. This dichotomy defines the bias of anthropology in general due to its Eurocentric perspective on the ancient and native societies that already implied a hegemonic power structure and led to a similar biased knowledge about the observed group.

Beginning in the 1980s with the groundbreaking works of George W. Stocking Jr., numerous critical approaches on how to understand the discipline of anthropology have been written. Various works have begun to link the discipline of anthropology inherently to colonialism and imperialism and thus have started to question the validity of ethnography and its implications for the discipline of anthropology in general.[17] Their main criticism is that as the anthropological observations are filtered through Eurocentric lenses, the results cannot be unbiased. One of the problems with early anthropological studies was that they tried to preserve "pure" non-Western cultures before they were extinct through the continuous progression of Western cultures. More theoretical studies that questioned this "progression" in general were never undertaken. Although the scholars were aware of the exploitative circumstances under which these cultures lived, they never theorized them.[18]

Talal Asad also criticizes the discipline of anthropology profoundly. He argues clearly that anthropology was born out of Western colonialism. As tool of imperialism, it served to investigate, classify, and categorize non-European people: "concerned at first to help classify non-

European humanity in ways that would be consistent with Europe's story of triumph as 'progress,' anthropology then went out from Europe to the colonies in order to observe and describe the particularity of non-European communities, attending to their 'traditional' cultural form or their subjection to 'modern' social change."[19]

Anthropology furthered the political hegemony of a few European states, while it led colonized societies into economic and political dependency. As Woodruff D. Smith's definition of "imperialism" points out, the attitude of racial superiority was an essential part in the imperial power relationship.[20]

While studies on "empire" and its implication have been popular especially regarding the British, French, and American colonialism for the past two decades, scholars on German colonialism have only in the past few years begun to develop investigations on the German empire and its implications. This was on the one hand due to the insignificance of the German empire[21] (including its short duration and its late start) in contrast to British, French, and American colonial holdings, and on the other hand due to the particularities of German history and its impossibility after World War II to compare it to the history of other nations. The slowly growing scholarly literature on the German empire usually centers on regions of direct German colonialism. In Latin America in general and in the Andes in particular, German economic presence was never vital, and the number of German immigrants to the region was comparatively small. Although a few studies of German influence in Latin America do exist, they are usually limited to the economic realm and the region of Central America as well as Venezuela.[22]

This paper approaches the imperial context with a nonconventional interpretation. Here, "imperialism" (understood in Michel Foucault's terms), defines the establishment of an intellectual power structure developed by Germans over the Andean people and its implications. In this context, an "intellectual conquest" or "intellectual imperialism" occurred that manifested itself in an "intellectualization" or intellectual appropriation of the high-cultured Inca civilization. The "collecting" and "confiscating" of their artifacts and the systematic production of knowledge about them implies the existence of a hierarchical power structure between the observing anthropologists and the observed natives. The theoretical discourse about the findings that followed was held mostly in the German language with a Eurocentric understanding of the foreign culture.[23] From the Andean perspective, the reconstruction of their history through Germans has to be regarded as an alienation or misappropriation of their own past. For the Germans, in con-

trast, the "intellectualization" and display of foreign high-culture artifacts in their national museums was a competitive enterprise that
helped to construct a specific German identity and served as a source
of national pride.

Due to the lack of literature specifically on the Andean context, a
number of works analyzing German archaeological endeavors in others parts of the world have to be integrated. Here, the intellectual
appropriation of ancient Greece by Prussia can serve as a guide, especially through Martin Bernal's brilliant work, *Black Athena*. Bernal critically analyzes German archaeology in Greece, explaining its racially
biased roots and Germany's particularity. He argued that the Western
ideal of Greece was artificially constructed while Greece's actual African
roots were negated. Simultaneously Germany, he argued, needed to
create a unifying national heritage that had the power to include all its
innumerable separate political entities. The fabrication of the antique
routes of "Germanness" served exactly this purpose. This movement
emphasized the distinctions and uniqueness of innate "Germanness,"
which led to a strong feeling of brotherhood among Germans, but also
evoked feelings of superiority toward other cultures. With the creation
of the German nation on these presumptions, people from different
backgrounds were systematically excluded. In the end being Teutonic
implied being superior.[24]

Similarly, Suzanne Marchand's interesting article on German archaeology in Asia Minor, arguing that these state-sponsored archaeological
endeavors had strong political and imperial implications, must be
addressed as well.[25] Both studies demonstrate how archaeology served
as an imperial tool that helped to establish links between German culture and ancient high-cultured civilizations that the German scholars
rediscovered and intellectualized in their writings.

The anthropological documents used here will be placed into the
context of the construction of theories of racial superiority in Europe
of the mid-nineteenth century. As Samir Amin points out, theories that
justified conquest, colonialism, and racism developed in the Renaissance in Europe as a result of the universalization of religion and culture.[26] Historical myths of racial superiority more formally developed
in the nineteenth century served as justifications for imperialism and
the existing global sociopolitical structure.[27] As Edward Said has
pointed out, people of different ethnic backgrounds were simply cate-
gorized and evidence for their physical and intellectual inferiority was
constructed.[28] The theories of Arthur Gobineau became the basis for
the development of German racial thought. He was the first to claim

that among the Caucasian races, the Aryan race was most superior. Scholars who supported this thesis used physical evidence in the form of the allegedly larger size of skulls to claim the superiority of the Aryan race.[29]

Ludwig Woltmann is especially important, first, because he established a connection between cultural and racial ideas, and second, because he played a prominent part in disseminating his beliefs into the "common knowledge" of German society. Woltmann wrote: "Based on pure morphological and biological considerations, one must (...) conclude that the tall, large-headed individual with . . . light pigmentation—the north European race—is the most complete representation of the human species and the highest product of organic development . . . this race is characterized by its high cultural species."[30] He was not only convinced that the concept of human equality was a myth,[31] but he also argued that the Germanic traits in people, which he saw embodied in the superior size of the head that related directly to a larger brain capacity, had produced "all great men."[32] He saw the Germanic race destined to rule the world and promoted his theories actively. Six decades later, Adolf Hitler reiterated Woltmann's argument.[33]

German anthropologists of the Andes were not free of these racial preconceptions, which became more formally developed and more publicly disseminated in the late nineteenth century. Instead, they were highly respected, high-ranking citizens who had been exposed to and played an active role in the traditional German academic environment, in which they had earned their PhD degrees. Their writings verify Charles Mills's "racial contract" in German perception. The scholars show a deep belief in a natural order of human society, which would naturally be led by the white races, particularly white men. They thought of themselves as naturally superior to all Andean people in racial, physical, and intellectual terms. In their view, even the white Creoles (Spanish-born people of the New World) were in no way comparable to any person of Germanic descent. From their Eurocentric perspectives they viewed themselves as being advanced, civilized, educated, and above all, German, which by definition implied strong discrimination against people who were non-German, non-Western, and even stronger racial and general aversion against those who were non-white.

Looking through their Eurocentric filter, Andean peoples were viewed as not only lacking progress and education, both of which were regarded as essential pillars of modernity in Europe, but also lacking "proper and civilized behavior." Middendorf's writings reflect a high awareness of class and race divisions in the Peruvian and Limanese society. He was especially interested in race differences, because the societies of Western Europe at that point were largely monoracial. His work, *Peru: Beobachtungen und Studien ueber das Land und seine Bewohner waehrend eines 25jaehrigen Aufenthalts* (Peru: Observations and Studies about the Nation and Its Inhabitants during a Twenty-five Year Residence), contains an entire section on the races in Lima. He treated each race in a separate chapter and went into detail about the distinct features, characteristics, and customs of each specific race. In it, he strongly objectified the people he described. This becomes most obvious when he explains the process of mixing races, and specifically the "racial outcome" of a Chinese-African couple in Lima to the reader, giving Charles Darwin's experiment with grapes ("Edeltraube") as a comparative example.[34]

Generally speaking, Middendorf perceived the heterogeneous Peruvian society as impure and strongly inferior to the Caucasian or Teutonic races. Applying the specific German definition of "Volk" (an entity with identical racial roots, traditions, culture, customs, history, and language) to Peru, Middendorf claimed "so far as the racial mixing is not completed and a homogenous population has not emerged, the Peruvians cannot be called 'Volk.' They simply qualify as population."[35]

For Middendorf, the uncivilized nature of the white Limanese society became apparent in their lack of cleanliness, responsibility, punctuality, and their constant "bragging, which is like a kind of physical need to these people," and their unwillingness to work.[36] His belief in his own highly superior race was so strong that he praised "certain hard-working, responsible, truth-loving, and enlightened men, who—since they notice the diseases of their compatriots without biases—are not against the foreigners who have their respective advantages. These men want to use these (white) foreigners as welcome helpers for the improvement of their race and for the improvement of their habits and customs."[37]

The writings of Uhle also indicate the mentioned notion of racial and intellectual superiority. He insisted that "progress" was very important for the development of the sciences and that Peru and Bolivia lacked both.[38] The Andean people were generally identified as "uncivilized."[39] Uhle thought that Peruvian officials were not even intellectually capable of conceptualizing their own museums. In fact, he wrote quite frankly about it: "And even if there was life in the Institute, in the entire nation of Bolivia there is a lack of adequate academic guidance.

Nobody would be able to establish a collection that would go beyond one gathered by a lover of curiosities."[40]

The German scholars were not only proudly aware of their supposed superior intellectual abilities, but also of their political significance as whites in a mostly non-white society. Middendorf clearly stated: "If the white foreigners were missing and would be forced to leave the country, their worst enemies would realize that presently the white foreign populations builds an essential pillar, without which the white Peruvians would not be able to remain in power against the much more numerous lower ranking races."[41]

Middendorf's observations about the Afro-Peruvians were extremely biased, full of contempt, and displayed the range of prejudices that existed against them. He claimed that the general racial character of the "Negroes" was the same everywhere in the world. He portrayed them as being physically ugly, lacking any sense of proper behavior, and acting savagely and cruelly. He often described them as childlike creatures, who were driven by "wild instincts, talkative, happy, laughing, and blustering."[42] Perceived as being incapable of thinking about the future,[43] German scholars also characterized Afro-Peruvians as mindless and stupid,[44] and as "always eager to copy their patron or the white people whose society they lived in."[45]

For German scholars racial inferiority encompassed both intellectual and physical inferiority and was manifested in physical attributes. Middendorf thought, for example, that "The throat of the Negro is mostly too thick to articulate the Spanish properly, but he always opens his big mouth widely, shouts, cheers, and is hardly capable of speaking softly."[46] Physical beauty was strictly measured by European features: "The eyes of the Negroes are not beautiful, because the white is usually suffused with blood or dirty, and the brown is so dark that one cannot see the pupil clearly."[47] As soon as Caucasian blood was joined with Afro-Peruvian blood, however, Middendorf perceived them as much more beautiful: "For the zambas the eyes become more pure the brighter the color and then usually sparkling and full of expression."[48]

The scholars made direct correlations between skin color and behavioral patterns. Generally, they perceived people of lighter skin colors to be behaving more civilized and proper than the darker and impure races. He wrote: "the dark and old women are the ugliest thing that you can possibly imagine . . . it seems that you see the garbage of the human race passing by."[49] Another correlation made by Middendorf was the one between skin color and violence. The darker and more impure the person, it was assumed, the less capable they were of having compassion for others. Middendorf stated that "compassion with animals is only to be found in the white population and the pure Indians; the Negro and the dark mixed races treat animals ruthlessly and violently."[50]

Middendorf even went so far as to say that many of the aesthetic evils and impurities of Limanese society were viewed as the consequence of the contact with people of African descent turning the Afro-Peruvians into scapegoats. He wrote, "also were you once in a while surprised to find very fragile looking persons [meaning whites] to have rough and deep voices. That might have resulted from the fact that the children grew up in the companionship of their black servants or slaves and without intending or even knowing would adopt their rough voices."[51]

As we see here, the definition of "people" included only persons of Caucasian descent. Whenever people of other races were referred to, it had to be added explicitly, since the general definition of people did not include them. Middendorf ended his chapter on Afro-Peruvians with the conclusion that "for the black race in its pure stage civilization is unattainable." The only positive aspect he saw in their race was that—before they would be extinct in Peru—they might be able to contribute their physical strength and heat resistance to the creation of a new and better Peruvian race.[52]

The sources of the German scholars reveal a deep-seated disrespect about people from "impure" or mixed racial backgrounds. Racial purity had become such a high-held ideal in Germany that these scholars had a hard time placing it. Uhle's correspondence reveals this uneasiness and the profound disrespect for *mestizos*, when he repeatedly termed the Bolivian administrators as "uneducated native cholos"[53] and strongly generalized their behavior. He wrote, "The chief characteristics of the "servanos" are, however, secrecy, treachery in their dealings, suspicion, and the unbounded selfishness, which always sees its own injury in the advantages gained by others; and from these result an absolute indifference to intellectual development or progress."[54]

Although the general correlation between skin color and behavior existed, exceptions were always made for the descendants of the ancient Inca, who were considered of noble blood and thus were naturally perceived as behaving civilized and proper. When describing the Amerindians they came into contact with, the scholars clearly distinguished between the average inferior Indian and the good descendants of the noble Inca. The contemporary Indians were generally viewed as racially, physically, and intellectually far inferior to the perceived "white and pure" ancient Indian races. The contemporary Indians were generally characterized as shy, reserved, distrusting and suspicious, gloomy and taciturn.[55]

Middendorf pointed out that "the Inca were unique in terms of physical composure and mental capabilities and in comparison to other tribes of the highlands of superior lineage."[56] "To have a lot of Indian blood does not necessarily lessen the self-esteem of a person, since it could have been the blood of the Inca and prove the descendence from the early aristocrats and rulers of the country."[57]

Although Uhle's publications display a deep fascination with the ancient Andean civilizations, he also made sharp distinctions between the noble Inca race of the past and the contemporary Andean population, for which he had little respect. He often contrasted the ancient high cultures to the contemporary "largely barbaric" cultures[58] and looked down upon native religions, characterizing them as mere "superstitions."[59]

After reviewing Middendorf's and Uhle's writings, it becomes most obvious how strongly they differentiated the ancient noble race and the high-cultured Inca civilization from the contemporary Andean cultures that they personally came in contact with. In their perceptions, the Incas had had a strong empire, were well organized, had nobility, and consisted of a homogenous populace. All this made it easy for these scholars to identify with them and to respect them.

In contrast to these established links by association between the Germans and the ancient high-cultured Inca, Cunow developed theories that linked Germans and Incas together even more directly. He compared the ancient Incas to the Germanic cultures and found various similarities. Not only did he observe similar social structures and a similar agrarian constitution, but he also claimed that the Inca administration resembled the German or Prussian bureaucracy: "It might surprise some readers and even some anthropologists that two peoples of such different character like the ancient Peruvians and our ancient ancestors are believed to have created the same agrarian legislation and institutions."[60]

Cunow shared the opinion that the investigation of Inca society would not only enhance German knowledge about other parts of the world, but that due to the similarities between the civilizations, such knowledge might even help the Germans to gain some new insights about their own past. The central issue of comparison for him was the agrarian constitution and the usage of communal land in Germanic village communities and the social organization of the Inca. "The institutions of the Inca emperors were nothing less than the agrarian communism that we knew from the tribal and village constitutions of the old Amerindians and Japanese, Germans and Celts," Cunow claimed.[61]

These German scholars transferred knowledge about the ancient and contemporary Andean civilizations to Germany, which their numerous publications in various journals and monographs helped to disseminate. They collected, appropriated, and shipped these artifacts to Germany in order to exhibit them in national museums, which supported their anthropological enterprises financially. Surprisingly enough, already in the 1830s, the Andean and other American artifacts were collected in Berlin in the "Kunst und Rartiaetenkammer" (Cabinet of Art and Curiosities) under the Grossherzog von Brandenburg. Under the direction of Adolf Bastian, the collection grew so rapidly that it had to be moved into a separate building near the "Potsdamer Platz."[62] Simultaneous with the increasing display of artifacts in museums, the German academic curricula also began to incorporate more and more Andean themes. The study of various Andean languages and cultures became a fixed part of German higher education. In 1892, Josef Koehler founded the field of ethnographic jurisprudence at the law faculty of Berlin University, where he offered comparative courses on Inca, Aztec, and German law.[63]

Alongside the archaeological treasures, the observations and images of the Andean people were transmitted to Germany, where various scholarly and popular journals, monographs, and scholarly conferences helped to disseminate them. At the end of the nineteenth century Germany had developed into the leading research environment for Peruvian and Andean studies. When valuable artifacts of the noble Incas began to be exhibited in national museums in Berlin and more and more Andean themes were incorporated into the German university curricula, the racial images of the pure Inca civilization and the darker colored and impure Andean people began to be spread likewise.[64]

CONCLUSION

In conclusion, we can presume that although Germany did not have official colonies in the Andes and was not the dominant economic investor in the region, the works of German anthropologists furthered the nation's intellectual claims to the area. By developing a continuous stream of popular and academic literature on the Andes from the seventeenth century onward, Germany did in fact appropriate the Andes as a permanent theme in its literature and academia.

The scholar's sharp distinction between the evil contemporary population and idealized ancient civilizations made it easy for them to identify with the ancient society, to which they linked themselves implicitly and, as Conow's work indicates, explicitly. The continuing investigation of the topic triggered a specific German intellectual discourse, which mirrored the hegemonic relationship and recreated the Andean past in Germany. The collections of artifacts and their display in national museums in Germany substantiated this process and in connection with the writings of all four German anthropologists they give evidence to the occurring process of "intellectualization."

Either while receiving funds from national German museums or other governmental institutions or simply by shipping their artifacts back home, the scholars consciously served as agents of national imperial endeavors. Their academic work helped to initiate and reproduce an anthropological discourse on the Andes and the growing collections of artifacts furthered German national pride in the climate of Western imperial competition. The scholars also helped to create a more unified German nation and to construct a perceived "superior" German identity.

The writings of the German scholars also suggest that the "racial contract" that Charles Mills detected as a hidden racial, economic, and legal system that assists white people to remain in their dominant positions was also part of the thinking of the German anthropologists and archaeologists. They clearly perceived white European men as the "ideal people" and measured the people they described in the Andes as naturally inferior to them. Seeing themselves as white, European, and modern turned them by definition into the "more valuable people" who were racially, physically, and intellectually superior to all the Andean peoples they came in contact with. During their residence in the New World, they connected racial attributes with cultural features and constructed racial images of the Andean people. Thus, they reinforced the already existing image of the "stupid Negro," the "treacherous Indian," and the "ugly mestizo" and ultimately helped to legitimize the existing global sociopolitical hierarchy or to use Mills's term, the "global racial contract." The sources indicate that they perceived themselves as rightfully deserving of the highest places in the social world order, while people of different darker and "impure races" were "naturally" placed beneath them. Even the definition of "person," as Middendorf's works indicate, only included people of white racial origin. Specific physical features, racial traits, as well as cultural behavior patterns were systematically used to fabricate the superiority of whites, especially Aryans and the inferiority of all other races. This means that the construction of "the Andean" occurred simultaneously with the formation of a specific "German identity" that took shape in stark contrast to the construction of the inferior people of the Andes. By creating mythical and intellectual links with the ancient high-cultured Inca civilizations that we observe in the writings of Cunow, these Germans implicitly claimed to be of the same type as the Incas had been: of noble blood, superior ancestry, high physical and intellectual capacities, and with the destiny to create a strong empire and leave their mark on history.

NOTES

1. Daniel G. Blackburn, "Why Race Is Not a Biological Concept," 3.

2. See Carl N. Degler, *Neither Black Nor White: Slavery and Race Relations in Brazil and the United States* (New York: University of Wisconsin Press, 1971); Emilia Viotti da Costa, *Brazilian Empire, Myths and Legends* (Chicago: University of Chicago Press, 1985); Manuel Moreno Fraginals, *Africa en América Latina* (Paris: UNESCO, 1977); George Reid Andrews, *Blacks and Whites in São Paulo, Brazil 1888–1988* (Madison: University of Wisconsin Press, 1991); Alejandro de la Fuente, *A Nation for All: Race, Inequality, and Politics in Twentieth-Century Cuba* (Chapel Hill: North Carolina Press, 2001); Susan D. Greenbaum, *More than Black: Afro-Cubans in Tampa* (Gainesville: University of Florida Press, 2002).

3. See François Chevalier, "Official Indigenísmo in Peru in 1920: Origins, Significance, and Socioeconomic Scope," in *Race and Class in Latin America*, ed. Magnus Moerner (New York: Columbia University Press, 1970); Pierre Van den Berghe, ed., *Class and Ethnicity in Peru* (Leiden: Brill Publishers, 1974); Marisol de la Cadena, *Indigenous Mestizos: The Politics of Race and Culture in Cuzco, Peru, 1919–1991* (Durham: Duke University Press, 2000); José Luciano and Humberto Rodriguez Pastor, "Peru," in *No Longer Invisible: Afro-Latin Americans Today*, ed. Minority Rights Group (London: Minority Rights Group Publication, 1995).

4. See Immanuel M. Wallerstein, *The Modern World-System: Capitalist Agriculture and the Origins of the European World-Economy in the Sixteenth Century* (New York: Academic Press, 1976) and Charles M. Mills, *The Racial Contract* (Ithaca: Cornell University Press, 1997).

5. See Samuel Fritz, *Karte von dem Laufe des Maragnon oder grossen Amazonas Flusses im Jahre 1743–1744* (Germany, 1744); Wolfgang Beyer, *Reize naar Peru: von ihm selbst beschrieben*. Nürnberg: Zeh, 1776).

6. See Anton Zarachias Helms, *Diario de mi viaje al Peru desde Buenos Aires a Lima, via Potosi: 1788–1792* (Lima: Mass Comunicacion SRL, 1994).

7. John Howland Rowe, *Max Uhle, 1856–1944*, 2.

8. Ernst W. Middendorf, *Gramatica Keshua*, xiv–vi.

9. Rowe, *Max Uhle, 1856–1944*.

10. Benoit Massin, "From Virchow to Fischer," 83.

11. Wolfgang Haberland, "Enrique Bruening," 5.

12. Max Uhle, Letter to Report to Department of Archaeology, March 1895.

13. See also Corinna Raddatz, ed., *Fotodokumente aus Nordperu von Hans Heinrich Bruening, 1848–1928* (Hamburg: Selbstvlg. d. Hamburgischen Museums für Völkerkunde, 1990); Estuardo Nuñez, *Viajes y Viajeros Extranjeros por el Peru: Apuntes documentales con algunos desarrollos historico-biographicos* (Lima: Tall. Gráf, Villanueva, 1989); Gerdt Kutscher, *Berlin Como Centro Estudios Americanistas: Ensayo Bio-Bibliographico* (Berlin: Gebr. Mann Verlag, 1976).

14. Richard Schaedel, "Der Bruening Nachlass," 36.

15. See Doig Federico Kauffman, *La Obra de los Archealogos Alemanes en el Peru* (Hamburg: FriedrichPörtner, 1963), and Estuardo Nuñez Hague, *Viajes y Viajeros Extranjeros por el Peru* (Lima: Tall. Gráf. Villanueva, 1989).

16. Gabriele Koch-Weithofer, *Peru im Spiegel deutschsprachiger Reiseberichte (1790–1860)*, 3.

17. See, for example, George W. Stocking Jr., *Colonial Situations: Essays on the Conceptualization of Ethnographic Knowledge* (Madison: University of Wisconsin Press, 1991), and *Volksgeist as Method and Ethic: Essays on Boasian Ethnography and the German Anthropological Tradition* (Madison: University of Wisconsin Press, 1996); Sandra Harding, *The "Racial" Economy of Science: Toward a Democratic Future* (Bloomington: Indiana University Press, 1993).

18. Mina Davis Caulfield, "Culture and Imperialism," 184–85.

19. Talal Asad, "From the History of Colonial Anthropology," 314.

20. Woodruff D. Smith, *The German Colonial Empire*, 20.

21. The German empire consisted of areas in Africa (German South West Africa, Togo, Tanzania, Cameroon) and in the Pacific (northeast New Guinea, part of Samoa, the Bismarcks, the Marshalls, the Carolines, the Marianas, and Kiachow on the Shantung Peninsula in China).

22. See Thomas Schonhoover, *Germany in Central America: Competitive Imperialism, 1821–1929* (Tuscaloosa: University of Alabama Press, 1998) and Nancy Mitchell, *The Power of Dreams: German and American Imperialism in Latin America* (Chapel Hill: University of North Carolina Press, 1999).

23. Massin, "From Virchow to Fischer," 83.

24. Martin Bernal, "Black Athena," 53.

25. See Suzanne Marchand, "Orientalism as Kulturpolitik: German Archaeology and Cultural Imperialism in Asia Minor", in *Volksgeist as Method and Ethic. Essays on Boasian Ethnography and the German Anthropological Tradition*, ed. George W. Stocking, Jr. (Madison: University of Wisconsin Press, 1996).

26. Samir Amin, *Eurocentrism*, 35.

27. Blackburn, "Why Race Is Not a Biological Concept," 6.

28. See Edward W. Said, *Orientalism* (New York: Vintage Books, 1979).

29. Eric H. Vieler, *The Ideological Roots of German National Socialism*, 64–65.

30. Ibid., 67.

31. Ibid., 71.

32. Ibid., 68.

33. Ibid., 73.

34. Middendorf, *Peru*, 235.

35. Ibid., 233.

36. Ibid., 207–10.

37. Ibid., 219.

38. Uhle, Letter to Department of Anthropology, August 28, 1896.

39. Ibid.
40. Uhle, Letter to Department of Anthropology, July 3, 1895.
41. Middendorf, *Peru*, 219–20.
42. Ibid., 232.
43. Ibid., 231.
44. Ibid., 236.
45. Ibid., 231.
46. Ibid., 232.
47. Ibid., 240.
48. Ibid.
49. Ibid.
50. Ibid., 219.
51. Ibid., 212.
52. Ibid., 232–33.
53. Uhle, Letter to Department of Anthropology, May 12, 1895.
54. Uhle, Letter to Department of Anthropology, January, 1896.
55. Middendorf, *Peru*, 232.
56. Ibid., 226.
57. Ibid., 235.
58. Uhle, Letter to Department of Anthropology, October 18, 1895.
59. Uhle, Letter to Department of Anthropology, May 12, 1895.
60. Heinrich Cunow, *Die Soziale Vergassung der Inkareiches*, v.
61. Ibid., 7.
62. Gerdt Kutscher, *Berlin Como Centro de Estudios Americanistas*, 9–12.
63. Ibid., 12.
64. Ibid., 9–12.

BIBLIOGRAPHY

Amin, Samir. *Eurocentrism*. New York: Monthly Review Press, 1989.

Asad, Talal. "From the History of Colonial Anthropology to the Anthropology of Western Hegemony." In *Colonial Situations: Essays on the Contextualization of Ethnographic Knowledge*, edited by George W. Stockings, Jr. Madison: University of Wisconsin Press, 1991, 314–24.

Bernal, Martin. *Black Athena: The Afroasiatic Roots of Classical Civilization*. Vol. 1, *The Fabrication of Ancient Greece*. London: Free Association Books, 1987.

———. "Black Athena: Hostilities to Egypt in the Eighteenth Century." In *The "Racial" Economy of Science*, edited by Sandra Harding. Bloomington and Indianapolis: Indiana University Press, 1993, 47–60.

Blackburn, Daniel G. "Why Race Is Not a Biological Concept." In *Race and Racism in Theory and Practice*, edited by Berel Lang. New York and Oxford: Lanham, 2000, 3–26.

Bruckner, Sierra Ann. *The Tingle-Tangle of Modernity: Popular Anthropology and the Cultural Politics of Identity in Imperial Germany*. 2 vols. Ames: University of Iowa Press, 1999.

Caulfield, Mina Davis. "Culture and Imperialism: Proposing a New Dialectic." In *Reinventing Anthropology*, edited by Dell Hymes. New York: Pantheon Books, 1969, 182–212.

Cunow, Heinrich. *Die Soziale Verfassung der Inkareiches. Eine Untersuchung des altperuanischen Agrarkommunismus.* Stuttgart, 1896.

Haberland, Wolfgang. "Enrique Bruening—ein deutscher Forscher in Perú: Apuntes Documentales con Algunos Desarollos Histórico-Biográficos (Lima: Tall. Gráf. Villanueva, 1989).

Koch-Weithofer, Gabriele Maria Gertrud. *Peru im Spiegel deutschsprachiger Reiseberichte (1790–1860).* PhD Dissertation, Tübingen, 1993.

Kutscher, Gerdt. *Berlin Como Centro de Estudios Americanistas: Ensayo Bio-Bibliographicos.* Berlin: Gebr. Mann Verlag, 1976.

Massin, Benoit. "From Virchow to Fischer: Physical Anthropology and 'Modern Race Theories' in Wihelmine Germany." In *Volksgeist as Method and Ethic: Essays on Boasian Ethnography and the German Anthropological Tradition,* edited by George W. Stockings, Jr. Madison: University of Wisconsin Press, 1996, 79–154.

Middendorf, Ernst W. *Gramatica Keshua.* Madrid: Aguilar, 1970.

———. *Peru. Beobachtungen und Studien ueber das Land und seine Bewohner waehrend eines 25-jaehrigen Aufenthaltes.* Berlin, 1893–95.

Mosse, George L. *The Crisis of German Ideology: Intellectual Origins of the Third Reich.* New York: Grosset & Dunlap Publishers, 1964.

Rowe, John Howland. *Max Uhle, 1856–1944: A Memoir of the Father of Peruvian Archaeology.* Berkeley: University of California Press, 1954.

Schaedel, Richard. *"Der Bruening Nachlass und seine Wiederentdeckung."* In *Fotodukumente aus Nordperu von Hans Heinrich Bruening, 1848–1928,* edited by Corinna Raddatz, 29–35. Hamburg: Hamburger Museum fuer Voelkerkunde, 1990.

Smith, Woodruff D. *The German Colonial Empire.* Chapel Hill: University of North Carolina Press, 1978.

Uhle, Max. *Letter to Department of Archaeology,* May 12, 1895. Museum of Archaeology and Anthropology, University of Pennsylvania, Philadelphia.

———. *Letter to Department of Archaeology.* March, 1895. Museum of Archaeology and Anthropology, University of Pennsylvania, Philadelphia.

———. *Letter to Department of Anthropology,* October 18, 1895. Museum of Archaeology and Anthropology, University of Pennsylvania, Philadelphia.

———. *Letter to Department of Anthropology,* January, 1896. Museum of Archaeology and Anthropology, University of Pennsylvania, Philadelphia.

———. *Letter to Department of Anthropology,* August 28, 1896. Museum of Archaeology and Anthropology?, University of Pennsylvania, Philadelphia.

———. *Report to Department of Archaeology,* July 3, 1895. Museum for Archaeology and Anthropology, University of Pennsylvania, Philadelphia.

Vieler, Eric H. *The Ideological Roots of German National Socialism.* New York: Peter Lang, 1999.

Cinematic Representation of the Yellow Peril:
D. W. Griffith's *Broken Blossoms*

Lan Dong

In the year 2000, the Directors Guild of America (DGA) retired its prestigious D. W. Griffith Award "because of the racial stereotypes the filmmaker portrayed in his movies, most notably in his 1915 film, *The Birth of a Nation*."[1] Regardless of the acknowledgment of Griffith being a "brilliant pioneer filmmaker" whose innovations have led the way for generations of directors to follow, DGA president Jack Shea states that Griffith "helped foster intolerable racial stereotypes."[2] Such a provocative action is confirmed by the National Association for the Advancement of Colored People (NAACP) whose president, Kweisi Mfume, asserts, "this award should have never been given under the name of D. W. Griffith."[3] As a matter of fact, right after its release Griffith was confronted with critiques and accusations concerning his racist attitudes. Griffith's cinematic works have come to represent a strongly problematic depiction of African Americans that persists today.

Indeed, there is little doubt that Griffith still should be credited as a great filmmaker owing to his distinguished contribution to the development of narrative film in early American cinema. Many viewers have taken Griffith's film *Broken Blossoms* (1919) as his retreat from the criticism of *The Birth of a Nation*. Scholars such as Michael Rogin tend to interpret this film as Griffith's withdrawal from political engagement to "an elegiac mode of pastoralism and tradition," through which he "embraced an aesthetic of victimization,"[4] in a narrative form. In the sense of constructing and developing a melodrama, *Broken Blossoms* surely is one of Griffith's feature masterpieces.[5] The storyline set up by the script and the cinema techniques including usage of the close-up, cross-cutting (parallel action) and flashback strengthen feelings, atmosphere, and tension, and thus work together to facilitate and propel the melodramatic narrative in this film.

Some reviewers and critics consider *Broken Blossoms* as Griffith's response to the accusation of racism against him through its sentimental plea for racial tolerance.[6] Yet the film also has been interpreted as another Hollywood anti-Asian narrative, which popularizes racial stereotypes, thus reinforcing his position as a racist filmmaker.[7] Recently a list of comments posted on the World Wide Web cover the two oppositional perspectives. Roger Ebert considers *Broken Blossoms* "not as important as" *The Birth of a Nation*, but "neither is it as flawed": "[I]n *Broken Blossoms* he [D.W. Griffith] told perhaps the first interracial love story in the movies—even though, to be sure, it's an idealized love with no touching. . . . Griffith's film was nevertheless open-minded and even liberal in the context of his time and audiences. . . Films like this, naïve as they seem today, helped nudge a xenophobic nation toward racial tolerance (notes added)."[8] Another review posted at *The DVD Journal* Web site presents an almost contradictory point of view in its following observation: "D. W. Griffith's reputation as a brilliantly racist filmmaker receives some dubious reinforcement from this excellent 1919 melodrama about interracial love. . . . [It] can be reasonably argued that on an unintended level *Broken Blossoms* is not a tragic romance, but rather an allegory of Asian self-loathing, and, much like a subplot in [*The*] *Birth of a Nation*, a testament to the universal, yet forbidden and unrequited, desirability of white women to other races."[9] Yet another reviewer holds the following opinion: "*Broken Blossoms* is often regarded and dismissed as Griffith's apology for his alleged celebration of the Klu Klux Klan in [*The*] *Birth of a Nation* . . . despite being the creation of a man who was very much a product of his time. Because *Broken Blossoms* is so earnest a portraiture of an impossible love between the races, it's easy to accept Griffith's claims that he didn't mean any harm with [*The*] *Birth of a Nation*."[10]

Given such highly controversial and divergent critical responses toward the melodramatic silent film *Broken Blossoms*, from its release until the present, this essay intends to examine this work's cinematic representations, in this case that of the Yellow Peril[11] embodied particularly by Asian men. Before embarking on an analysis of the film, I shall conceptualize the Yellow Peril in cinema as a visual manifestation of orientalism and situate my research in the discussion, which explores cultural (mis)representation of the East in the West, initiated by Edward Said's pivotal work *Orientalism* (1979). In the argument to follow, I shall examine how Griffith adapts an interracial love tale from Thomas Burke's short story "The Chink and the Child" (1917) but in the process transforms it to accommodate the widely accepted perception of Asian, especially Chinese, male immigrants that originated in American popular culture in the specific social and historical context when the film was released. In the light of adapting the Yellow Peril theme and orientalizing the film's design and chorography, I want to examine how Griffith's cinematic representation perpetuates the racial stereotypes and discriminative restrictions against miscegenation in the United States in the early twentieth century.

After his investigation of Chinese Americans in U.S. fiction during a time span of ninety years, William Wu calls for scholarly attention to literature by Chinese Americans in order to examine the challenges raised by and the influences of their writings.[12] After scrutinizing the orientalist perspective perpetuated in *Broken Blossoms*, I would like to extend this focus on media racism to a brief review of films and videos directed or produced by Asian Americans and their critical aftermath in the past decades, in order to explore further how the Yellow Peril is problematized, reconsidered, and represented in more recent cinema, video, and other visual arts.

Even though the emergence of "Asian American cinema" is closely yoked to the political struggles and cultural practices of the 1960s and 1970s, the representation of Asian immigrants in American cinema as well as in other art forms predates contemporary self-representation of Asian Americans in films. Therefore, the study of Asian representation in early American cinema will proffer an indispensable background to the self-conscious Asian American cinematic theory and practice which assert themselves against the marginalization and exclusion of the "Yellow people" in the United States and try to provide a countervisual scenario.[13] One of the distinctive contributions as well as goals of Asian American cinema in representing Asian Americans is to create "alternatives to Hollywood's master narratives" "in front of and behind the camera."[14] Therefore, it is worthwhile to reexamine the supposedly authoritive "mainstream" American cinema and at the same time to review the impact of racial inequality and discrimination on the minority communities of Asian ancestry during and after that historical period. With a deeper understanding of the problematic images of Asian Americans in the past, the challenge to and redress of their invisibility or misrepresentation in American history and culture will provide a stronger and more effective case.

My analysis of the film *Broken Blossoms* departs from the past explorations of solely one side of the Yellow Peril: I will examine also the leading character of Cheng Huan (identified as the Yellow Man in the film, Richard Barthelmess), in terms of his fantastic love for and accidental contact with the white girl Lucy (Lillian Gish) in order to demonstrate the film's rather effeminate portrayal of an Asian man in addition to its more traditional stereotype of the evil Yellow Peril. Throughout the film, Cheng Huan's image as the Yellow Man appears to be feminine, consistent with the popular image of the emasculated Asian male in American cinema and fiction in the early twentieth century. Yet the final scene in which the passive Cheng Huan pulls the trigger and shoots to death Lucy's murderous father—Battling Burrows (Donald Crisp)—ends the film with the picture of a violent yellow villain. A supplemental and complementary role as he is, the character named the Evil Eye (Edward Peil Sr.) not surprisingly confirms the social perception of the Asian male as viciously evil, the other side of the Yellow Peril, through his overt desire for and threat to the purity of white womanhood embodied by Lucy. These conflicting qualities within one character, embodied by the Yellow Man and supplemented by the Evil Eye—effeminate and violent—demonstrate a representation of the Yellow Peril in both implicit and explicit ways. Thus such depictions as the Yellow Man's feminized body, his relationship with Lucy, and the intensified confrontation of the white (Burrows) and the yellow (Cheng Huan) men at the end demand further examination.

Moreover, the film links the issue of race most notably to skin color. As Robert Lee states, "the designation of yellow as the racial color of the Oriental is a prime example of this social constructedness of race."[15] Contextualizing Griffith's characters Cheng Huan and the Evil Eye specified by their skin color within the broader stereotypes of the Asian in the United States in the early twentieth century,[16] I propose a duality portrayed in the embodiment of the Yellow Man: on the one hand, he is an effeminate villain while on the other, he exemplifies the yellow race's hidden danger to white society.

Other scholars provide evidence of such racial stereotyping in early film media. Considering orientalism as an "ideological form" in the silent film period, Nick Browne details the reprehensible ways early American cinema, film criticism, and designs of theater performances incorporate racial stereotypes.[17] The process of stereotyping is, however, as Homi Bhabha observes, "not a simplification because it is a false representation of a given reality. It is a simplification because it is an arrested, fixed form of representation that, in denying the play of difference . . . constitutes a problem for the [sic] *representation* of the subject in signification of psychic and social relations."[18] Following Bhabha's lead, I tend to view Griffith's cinematic narrative as a product that is inseparable from its historical and social context and that is developed in a contingent way so as to be accepted by the audience at that time. Thus, it is necessary to address the central theme of this essay—cinematic representation—in relation to Asian immigrants' history in the United States and the perceptions of them as dangerous "Others" in American culture from the late nineteenth century to the early twentieth century.

In observing orientalism as it "responded more to the culture that produced it than to its putative object which was also produced by the West," Said demonstrates the impossibility for representation—scholarly, scientific, or artistic—to be apolitical or to be created apart from a social context.[19] Since "racialized discourses of subordinate social identity must be accounted for historically and politically,"[20] the duality represented by Fu Manchu and Charlie Chan and by Cheng Huan and the Evil Eye, relies heavily on the distorted interpretation of Chinese Americans in American history. Preceded and followed by a variety of local and state laws and regulations targeting immigrants, the Chinese Exclusion Act, approved by the Congress in 1882, prevented working-class Chinese from entering the United States. Those who already had been living in America were not allowed to become naturalized citizens, no matter how long they stayed and where they were born. This act, together with its amendments, was valid for a significant time span, and was not lifted until 1943. To some degree, it was effective in decreasing the population of Chinese immigrants in the United States. But most importantly, it had considerable influence on the immigrants' life in America and legitimated the hostility toward them from American society. The Immigration Regional Restriction Act of 1917 excluded all Asian groups from American society, except for Japanese Americans. All school-aged children of Asian origin, except for those of Japanese heritage, were prohibited to go to white schools. They had to go to a limited number of "Oriental schools" and were kept distant from white children. In 1919, miscegenation between different races was widely considered as a crime. The California law against miscegenation defined it as interracial marriage between the white race and the "Negro, mulatto, or Mongolian."[21] According to the Immigration Act of 1924, any American woman who married a Chinese man lost her citizenship and so did American men who married women of Chinese ancestry. Besides those national acts, many states also instituted antimiscegenation laws and rules around this period to exclude immigrants, particularly Asian men.

In approaching *Broken Blossoms* within its historical context, I choose to draw upon behind the scenes, technical aspects as well as its thematic representations; to be more precise, I shall discuss not only the Yellow Man's hopeless affection for Lucy that is destined to be tragic, but also the cross-racial casting for the film that incorporates the social ethics and filmmaking conventions active in the early twentieth century.

THE STEREOTYPE OF THE YELLOW PERIL: A MANIFESTATION OF ORIENTALISM

Before exploring further the portrayal of the Yellow Peril in the film *Broken Blossoms*, we need to understand the evolution of the stereotype itself. In my view, the Yellow Peril, as a politically involved phenomenon is a reflection of orientalism in the media. In defining orientalism, Edward Said employs the notion of discourse in Michel Foucault's sense to refer to "a Western style for dominating, restructuring, and having authority over the Orient." Orientalism, hence, "depends for its strategy on this flexible [*sic*] *positional* superiority, which puts the Westerner in a whole series of possible relationships with the Orient without ever losing him the relative upper hand."[22] Inaugurated as such, the demarcation between the Orient and the Occident, as discursive constructions, is questionable from its very beginning. "The Orient," Said wrote, "was almost a European invention, and had been since antiquity a place of romance, exotic beings, haunting memories and landscapes, remarkable experiences."[23] That is to say, the very concepts of Orient and orientalism are social constructs invented, standardized, and repeated by the European and American ideology. Although Said focuses on writing as the primary source materials to structure his seminal work, he also refers to television, films, and media resources as the means that have "intensified" the circulation and popularity of the cultural stereotypes and in the process have helped to build up the "imaginative demonology of 'the mysterious Orient.' "[24] In the light of media production, Hollywood's creation of the East as an imaginary territory exemplified and popularized the idea of Orient that was generated by the Occident, in Said's sense.

Such portrayals of Asia and Asian characters have enjoyed a long history in the American film business. The American film industry sought out Asians as subjects in cinema as early as 1896.[25] As Nick Browne has noticed, "[w]ithin the years of the embourgeoisment of the cinema, 'the Orient' was dispersed into the multiple sectors of the film institution—notably as an investment in theater design, in the exoticism in films themselves, and in theory."[26] Similarly, in his notes on the ethnic dimension in silent films, Edward Ifkovic bridges the limited representation of immigrants in early American cinema with the widespread fear of the "Others," whose intrigues are depicted to "romanticize" or "sentimentalize" Asian Americans as the "one-dimensional evil forces or buffoons."[27] What is particularly significant for discussion in this essay is the peculiar form of orientalization that was undertaken by the film institution at the beginning of the twentieth century.

One of the approaches that emergent film scholarship during the past decades has used in exploring this Hollywood orientalism is to analyze the representation of interracial sexual relationships, in a direct or symbolic way, in selected films. As an illuminating example, the second chapter in Gina Marchetti's book, *Romance and the "Yellow Peril"* (1993), juxtaposes Cecil B. DeMille's *The Cheat* (1915) and Griffith's *Broken Blossoms*, in order to suggest that the ideological implications of Hollywood's cinema arise from the "fantasy of the violation of the white woman by a man of color."[28] Marchetti's emphasis on the "rape fantasy" in *Broken Blossoms* seems to imply a masculine sexuality of the Yellow Man. In my view, however, the leading character Cheng Huan's most dominant driving trait is his effeminacy: his intoxication with Lucy is derived more from fetishism than from libido. The Yellow Peril for white womanhood and for the larger social order as symbolized by the Yellow Man is described mostly as a hidden danger in the film; namely, it is more implicit than explicit. Such a peculiar form of orientalization as well as the interracial relationship between Cheng Huan and Lucy provide a fascinating arena within which to explore the Yellow Peril theme in this essay.

Before Said embarks on the argument on orientalism, he addresses the multiple readerships he is writing for: his expected readers include students of literature and criticism, contemporary students of the Orient, from university scholars to policymakers, and readers in the so-called Third World.[29] Indeed, cultural critics and theorists have taken up his lead to continue the compelling discussion.[30] My particular positions—as a student of "literature and criticism" (due to my professional affiliation and the interdisciplinary scope of my research) and as a representative of the "so-called Third World" (based on my nationality and cultural roots)—enable me to take the perspective of more than one of Said's readerships and in the process to challenge and revise orientalism, in this case through an exploration of the Yellow Peril theme reflected in early American cinema, specifically in *Broken Blossoms*.

William Wu, in his study on the Yellow Peril as an overwhelmingly dominant theme in American fiction about Chinese Americans between

1850 and 1940, defines the term as "the threat to the United States that some white American authors believed was posed by the people of East Asia."[31] As a cultural subject matter, the fear of the Yellow Peril takes on a variety of forms with different foci in literary and media expressions, one of which is "the potential genetic mixing of Anglo-Saxons with Asians, who were considered a biologically inferior race by some intellectuals of the nineteenth century."[32] Among the emblems of the racially problematic themes in cinema, one of the most potent aspects of the Yellow Peril discourse in American popular culture is the predatory sexual desire from the yellow race that endangers white womanhood and consequently threatens the racial purity of white American society.

In terms of the history of film analysis, there has been a strong interest in this premise of miscegenation in Hollywood's orientalist films.[33] From *The Cheat* to *The Bitter Tea of General Yen* (1932), the portrayal of such a concern has barely changed. Along the trajectory of such commonly perceived cinematic representations in interracial contact, Asian men are usually depicted as two major types. First, they are rapist villains who embody visible sexual intimidation. The mysterious Burmese merchant Tori (Sessue Hayakawa) in *The Cheat* and the notorious Dr. Fu Manchu in fiction, TV, and film series are prominent examples in this category. Second, some yellow men appear as emasculated figures who have been domesticated; it is their assimilation into Caucasian society that controls their evil nature and thus the potential danger for American society. In this category, the detective Charlie Chan in both fiction and media provides a renowned instance. In terms of discriminatively representing the yellow people marked by their skin color, Griffith's 1919 film *Broken Blossoms* participates in Hollywood's orientalist narrative and complicates the Yellow Peril theme through not only its leading character—the desexualized yet dangerous Yellow Man—but also through the love fantasy between people of different skin colors that is doomed to fail in the film.

In his aforementioned book, Wu elaborates the phenomenon of the Yellow Peril in American popular culture as well as the complex implications of the well-known Asian figures in the 1920s to 1940s: the evil Dr. Fu Manchu and the docile detective Charlie Chan. From 1913 to 1959, British writer Sax Rohmer published a series of novels and novellas that won him prestige both in Britain and abroad and introduced the vicious and mysterious Dr. Fu Manchu to a broad readership.[34] "[I]magine that awful being, and you have a mental picture of Dr. Fu-Manchu, the yellow peril incarnate in one man."[35] As an evil genius that

embodies the Asian threat, the Fu Manchu character in British literature preceded his film embodiment created in the United States.
Nevertheless, the popularity of the filmic adaptations of the Fu Manchu
stories is what catapulted him as the "archetypal Asian villain" among
the American audience.[36] Charlie Chan was shaped also by British literature; he was originally a character in Earl Derr Biggers's six mysteries published between 1925 and 1932. The detective too went on to
attract much attention among American audience through a total of
forty-seven serial and feature films between the 1930s and 1940s[37] and
became the second celebrity in yellow skin in American media. Perceived as a contravention of Fu Manchu, the detective Charlie Chan is
a symbol of the tamed and desexualized Yellow Peril that evolved as a
result of assimilation. Given their prevalence among and influence on
U.S. audiences, Fu Manchu and Charlie Chan exemplify the two
extremes of the representations of Asian men in American fiction and
media before the 1940s.[38]

Inspired by such juxtaposition, I examine the characters of the Yellow Man and the Evil Eye in *Broken Blossoms* using a comparative
methodology. Nevertheless, through discussing in detail the visualized
stereotypes of Asian men, I consider the two images in Griffith's film
as orientalist representations of complication and subtleness. The Yellow Man and the Evil Eye function as complementary counterparts in
the film: a feminized obedient merchant as the leading role versus a
wicked villain as the supportive figure. As a particular cinematic design
feature, both men's gazes are directed to the white girl Lucy and in the
process indicate the potential threat (in Cheng Huan's case) and the
direct threat (exemplified by the Evil Eye) to the Caucasian female from
the yellow community. The duality embodied by them "is therefore
created specifically by certain values and beliefs of white supremacy.
These include a belief in the Yellow Peril."[39] The two characters com-
bine the commonly accepted clichés of Asian men in American popular culture through contrasting images: the desexualized civilian who
represents the potential Yellow Peril to American culture underneath
his domesticated demeanor and the yellow villain who threatens white
racial purity as a whole. Through such analysis, I suggest that the peril
indicated in Griffith's film is a manifestation of Hollywood orientalism
ideology within specific historical and social contexts.

If Rohmer incarnates the Yellow Peril through the body of Fu
Manchu, branded and remembered peculiarly by his skin color and by
mysteries grounded in his Oriental cultural roots and fostered in Chinatown, films like *Broken Blossoms* bring the warning to white households

through incorporating the racialized theme within a family drama. This particular cinematic representation shows the threat implied in the Fu Manchu stories and calls for more caution on the part of white society toward the yellow race. The film makes it clear to the (presumably white) viewers, at the time of its release, that the danger of the yellow men not only resides in Chinatown, but also extends to the endangerment of white homes and social stability at large. In focusing his story on romantic relationships, Griffith extracts the potential love and sexuality between a Yellow Man and a Caucasian child-woman from Burke's story but relegates the passion to a spiritual level and transforms the tale into a broken romance: namely, the Yellow Man's affection toward Lucy is presented as sensual love in Burke's narrative yet heightened into a form of holy worship in Griffith's film. The cinematic version thus limits the interracial relationships to an acceptable scope for the white American audience and in the process reflects the social perceptions of immigrants at the time.

As I mentioned earlier, beyond adapting the leading character of Cheng Huan from Burke's story, Griffith also creates a supporting role in *Broken Blossoms*, the Evil Eye, who expresses Asian males' sexual desire for and visible threat to white women in a more direct way. Through the duality, the film highlights the great danger from the yellow race, in both potential and palpable means. Even though Lillian Gish's marvelous portrayal of the pathetic figure Lucy empowers *Broken Blossoms* with sentimental elements, the film, as a whole, participates in the media's tendency toward orientalist representations of Asian male immigrants.

DUAL PORTRAYAL: HIDDEN PERIL IN THE EFFEMINATE VILLAIN

Based on Burke's fiction, the storyline of *Broken Blossoms* is set during the First World War in the Limehouse district—where the oriental neighborhood is located in London. The introductory subtitles in the film narrative address some of the important themes in Griffith's silent film at the point of departure. "It's a tale of temple bells sounding at sunset before the image of Buddha. It is a tale of love and lovers. It is a tale of tears."[40] Ostensibly, it is self-identified as a representation of the oriental culture embodied by temple bells and Buddha and as a sentimental melodrama about love and tragedy. An exotic Orient populated by Asian women, fortune-tellers, and crowded streets introduces the opening of the film, where Cheng Huan, wearing a decorated fine silk robe, enters the stage as one of the educated elite in China.

Cheng Huan initiates his journey to the West with a lofty ideal that he is about to enlighten the savage masses by taking "the glorious message of peace to the barbarous Anglo-Saxons, sons of turmoil and strife." His mission of uplifting the "uncivilized" and xenophobic British is soon smashed to pieces in the cruel reality, as the film cross-cuts to a scene on an "early morning in the Limehouse district of London, some years later. He is no longer the Buddhist advocate who tries to stop other people's quarreling and fighting on the street but an opium addict; his humble image almost merges into the heavy fog and darkness in Limehouse. His means of making a living in England is running a small oriental store. Not only the merchandise downstairs around the shopping counter sends forth Asian smells, but his living quarter upstairs is also filled with various items commonly taken as oriental: a small statue of Buddha, an incense burner, the scented tea, the ceramic cups, and the silk wall hanging, among others. The particular locus of identification leads the audience to the image of an exotic and (un)familiar East in London's Chinatown—the overly rehearsed trope and headquarters for the Orientals. The caption of the movie, as the side narrative, posits the Yellow Man as a "Chink shopkeeper." In point of fact, his name, "Cheng Huan," is never introduced by the film narrative or used by other characters to address him, but it is shown only on the sign on the wall outside his shop. To put in another way, his personal identification does not matter here; instead, always being referred to as the Yellow Man, his skin color is what matters the most.

Secluded as he is, the Yellow Man does not stand out as a single image of the Orient in Griffith's film. Rather, the yellow "Others" appear in groups at the opium den the leading character frequents: "Chinese, Malays, Lascars, where the Orient squats at the portals of the West." The Yellow Peril idea enjoys considerable currency in the films of this period; Chinatown or a district as such usually serves as the backdrop to impressions of evil and mystery: "the ominous shadow of an Oriental figure thrown against a wall, secret panels which slide back to reveal and inscrutable Oriental face, the huge shadow of a hand with tapering fingers and long pointed fingernails posed menacingly, the raised dagger appearing suddenly and unexpectedly."[41] In Griffith's film version, Limehouse is the region where the Asians live and entertain in compact space and the location where Lucy is fetishized by the Yellow Man and attacked by the Evil Eye.

Cheng Huan, the Yellow Man, is depicted as a mixture of the stereotypes of an emasculated Asian man. His appearance, demonstrated through his oriental dressing style, his timid gesture while he wanders on the foggy narrow streets, his frail figure, his pale face under the skullcap, and his dreamy facial expression with slant eyelids, enables him to be easily recognized as an emasculated yellow "Other." He embodies "the 'feminine' qualities linked in the Western imagination with a passive, carnal, occult, and duplicitous Asia."[42] The issue of the feminization of the Orient in cultural representations in the West has been raised by Said in 1979.[43] In 1985, Said reiterated orientalism in terms of gender more explicitly: "We can now see that Orientalism is a praxis of the same sort, albeit in different territories, as male gender dominance, or patriarchy, in metropolitan societies: the Orient was routinely described as feminine, its riches as fertile, its main symbols the sensual woman, the harem and the despotic—but curiously attractive—ruler. Moreover, Orientals like Victorian housewives were confined to silence and to unlimited enriching production."[44] The image of the Yellow Man is always shot with the Sartov long lens technique or with diffusing light to soften the lines of his face and body in order to portray an effeminate character. Moreover, his actions, such as walking back and forth on the street in a hunchbacked fashion, standing by the sidewalk with folded arms, and leaning on the wall huddling up, all weaken the sense of his masculinity. In striking contrast to the extremely masculine and patriarchal boxer, Battling Burrows, Cheng Huan is schematized to embody a desexualized image. His slender and delicate appearance as well as his timid attitude embodies what Renan defines as the image of the Asian male—"like those individuals who possess so little fecundity that, after a gracious childhood, they attain only the most mediocre virility."[45] Such a visual design perpetuates the commonly identified effeminacy of Asian man in American popular culture at that time. In this sense, I agree with Rich DeCrox's assertion that Richard Barthelmess's performance as the Yellow Man "who constantly squints his eyes and walks pigeon-toed for a so-called natural effect" is stereotypical and "almost embarrassing at times today."[46]

In *Broken Blossoms*, the Yellow Man's contact with Lucy is elucidated by his gaze at her. After her father goes drinking at the tavern, the abused girl timidly leaves their gloomy slum and ventures out for a shopping trip. At fifteen years old, she has to take care of all household chores and be a servant and a "punching bag" for her brutal father. Lucy is thrown into Burrows's life in a bundle of rags by "one of his girls." At home, there is no trace of parental love and care for her from her father, a tyrant prizefighter. Stepping out of the door of the cold and miserable hovel, Lucy has nowhere to escape her unfortunate destiny either. Her aunt shows her the hopeless abysm in marriage for women. "Whatever you do, dearie, don't get married." At the same time, the aunt herself is washing clothes, looking after the crying kids, and bearing her husband's reprimand. On the streets, the women of the night strongly warn Lucy against prostitution. Moreover, the Evil Eye strengthens the hostility and danger for Lucy from the society around her. Such a "child-woman" role, "victimized by her surroundings" is Lillian Gish's typical role in Griffith's films.[47] Between these parenthetical shots, the relatively deserted mises-en-scène on the street where Lucy is wandering further emphasizes her despair and lack of options.

It is at the window front of his shop that Lucy and the Yellow Man are framed in the same picture for the first time. This shot initiates the Yellow Man's fetishization of Lucy. Through the window, Cheng Huan, with a dreaming face, stares at her in an intoxicated way. The title tells us, "the Yellow Man watched Lucy often. The beauty which all Limehouse missed smote him to the heart." The Yellow Man is obsessed with his fantasies while Lucy, metaphorically embodied as the "small white blossom," functions as the object of his worshiping gaze. At this point, his emasculated body is still able to assure the audience of the purity of his love and avoids the transgression of lusty desire. At the same time, Lucy's vision is attracted by the doll displayed in the window. In my understanding, her gaze at the doll signifies a double meaning. On the one hand, it functions as a self-reflection, since she herself is a doll who exists passively for the purpose of being looked at. On the other hand, her adoration of the doll confirms the purity and innocence of her role as a child-woman in the film.

After Lucy's first appearance in her shopping trip around the oriental district, the film cuts back to the hovel where Lucy and her father live. After Burrows comes back from the tavern tempered by his manager's criticism of his involvements in alcohol and women, he finds an excuse to whip Lucy—the usual way for him to release anger or a grudge. Heavily beaten and having no asylum to which to turn, Lucy stumbles onto the dusky street before she loses consciousness at the counter in the oriental shop. The next shot is of Cheng Huan, who sits near the counter smoking after he returns from the noodle store for dinner. When he first notices Lucy lying on the floor, he takes it as one of his dream images. Then the camera provides a close shot of how he rubs his eyes, looks again carefully, and is shocked by the incredible reality: Lucy is right in front of him. He goes down on his knees near Lucy, who has just come back to consciousness, and tends her wound with water and tenderness. Without any trace of conversation or communication between them, the film features an intriguing flickering shot in which the Yellow Man, kneeling down beside Lucy, with his hands clasped, moves his torso toward Lucy. It seems that he attempts to kiss her, yet he retreats very quickly while she shows no awareness of his intention. Heretofore in the film, the plot confirms that the Yellow Peril is under control and it has been regulated within a moral scope of the ethics at the time. Nevertheless, it also presents a hint of the danger underneath. Given the fact that the Yellow Man's gaze targets a white child-woman and he even ventures to kiss her, his docility is not entirely deprived of the possible peril in this plotline. Even though he is represented as being effeminate in Griffith's cinematic narrative, his yearnings toward the young white woman remain, which implies, at a certain level, a tamed yet potential jeopardy to Caucasian society. To express such an indication as the Yellow Peril in a more explicit way, the film features another scene in the narrative where the Yellow Man endeavors to kiss Lucy, his second attempt. Being saved and sheltered by Cheng Huan, Lucy takes refuge for a short while at his small living quarter upstairs, where she encounters "the first gentleness she has ever known."

In this attic full of oriental scent and decorations, a particularly fascinating scene takes place. In this scene, Lucy is sitting in bed, wearing a fine silk robe and beautiful ribbons with a variety of oriental ornaments decorating her. She is treated as a princess here; her hidden beauty and glory shine in the narrow space. There seems to be no proper way to adequately express the Yellow Man's ecstasy. "Oh Lily flowers and plum blossoms! Oh silver streams and dim-starred skies!" To present an angelic image of the child-woman, the camera always shoots Lillian Gish from above. For the second time, the doll as a symbolic self-reflection of Lucy functions to emphasize her innocence and purity. After the Yellow Man hands Lucy the doll, which she had yearned for from the window display, the thrilled child-woman asks: "why are you so kind to me, Chinky?" Ostensibly, she is not aware of the sexual threat a male might impose on her but she does identify Cheng Huan as an "Other" marked by his skin color. After transforming Lucy into his "oriental" princess, Cheng Huan, standing beside the bed, arches his body toward Lucy as if he intends to kiss her. Here, the camera shows a close-up of Cheng Huan's fascinated face looming closer and closer to Lucy, who is sitting in his bed holding a doll in her hands. Lucy's reaction is to withdraw to the other side of the room. We can see her wide-open eyes and her terrified face. Soon the camera pulls away. Cheng Huan retreats from the girl and ends up kissing only the hem of her sleeves: another aborted trial. The subtitles further assure the audience of his pure intention and restrict his love to a "platonic level." They tell us that in the Yellow Man's romantic fantasies, Lucy is idealized as his goddess and the purist "White Blossom," rather than as a sexually attractive female body. Huan admires her and serves her humbly. In my view, the film represents his obsession with Lucy more as fetishism than as love.

If the Yellow Peril is indicated in an implicit and at times paradoxical way through the leading character of Cheng Huan, it is expressed on a more tangible level through the supporting role, the Evil Eye. The character Cheng Huan in the film is adapted, though transformed, from Burke's short story, whereas the Evil Eye is Griffith's original creation in the cinematic representation. The supplemental but also significant role serves as a counterpart to the feminized character Cheng Huan.

Being complementary to the potential yet domesticated danger represented by Cheng Huan, the Evil Eye, like a descendant of Dr. Fu Manchu, signifies the direct sexual threat to Caucasian women from the yellow race. Not only does this figure notice Lucy, the wretched pretty girl without protection in Limehouse, but he also targets her as a sexual object that he may take advantage of. The Evil Eye's appearance on screen starts with his malicious gaze at the white female teenager when she walks down the street alone. His vision follows Lucy's steps in her grocery shopping to the florist's shop where she yearns for the small blossoms but lacks enough tinfoil to trade for one. The gender dynamics between the subject and the object of his gaze, namely the active and the passive, are interwoven with the subplot of the threat imposed by yellow men on white womanhood. Indeed, the Evil Eye functions as one of the elements that formulates Lucy's despairing situation in Limehouse. The cliché-ridden devices of stage and costume design intensify the danger surrounding Evil Eye as the yellow villain who reminds the audience of the jeopardizing "Others" with his different skin color. In this sense, Griffith exaggerates the peril surrounding Lucy's social environment through positioning the poor helpless Caucasian girl as the target of the oriental's sexual desire.

At the shopping scene when Lucy timidly walks on the gloomy street, she is followed by the Evil Eye. His vicious gaze trails her with the slight malignant smile at the corner of his mouth. Boldly, he blocks her way on the sidewalk, disrupts her, and plays with the hem of her clothes tantalizingly. The girl feels caught in trouble and panics, not knowing what to do. The tension is resolved by the Yellow Man's interceding between the Evil Eye and Lucy that releases the girl from the Evil Eye's villainous intention and action.

In her encounter with the two yellow characters, Lucy is repeatedly connected to white blossoms. The tiny white flower represents the female teenager in a symbolic way: pretty and frail. The Evil Eye's action of toying with a branch of the white blossom, an embodiment of the young girl, contains a visible assault on her. To put it another way, through the cinematic design, where the virginal blossoms are played with in the Evil Eye's hands, the movie shows the Evil Eye's motive and sexual attack on Lucy in a metaphorical way. The pure white blossoms here echo those in the scene where Cheng Huan imagines his holy love for his sacred virgin Lucy in his attic. As a symbol of the girl, the blossoms are admired by Cheng Huan, yet almost trampled by the Evil Eye. Thus in *Broken Blossoms*, Griffith's portrayal of the two yellow characters, Cheng Huan and the Evil Eye, reflects and simultaneously resonates with white American perceptions of Asian men. The cinematic representation of Asian immigrants has roots in the particular historical and political context of that time period while its own creative output too is consistent with and reinforces the social phenomenon of racial discrimination.

When Lucy's father, Battling Burrows, is informed by a spy of his daughter's whereabouts, he is infuriated. "He discovers parental rights. A Chink after his kid! He'll learn him!" Through these subtitles, the social taboo against miscegenation is raised in an explicit way and brought to the forefront of the tension. After Lucy's tyrant father finds her at the "Yellow Man's" place, he smashes everything into pieces in a rage, strips off Lucy's silk robe, and forces Lucy to change back to her rags. Full of fear, Lucy cries out, "T'ain't nothing wrong?" "T'ain't nothing wrong?" Even this seemingly naïve young girl shares awareness of the great danger of the social taboo—miscegenation. Her staying at Cheng Huan's place implies, at least for her, that a "Chinky" poses no sexual threat, since the yellow figure is emasculated. To this extent, Griffith intrigues the audience with the exotic fantasy and possibility of the unusual relationships between Cheng Huan and Lucy but keeps the love tale on a spiritual level, thus assuring that his narrative remains within the acceptable moral boundaries at that time.

Toward the end of the story, the film further intensifies the drama through a series of crosscutting: while Burrows is shattering everything in Cheng Huan's living quarters in outrage, the Yellow Man is out on the street purchasing flowers for Lucy; when Burrows is dragging his daughter along the foggy street back to their hovel, the Yellow Man throws himself down to the floor among the debris in his attic crying for the loss of his "Lily flower"; when the father is beating helpless Lucy to death, Cheng Huan pulls out a pistol from his suitcase and hurries to rescue his princess.

Yet instead of portraying the Yellow Man as a hero who is able to reclaim the female protagonist and win back her heart, the film ends tragically. The first and only direct confrontation between the white and the yellow happens in the hovel with Lucy's body lying beside them. Regardless of their contrasting physical strength—Burrows's angular masculinity and Cheng Huan's soft femininity—the Yellow Man pulls the trigger and shockingly executes the white working-class patriarch. After carrying Lucy's body to his attic and performing Buddhist worship for his deceased beauty, Cheng Huan commits suicide by the side of Lucy, which forms the final cadence of the film. Before confronting the tyrant Burrows, Cheng Huan gets himself a gun, a perfect symbol of violence and danger: the lethal weapon hidden the whole time inside his suitcase in his home reinforces the concealed threat to the larger society from the yellow race. Domesticated and subservient as the Yellow Man might be, the peril branded into his yellow skin never disappears.

CROSS-RACIAL CASTING, FILM ADAPTATION: SOCIAL CONTEXT

The problematic "visual racism" of the film *Broken Blossoms* begins with the fact that Griffith cast two Caucasian actors to play the Yellow Man and the Evil Eye. Both Richard Barthelmess and Edward Peil Sr. perform the roles of stereotypical Asian male characters through their dress style and certain ways of behavior. Both characters wear oriental-styled jackets, skullcaps, and cloth shoes. They usually walk with their hands folded inside their sleeves and their backs hunched. Thus the designs of costume and stage property are branded by racial stereotypes. Moreover, through employing such choreography consistent with the social perception of Asian males from this historical period and from the loci around London's Chinatown of the 1910s, these Caucasian actors can be recognized as Asians by the audience at the time. Given the fact that during that period most American natives had little opportunity to meet Asian-immigrants who usually lived in their own ethnic communities isolated from mainstream American society, it is reasonable for the film audience of the times to interpret the characters on screen as the yellow "Others."

The cross-racial casting in *Broken Blossoms* provides a strand to challenge the racial discrimination in early American film production. In fact, the stratification between white actors and those of color is by no means a distinct phenomenon in Griffith's film production. Most of the well-known Asian characters in early American cinema, including Fu Manchu and Charlie Chan, are played by Caucasian actors. There were a few actors and actresses of Asian heritage who pursued their career in show business during the silent film era, but most of them had little opportunity to play the leading roles. "In the film industry there is a race-specific consciousness which segregates roles per se into those for whites, on the one side, and those for Asians, on the other side."[48] As an exception, Sessue Hayakawa, an actor of Japanese origin, played leading roles in American films during that period. The common situation, however, has been that "major roles or characters have been reserved for the whites and minor roles or characters often open to, but not necessarily reserved for, the Asian actors."[49] The positions usually "reserved" for Asian and Asian American performers are limited to certain supporting or unimportant roles in the movies. In choosing a cross-racial cast for *Broken Blossoms* to represent the two "yellow" men and the danger their existence poses for white society, Griffith becomes one of the partakers in the casting division according to skin color. Viewed from this perspective, this film participates in Hollywood orientalism in the light of the racial restraint shown in its casting.

Also, Griffith's choice of cast is consistent with the filmmaking conventions in the early twentieth century that forbade physical intimacy between a Caucasian and an Asian on screen. In keeping with the taboo against miscegenation, Griffith also made considerable revisions in the film narrative during the process of adapting the love tale from Burke's story. Orphaned in infancy, Burke himself spent several years near the Limehouse district where he was fascinated by street life. Based on his acquaintance with an old Chinese man as a youth, Burke gained knowledge of what he called, "all the beauty and all the evil of the heart of Asia; its cruelty, its grace and its wisdom."[50] His attitude toward and the debatable accuracy of the depiction of Chinese immigrants in London reflected in his writing will lead to another full-length analysis.

What is of importance for my argument here is Burke's telling of an audacious interracial romance in the short story that opens his collection *Limehouse Nights: Tales of Chinatown* (1917) and that Griffith reshapes into a more ethereal melodrama in response to the social restrictions and the customary rules in film production of the early twentieth century. In the original text, Burke emphasizes the emotional communication between the Yellow Man and Lucy, even though the Yellow Man speaks broken English and they have no effective linguistic vehicle to converse with each other. Given the hindrance in language, Burke emphasizes the physical contact and mutual understanding between the two characters in his fiction. The Yellow Man finds Lucy on a divan after she's been flogged and locked out of doors by her drunken father and led into the scene by girls "in that region": "He sat by her. He looked at her—reverently yet passionately. He *touched* her—wistfully yet eagerly. He locked a finger in her wondrous hair. She did not start away; she did not tremble. . . . She *clung to* him, and he to her. She held his strong arms in both of hers as they *crouched* on the divan, and *nestled* her cheek against his coat" (emphasis added).[51] This is the first time in the story where the Yellow Man and Lucy appear in the same frame in Burke's story. Barely speaking English, the Yellow Man is able to ask Lucy's name and age and tell her his own experiences. They chat in the tavern while leaning on the cushion and cuddling before they mount the stairs to his room slowly and softly. After they reach his place: "[w]ith a bird-like movement, she looked up at him—her face alight, her tiny hands upon his coat—clinging, wondering, trusting. He took her hand and kissed it; repeated the kiss upon her cheek and lip and little bosom, twining his fingers in her hair. Docilely, and echoing the smile of his lemon lips in a way that thrilled him almost to laughter, she returned his kisses impetuously, gladly."[52] From such bold description of the physical intimacy of the Yellow Man and Lucy, Burke's version on the one hand presents a love romance crossing racial boundaries for the reader while Griffith's film adaptation on the other emphasizes Cheng Huan's wishful fantasy of love and aborted attempts for a kiss instead of mutual contact and communication with Lucy.

To juxtapose Burke's and Griffith's versions in a comparative framework, the film is an obvious and distinct transformation of the short story. To follow Frantz Fanon's statement that "[t]he white man is sealed in his whiteness" and "[t]he black man is in his blackness,"[53] I propose that the yellow man is sealed in his yellowness in *Broken Blossoms*. Griffith has the awareness to protect, or at least to follow, such a racial division in American society in the early twentieth century. From this point of view, the film is "a drama of impossible desires" that "can only end in death."[54] The transgressive actions of the leading characters—the Yellow Man's fantasizing about a white girl and Lucy's trusting and taking refuge with a chink—predestine the tragedy of the story. Given the historical and social background around 1919, the film is a product of its time as well as a reflection of the social perception of a certain ethnic group, here Asians and Asian Americans.

Regardless of its distinctive characteristics, cinematic theory and practice were undoubtedly influenced by the larger society's trends and taboos. In turn, films usually reinforced or distributed social norms and ethos of the times. It is from such a perspective that I consider Griffith's *Broken Blossoms* a film that belongs to Hollywood's orientalist narrative tradition and to "the system of signification that represents non-Western cultures to Western recipients in the course of Western imperialism and operates visually as well as narratologically to subject 'the Orient' to ideological manipulation."[55] In *Broken Blossoms*, Griffith transforms the stereotypical perceptions of the Asian "Other" into a sentimental melodrama. What his visual narrative presents to American viewers of the early twentieth century is their preoccupation with the idea that immigrants from Asia pose a yellow danger to white society. Yet Griffith fractures the Yellow Peril theme into two dimensions which represent Asian males either as submissive, feminized, and silenced (the Yellow Man) or as evil, threatening, and insidious (the Evil Eye). In the film, the former implies the menace under control but still harbors the potential to undertake an actual act of violence such as portrayed in the scene with the gun which Cheng Huan uses at the end. The latter action surfaces as a visible, explicit danger to Caucasian women. Thus the two brands of danger act as complimentary counterparts, which create a cinematic duality of the Yellow Peril. Thus, *Broken Blossoms* becomes, like its predecessor *The Birth of a Nation*, a film of "signification" that reflects stereotyped social perceptions of a racial group, in this case Asian immigrants, particularly male.

If scrutinizing the subtle portrayals of the Yellow Peril in *Broken Blossoms* is my way of participating in the scholarly challenge to orientalism, then the direction for further studies is to illuminate a brief overview of the anti-oriental productions in filmmaking and criticism during the past decades, loosely labeled "Asian American cinema." Such a reorganization and conceptualization of Asian American cinema grew out of the Asian American movement of the late 1960s and 1970s. On the one hand, "it is unrealistic to assume that the distorted image of Asian-Americans will be eradicated readily or overnight" since they "are embedded in people's minds through those socializing institutions which mold people's ideas."[56] On the other hand, Asian American communities demand, "the images of their lives and history be presented correctly, positively, with accurate historical perspectives through the mass media."[57] The institution of the media needs new contributions to redress the orientalist portrayals of the Yellow Peril in films like *Broken Blossoms*.

In her overview of the cinema culture inaugurated by Asian Americans in the 1970s, Renne Tajima observes Asian American cinema as "socially committed," created by people bound by race as well as "cultural and historical relations," and "a common experience of western domination."[58] Also in North America in 1990, Asian-Canadian artists organized an exhibition, entitled "Yellow Peril: Reconsidered," that includes "a diverse selection of experimental and documentary photo, film and video work produced by Asian Canadians."[59] With its title representing their visual portrayal of the orientalist stereotypes imposed on Asians living in North America, the collection is a "testimony" to the creation of counter visions. One of the participants of this event, filmmaker Midi Onodera, expresses the political stance she takes in her career: "I want to encourage and challenge myself and my audiences to reconsider our own prejudices concerning homophobia, sexism, classism, racism, and the 'Yellow Peril.' "[60] My analysis here is meant to provoke and to encourage more interrogation of orientalism in media and more critical engagement with Asian-American cinema.

NOTES

I am grateful to the editors of the collection: Elizabeth Crespo, Glyne Griffith, and Linden Lewis for their comments on an earlier version of this essay.

1. "Directors Guild Retires Griffith Award for Racial Stereotypes," *Jet*, January 10, 2002, 62.

2. Ibid.

3. Ibid.

4. Michael Rogin, "The Sword Became a Flashing Vision", D. W. Griffith's The Birth of a Nation," *Representations* 9 (Winter 1985) 150–95. For additional discussions on and reviews of *Broken Blossoms* as an "art film," see Dudley Andrew, *"Broken Blossoms:* The Art and the Eros of a Perverse Text," 81–90; Lewis Jacobs, *Rise of the American Film*, 389–90; Vance Kepley Jr., "Griffith's *Broken Blossoms,"* 37–47; Robert G. Lee, *Orientals*, 127; George C. Pratt, *Spellbound in Darkness*, 250–51.

5. The issue of melodrama has incurred considerable studies among film scholars. For the exploration of *Broken Blossoms* and melodrama, see Robert Lang, *American Film Melodrama*, 90–104. In this essay, I will focus on the problem of representing the marginalized people in terms of race, rather than employ a full study to examine the genre of Griffith's film.

6. Lee, *Orientals*, 128; Kepley, "Griffith's *Broken Blossoms,"* 39; Roger Ebert, *"Broken Blossoms,"* January 23, 2000.

7. Rick DeCrox, Review of *Broken Blossoms*, 94.

8. Ebert, *"Broken Blossoms,"* January 23, 2000.

9. *DVD Journal, "Broken Blossoms."*

10. Ed Gonzalez, Review of *Broken Blossoms.*

11. William Wu attributed the initiation of the term "Yellow Peril" to the Mongol invasions of Europe in the thirteenth century, led by Genghis Khan and his descendants (William Wu, *Yellow Peril Reconsidered* (Vancouver: On the Cutting Edge Productions Society, 1990), 9–10. In this essay I used the term in the context of Orientalism in contemporary scholarly discussion without tracing its genealogy in history.

12. Ibid., 209.

13. Darrell Y. Hamamoto and Sandra Liu, eds., *Countervisions*, 1.

14. Jun Xing, *Asian America Through the Lens*, 10.

15. Lee, *Orientals*, 2.

16. In his discussion on Asian Americans in American popular culture, Robert Lee defines the "Oriental" as "an alien body and a threat to the American national family" (8). He categorizes this group into six major images as racial paradigms—"the pollutant, the coolie, the deviant, the yellow peril, the model minority, and the gook," each of which further generates "a wide array of specific images" (8).

17. Nick Browne, "Orientalism as an Ideological Form," 23–31.

18. Homi Bhabha, "The Other Question," 75.

19. Edward Said, *Orientalism*, 10, 13–14.

20. Hamamoto and Liu, *Countervisions*, ix.

21. Ronald Takaki, *Strangers from a Different Shore*, 102.

22. Said, *Orientalism*, 3, 7.

23. Ibid., 1.

24. Ibid., 26.

25. Dorothy B. Jones, *The Portrayal of China and India*, 13.

26. Browne, "Orientalism as an Ideological Form," 29.

27. Edward Ifkovic, "Some Notes on the Ethnic Dimension," 13.

28. Gina Marchetti, *Romance and the "Yellow Peril,"* 16.

29. Said, *Orientalism*, 24–25.

30. Matthew Bernstein and Gaylyn Studlar, eds., *Visions of the East*, 2, 5.

31. Wu, *The Yellow Peril*, 1.

32. Ibid.

33. Eugene Franklin Wong, *On Visual Media Racism*, 22–23.

34. Eugene Franklin Wong, "The Early Years," 56–59; Wu, *The Yellow Peril*, 164–74.

35. Sax Rohmer, *The Insidious Doctor Fu-Manchu*, 1.

36. Wu, *The Yellow Peril*, 164.

37. Ibid., 174; Wong, "The Early Years," 59–61.

38. Wu, *The Yellow Peril*, 182.

39. Ibid.

40. All citations without source of origin in the essay are subtitles from *Broken Blossoms*, Griffith, 1919.

41. Jones, *The Portrayal of China and India*, 24–25.

42. Marchetti, *Romance and the "Yellow Peril,"* 35.

43. Charles O'Brien, "The 'Cinema Colonial' of 1930s France," 227 n. 10.

44. Edward Said, "Orientalism Reconsidered," 103.

45. Said, *Orientalism*, 149.

46. DeCrox, Review of *Broken Blossoms*, 94–95.
47. Richard A. Blake, "Lillian Gish," 14.
48. Wong, *On Visual Media Racism*, 11–12.
49. Ibid., 13.
50. "Thomas Burke, 1886–1945."
51. Thomas Burke, "The Chink and the Child," 24–25.
52. Ibid., 27.
53. Frantz Fanon, *Black Skin, White Masks*, 9.
54. Lang, *American Film Melodrama*, 91.
55. Rey Chow, "Film and Cultural Identity," 171.
56. Christine Choy, "Images of Asian Americans," 147.
57. Ibid., 155.
58. Renée Tajima, "Moving the Image," 12.
59. Wu, *Yellow Peril Reconsidered*, 6.
60. Midi Onodera, "A Displaced View," 31.

BIBLIOGRAPHY

Andrew, Dudley. "*Broken Blossoms:* the Art and the Eros of a Perverse Text." *Quarterly Review of Film Studies* 6, no. 1 (Winter 1981): 81–90.

Bernstein, Matthew, and Gaylyn Studlar, eds. *Visions of the East: Orientalism in Film.* New Brunswick, NJ: Rutgers University Press, 1997.

Bhabha, Homi, "The Other Question: Stereotype, Discrimination and the Discourse of Colonialism." In *The Location of Culture*, by Homi Bhabha. London: Routledge, 1994, 66–84.

Blake, Richard A. "Lillian Gish: A Passing." *America* 168, no. 10 (March 20, 1993): 14.

Broken Blossoms. Directed by D. W. Griffith. 1919; D.W. Griffith Corp. for United Artists.

Browne, Nick. "Orientalism as An Ideological Form: American Film Theory in the Silent Period." *Wide Angle* 11, no. 4 (October 1989): 23–31.

Burke, Thomas. "The Chink and the Child." In *Limehouse Nights: Tales of Chinatown*, by Thomas Burke. New York: Robert M. McBride & Company, 1917, 13–37.

Chow, Rey. "Film and Cultural Identity." In *The Oxford Guide to Film Studies*, edited by John Hill and Pamela Church Gibson. Oxford: Oxford University Press, 1998, 169–75.

Choy, Christine. "Images of Asian Americans in Films and Television." In *Ethnic Images in American Film and Television*, edited by Randall M. Miller. Philadelphia: Balch Institute, 1978, 145–55.

DeCrox, Rick. Review of *Broken Blossoms*. *Journal of Popular Film and Television* 22, no. 2 (Summer 1994): 94–95.

"Directors Guild Retires Griffith Award for Racial Stereotypes." *Jet* 97. 5. January 10, 2000, 62.

DVD Journal. "Broken Blossoms or The Yellow Man and the Girl." *DVD Journal Quick Reviews*. http://www.dvdjournal.com/quickreviews/b/brokenblossoms.q.shtml.

Ebert, Roger. *"Broken Blossoms." Chicago Sun-Times.* January 23, 2000. http://www.suntimes.com/ebert/greatmovies/brokenblossoms.html.

Fanon, Frantz. *Black Skin, White Masks.* Translated by Charles Lam Markmann. New York: Grove Press, 1968. Originally published in Paris, France, as *Peau Noire, Masques Blancs,* 1952.

Gonzalez, Ed. Review of *Broken Blossoms. Slant Magazine.Com.* http://www.slantmagazine.com/film/film_review.asp?ID=760.

Hamamoto, Darrell Y., and Sandra Liu, eds. *Countervisions: Asian American Film Criticism.* Philadelphia: Temple University Press, 2000.

Ifkovic, Edward. "Some Notes on the Ethnic Dimension in the Silent Film." *MELUS* 4, no. 2 (Autumn 1977): 13–14.

Jacobs, Lewis. *The Rise of the American Film: A Critical History.* New York: Teachers College Press, Columbia University, 1968.

Jones, Dorothy B. *The Portrayal of China and India on the American Screen, 1896–1955.* Cambridge, MA: Center of International Studies, MIT, 1955.

Kepley, Vance, Jr. "Griffith's *Broken Blossoms* and the Problem of Historical Specificity." *Quarterly Review of Film Studies* 3 (Winter 1978): 37–47.

Lang, Robert. *American Film Melodrama: Griffith, Vidor, Minnelli.* Princeton, NJ: Princeton University Press, 1989.

Lee, Robert G. *Orientals: Asian American in Popular Culture.* Philadelphia: Temple University Press, 1999.

Marchetti, Gina. *Romance and the "Yellow Peril": Race, Sex, and Discursive Strategies in Hollywood Fiction.* Berkeley: University of California Press, 1993.

O'Brien, Charles. "The 'Cinema Colonial' of 1930s France: Film Narration as Spatial Practice." In *Visions of the East: Orientalism in Film,* edited by Matthew Bernstein and Gaylyn Studlar. New Brunswick, NJ: Rutgers University Press, 1997, 207–31.

Onodera, Midi. "A Displaced View: What Are We Reconsidering about the 'Yellow Peril'?" In *Yellow Peril Reconsidered,* edited by Paul Wong. Vancouver, Canada: On the Cutting Edge Productions Society, 1990, 28–31.

Pratt, George C. *Spellbound in Darkness: A History of the Silent Film.* Greenwich, CT: New York Graphic Arts Society, 1973.

Rohmer, Sax. *The Insidious Doctor Fu-Manchu.* 1913. New York: Pyramid, 1961.

Said, Edward. *Orientalism.* New York: Vintage Books, 1979.

———. "Orientalism Reconsidered." *Cultural Critique* 1 (Fall 1985): 89–107.

Tajima, Renée. "Moving the Image: Asian American Independent Filmmaking 1970–1990." In *Moving the Image: Independent Asian Pacific American Media Arts,* edited by Rusell Leong. Los Angeles: UCLA Asian American Studies Center and Visual Communications, South California Asian American Studies Center, 1991, 10–33.

Takaki, Ronald. *Strangers from a Different Shore: A History of Asian Americans.* Boston: Little Brown, 1989.

"Thomas Burke, 1886–1945." Database University of Mass, Amherst, Contemporary Authors. http://web7.infotrac.galegroup.com/.

Wong, Eugene Franklin. "The Early Years: Asians in the American Films Prior to World War II (excerpt, with a new introduction)." In *Screening Asian Americans,* edited by Peter X. Feng. New Brunswick, NJ: Rutgers University Press, 2002, 53–70.

—————. *On Visual Media Racism: Asians in the American Motion Pictures.* New York: Arno Press, 1978.

Wong, Paul, ed. *Yellow Peril Reconsidered.* Vancouver, Canada: On the Cutting Edge Productions Society, 1990.

Wu, William F. *The Yellow Peril: Chinese Americans in American Fiction 1850–1940.* Hamden: CT, Archon Books, 1982.

Xing, Jun. *Asian America Through the Lens: History, Representations, and Identity.* Walnut Creek, CA: Altamira Press, 1998.

Past as Prologue: Rewriting and Reclaiming the Marked Body in Michelle Cliff's *Abeng* and Margaret Cezair-Thompson's *The True History of Paradise*

Carmen Gillespie

> . . . there be a mark set upon these people, which will hardly ever be wiped off . . . For what can poor people do, that are without Letters and Numbers, which is the soul of all business that is acted by Mortals, upon the Globe of this World.
>
> —Richard Ligon, *A True and Exact History of the Island of Barbados*, 1657

IN ONE OF THE EARLIEST TEXTS WRITTEN IN AND ABOUT THE Caribbean, *A True and Exact History of Barbadoes* [*sic*], Richard Ligon pens detailed descriptions of the enslaved African population. His account reveals the extent to which the black Caribbean body has been from the beginning a sight of ideological inscription: "there be a mark set upon these people, which will hardly ever be wiped off."[1] In Ligon's iteration, the black body bears the indelible narrative markings of inferiority and subordination. As he asserts earlier, "what can poor people do, that are without Letters and Numbers, which is the soul of all business that is acted by Mortals, upon the Globe of this World."[2] With his presumption of the primacy of literacy, Ligon misrepresents the African slaves as inherently incapable of participating in the meaningful commerce of the world and therefore as "near beast as may be."[3] They are, in Ligon's definition, without the capacity to write and therefore self-define. From Ligon's time onward the mark, the "diabolic die," of race becomes the central signifier in Caribbean discourses and the primary determinant of its various social, political, and economic hierarchies.[4]

As Du Bois noted in his controversial essay "The Conservation of Races," "the grosser physical differences of color, hair and bone go but a short way toward explaining the different roles which groups of men have played in Human Progress, yet . . . they have divided human beings into races, which, while they perhaps transcend scientific definition, are clearly defined to the eye of the Historian and Sociologist."[5] Perhaps Du Bois could have added novelist to his list of discerning visionaries. In their novels *Abeng* and *The True History of Paradise* Jamaican-born authors Michelle Cliff and Margaret Cezair-Thompson attempt to discern, define, and reread the marked body in the complex context of the Jamaican social landscape. Their characterizations represent an overt attempt to destabilize claims for truth made by "authorities" such as Richard Ligon, claims often asserted in the very titles of so-called historical accounts.

One of the characters in *The True History of Paradise*, an ancestor of the protagonist Jean Landing, directly confronts the authenticity of these narratives. "It is supposed to be a True History based upon some time . . . I am certain every word is a lie. . . . These books hurt me. They are cracked mirrors which break the paradise in my mind."[6] Cliff and Cezair-Thompson challenge the construct of Jamaica as island paradise through the internal and external reflections of their protagonists. The "paradise" in the minds of their characters bears little resemblance to those articulated by the early narrators of Caribbean life. The Jamaican settings created in both novels undermine traditional notions of paradise, while simultaneously establishing this postlapsarian world as spiritual, psychological, and physical home for the protagonists. The Jamaica of these novels deconstructs traditional Western polarities. "The history of our island is a history of hell. It is also a history of grace terrestrial."[7] The Jamaica configured in these novels and represented through the experiential realities of the protagonists exists simultaneously as heaven and hell—as the space in between.

Fragmenting the notion of history as monolithic and linear, *Abeng* and *The True History of Paradise* utilize fiction in order to dissect the hegemonic inaccuracy of the "objective" male gaze of narrators like Ligon and to reconfigure Caribbean histories through the physical subjectivities of the novels' female characters. Critics such as Alison Easton maintain that there is an important theoretical distinction between the metaphoric conception of the body as a site of inscription and the project and objective of fiction whose primary concern is with the literary (re)membering of black bodies within their historical contexts. According to Easton, writing the body as articulated by white feminist theorists such as Cixous and Irigaray becomes "problematic in the face of the material context of both slavery in the Americas and a tribal Africa which sold Africans to the slavers."[8] Analysis of the black and female Caribbean body is not "possible without first consciously and directly subverting the white traditions of signification and those narratives they call history."[9] Both Cliff and Cezair-Thompson deliberately foreground the black female body[10] as the terrain upon which the violence and disjuncture of Caribbean histories can most effectively be understood; however, they resist conceptualization of the black female body as object by providing a view from within that ruptured and rent, yet surviving, humanity.

Throughout the novels *Abeng* and *The True History of Paradise* the various corporeal characterizations that inhabit and give flesh to the texts function not only as metaphorization of the legacies of colonization, enslavement, and neocolonization, but also as signposts for a libratory, albeit fictive, reclamation of the lost selves—the histories—these physical bodies represent. In part, the project of these texts is rooted in an effort to excavate, to unbury, the forgotten, officially uninscripted black woman and to (re)tell her story. As conduit for the retelling of the lives of generations of Jamaicans, the protagonists of the texts are physically marked in a language that can only accurately be read through the genesis of an alternative to the interpretive lens ground and distorted by racialized constructions, class constraints, and misremembered memories. These texts engage what Katherine McKittrick calls "the chaotic in between-ness of black womanhood in order to embrace discourses and spaces of 'elsewhere' and possibility, while also acknowledging sites of racism, sexism, memory and struggle."[11] Although these texts are fictional, they represent an important interruption in the homogenizing and distorted discourses about race, gender, identity, and nationhood and contribute another plane, a black female subjectivity, to the multifaceted embodiments of Caribbean identities.

The protagonists of *Abeng* and *The True History of Paradise*, Clare Savage and Jean Landing are narrators who improvisationally weave together multigenre tapestries. Their stories "remind us that it is fanciful to believe that broken threads of human stories will rearrange themselves into a weave of comfortable social harmony."[12] Clare and Jean's fragmented renderings result in narratives that more closely approximate the polyvocality of the Jamaican past. As Cliff has asserted, the "work has to do with revising: revising the written record, what passes as the official version of history, and inserting those lives that have been left out."[13] Through creation of the protagonists' subjective consciousness within the racially, historically, and gender-marked body, Cliff and Cezair-Thompson contextualize, design, and "write the body in ways which are both new and yet related to culture and history."[14] Structurally these texts disrupt the premise of linear time and, through the texts' elliptical and cyclical presentation of temporality, render the individual and collective memories of both Clare and Jean as transcendent and representational.

Cliff and Cezair-Thompson's narrative structures also demonstrate Toni Morrison's definition of "rememory" as illustrated in her novel *Beloved*.

> my rememory. You know. Some things you forget. Other things you never do. But it's not. Places, places are still there. If a house burns down, it's gone, but the place—the picture of it—stays, and not just in my rememory, but out there, in the world. What I remember is a picture floating around out there outside my head. I mean, even if I don't think it, even if I die, the picture of what I did, or knew, or saw is still out there. Right in the place where it happened.[15]

The perceived realities and temporal fluidities of these novels provide access to familial and communal knowledge. This strategy enables a rewriting of history that allows for multiple subjectivities; subjectivities that are expressed through the protagonists' negotiations with their bodies vis-à-vis history, narrative, race, class, and gender. "Black women's subjectivities and bodies are processes, acts and enactments that are contested and conjunctural rather than oppositional and static."[16] Reinterpreting meanings of the imprinted historical experience on the bodies of the characters in *Abeng* and *No Telephone to Heaven* occurs most significantly as a result of the authors' textual renderings of physically oppositional parings. These pairings seed the protagonists' struggles against the predeterminacy of their marked bodies. Clare and Jean act to undermine the meanings imposed upon their lives by the hierarchies of history.

Both *Abeng* and *No Telephone to Heaven* center protagonists who are racially mixed. Indeed these women characters are a panoply of racial categorizations. Like Jamaica herself, they are at once black, white, Chinese, East Indian, Carib, and Arawak. Despite this constitutional hybridity, both Clare and Jean are caught in the midst of cultural obsessions with racial definition and categorization. Clare Savage, for example, uncomfortably inhabits the interstices between distinct racial classifications. "The Black or white. Both perhaps. Her father told her she was white. But she knew that her mother was not. Who would she choose were she given the choice? . . . She was of both dark and light. Pale and deeply colored. . . . The Black or the white? A choice would be expected of her, she thought."[17] Clare has the option of choosing to identify herself as black and, concomitantly, to accept marginality. Although Clare ultimately defines herself as black, the fact of her choice is a luxury that a person defined by appearance as black can never experience. Clare's mixed race heritage manifests in caste privilege.

Similarly, Jean Landing, the protagonist of *The True History of Paradise*, has a complex relationship with racial identification. Within her family she is subordinate because of her dark skin. Jean's mother, Monica, sees her as "scrawny and dark, darker than anyone in Monica's family."[18] Jean's eyes, however, reveal the myriad of races that inhabit her person. "People always commented on her eyes. They were slanted like Cherry's [her Chinese and black grandmother], but unusually large and hazel-colored, subtly changing from brown to green."[19] The chameleonlike mutability of Jean's eyes reflects the changing Jamaican landscape of the 1970s as well as her own variegated racial legacy, yet, Jean is considered to be black: "among the varying shades of white, yellow, and brown faces [of her family], . . .—Jean was the only one that could unquestionably be called black."[20] Jean and Clare occupy oppositional positionalities in the Jamaican intraracial class hierarchies. Grappling with the complexity of racial identity is one of the primary catalysts of both Clare's and Jean's quests for self-discovery. Both girls come to terms with the various significations of their skin color through intimate relationships with characters who are physically opposite in appearance, but who function as doppelgängers in their influential sculpting of both Clare's and Jean's identities.

Both Cliff and Cezair-Thompson partner their protagonists with best friends who, through their physical difference but developmental and psychological compatibility, motivate Clare and Jean's development of autonomy. Clare's doppelgänger and childhood best friend is Zoe. Through her relationship with Zoe, Clare begins to understand the historical and contemporary significations of her skin and the primary and deterministic role they play in her life.

This was a friendship—a paring of two girls—. . . and . . . their games and make-believe might have seemed to some entirely removed from what was real in the girls' lives. Their lives of light and dark—which was the one overwhelming reality. . . . To the girls, for a time, this was their real world— . . . The real world—that is the world outside country—could be just as dreamlike as the world of make-believe—on this island which did not know its own history.[21]

The dreamscape of the Jamaican country is a place where the histories represented by both Clare and Zoe are simultaneously invisible and visible, irrelevant and central. The girls cannot sustain the innocence and ahistoricity of their relationship beyond the confines of childhood. As Cliff herself has suggested, "there is no pure relational state that exists outside of social structures," and so inevitably the meanings of the differences that mark the girls intervene in their pastoral partnership.[22] These differences manifest as a series of conflicts, disagreements that occur primarily as physical confrontations.

The physical fights between Clare and Zoe are the kettle-whistle of the tension inherent in the differences their bodies represent. The process of sexual maturation exacerbates the girls' physical differences and introduces insurmountable obstacles to their friendship. Upon her grandmother's instructions, Clare disallows her friend access to her clothing, specifically her bathing suit. The bathing suit is emblematic as it is the thin layer between the emerging sexualities of the girls and the gaze of the world. Clare's refusal to share her extra bathing suit reminds Zoe of the social hierarchies her friendship with Clare ignores and affirms her suspicion that Clare believes that lighter skin embodies the purity and superiority endowed it by the dominant culture. She challenges this differentiation by asserting that, like her, Clare is also black. "Wunna is one wuthless cuffy, passing off wunnaself as *buckra*."[23] Clare's refusal to allow her friend to try on her bathing suit foreshadows the schism in the lives of the girls. Zoe will never be allowed to inhabit the same class markers, the suit, so to speak, that Clare inherits. Although Clare strikes the first blow in the girls' battle, Zoe understands that skin color privilege is the source of this discrimination and thus uses her body in order to defend against invisibility and erasure. "Zoe caught up with [Clare] as she was balancing over the rocks. Zoe pushed her down in the water until Clare sputtered and gasped for 'peace.' "[24] The setting of the girls' temporary reconciliation, the river, is a metaphor for Jamaica, land of wood and water.[25] Although they seem to achieve equality during their struggles in the river, Clare and Zoe attain a false "peace." Ultimately the river, as representation of the powerful currents of Jamaican history and tradition, is the site of their forced conformity to the cultural meanings imposed upon their bodies.

The bathing suit is a significant symbol of leisure, class, and female beauty and sexuality. On another day, in a seeming attempt to undo the power of this marker, Zoe and Clare bathe in the river without the outside signifier, the bathing suit, which divided them earlier: "They went straight to the river, to Annie's Hole, which was at a secluded place. . . . After their bath, the two girls lay back . . . . Brown and gold beside each other. . . . Pussy and rass—these were the two words they knew for the space-within-flesh covered now by strands and curls of hair. . . . Right now it could belong to them."[26] Although the name of the location on the river, Annie's Hole, suggests a safe womblike sanctuary in which to be naked—fetal—the watery orifice is violated by the gaze of a male cane-cutter who, like the marginalized yet patriarchal culture he represents, defines the nudity of the girls in sexual and color conscious terms. His gaze causes the girls shame and acute awareness of their color caste positions. " 'Two gals nekked pon de river rock.' . . . Clare looked up to see a man in khaki with a cutlass in his hand—a cane-cutter—who stood in front of the barbed wire. . . . She reached beside her for the rifle."[27] The rifle Clare has stolen from her grandmother's house remains by her side unreturned from an aborted hunt for a wild pig earlier in the day. "When she takes the gun to shoot the wild pig, she's really taking it through a male mode. She can't take it through a female mode because the power she's witnessed is always through a male mode."[28] For Clare, the hunt represents male adventure and possessing it is her unconscious attempt to transgress the parameters placed upon her as a result of the strict gender and class definitions dictating her behavior and subordinating her agency. When the cane-cutter discovers Clare and Zoe naked on the rock, Clare immediately asserts " 'Get away, you hear. This is my grandmother's land.' She had dropped her patois—she was speaking *buckra*—and relying on the privilege she said she did not have."[29] In an action that proves fatal not only to Old Joe, her grandmother's bull, but also to her friendship with Zoe, Clare exercises the power and dominance her body falsely represents and shoots at the man. Clare's shot triggers a series of reconfigurations of the alphabet of her reality. "Zoe. Property. Selfishness. 'Gal smaddy'[30] White Smaddy. Kingston Smaddy. . . . Different smaddy,' Nakedness."[31] Clare's new cognition reveals to her the concrete parameters dictated by her class and racial markings.

Clare's epiphany is intuitive knowledge to Zoe, who responds to the situation with self-recrimination. The assertion of male authority, while serious for Clare, could mean the loss of home and income for Zoe and her mother. "How could she let a *buckra* town gal lead her into this? . . . it would all be her fault—all because she had gotten too close to a *buckra* gal and had not kept to her distance and her own place."[32]

Following this event, the distance inscribed on the bodies of the girls from birth becomes determinative and permanent.

Even though the two are separated forever, the shadowy presence of Zoe remains a forceful reality in Clare's life. Exile illuminates for Clare the powerful cultural undertow that separates the girls and creates the social hierarchies that define their bodies as oppositional. Later in her life Clare is able to resist acquiescence to this imposed reading by validating the subjective experience, equality, and education the friendship provided. When Clare first gets her period, that symbolic and mysterious initiation is informed for her solely by the memory of Zoe's reassuring and essential knowledge. "All had happened as Zoe said it would."[33] Understanding and accepting Zoe as an authority frees Clare to transcend the conflicting and constraining narratives of her cultural nomos and to rewrite, or at least redefine, her own body.

Cezair-Thompson, like Cliff, uses a double or doppelgänger as a key to her protagonist's resistance to external definitions. Jean Landing, the central character in *The True History of Paradise*, discovers the various possible readings of the texts marking her body in large measure through her relationship with her best friend, Faye Galdy. The contrast between Jean and Faye is the opposite of that which separates Clare and Zoe. As previously mentioned, Jean is the darkest member of her family and the only one who is consistently perceived as black. Her foil, Faye, is phenotypically white. Faye is the epitome of the idealization of white Western girlhood as scripted in texts such as *Goldilocks and the Three Bears*. "She had startling, big blue eyes and straight blond hair cut in a pageboy style. Her skin was so translucent that her veins showed, and there were deep shadows under her eyes. Jean had never seen anyone so white. She assumed Faye was English, but when she spoke it was clear she was Jamaican."[34]

From their initial meeting, Faye disrupts Jean's linking of race and nationality. In an inversion of Clare's assertion of power and dominance through her use of standard English, Faye uses Jamaican English and establishes herself as kindred—as Jamaican—to Jean. Faye's voice, the sound of her authentic self, belies her racial marking. Notably, Jean's understanding of Faye as Jamaican arrives through auditory signification. One of the peculiar markings of Jean's physical self is her, perhaps supernatural, ability to hear and perceive the memories/narratives of her ancestors.

She has heard them all her life, these obstinate spirits desperate to speak, to revise the broken grammar of their exits. They speak to her, Jean Landing, born in that audient hour before daylight broke on the nation, born into the knowledge of nation and prenation, the old noises of barracks, slave quarters, and steerage mingling in her ears with the newest sounds of self-rule. On verandas, in kitchens, in the old talk, in her waking reveries and anxious dreams, she has heard their stories.[35]

Jean hears Faye's true self through sensorial channels independent of the racialized dictionaries of the dominant culture. Jean's audient perception of Faye dislodges the visual primacy of race and undermines the interpretative limitations of the girls' cultural context. In spite of her white appearance, Faye rejects the privileges afforded those occupying that racial designation and is fiercely determined to identify herself simply as one of the multihued populace of Jamaica. From the beginning of their relationship Jean unconditionally accepts Faye's defiantly scripted self-definitions.

In an unconventional use of representation, Cezair-Thompson pairs Faye and Jean as a sort of complementary integrated symbol of the polarities of Jamaican culture. The two share a room at boarding school with identical twins, a paring that suggests the zygotic relationship that eventually develops between Faye and Jean. As the two begin their relationship, Faye is physically debilitated with an unnamed "congenital disease."[36] In part, Faye's physical limitations reflect the handicaps of colonialism. At an early turning point in the girl's friendship Jean steals Faye's crutches.

> [Jean] hid behind the bushes with them. Faye's crutches! She examined them, noticing that the white rubber tops where Faye's weight rested were grimy and worn. Jean rested her own weight on the crutches. She lifted both feet off the ground. The mechanics of it eluded her. She tried to move forward but couldn't. With her weight upon them, the crutches sank into the damp soil. She was stuck, and she felt, not like Faye, but like a child with a circus toy. And then she heard Faye's cry.[37]

Ironically, Jean commits this hurtful act in order to secure Faye's dependence. The results of this betrayal are not only foundational for Faye and Jean, but represent a larger reality regarding the colonial status of Jamaica. Like Faye, colonial Jamaica, crippled by the congenital diseases of slavery and unsupported by the multilayered and oppressive histories embodied by Jean, cannot walk without crutches.

Significantly, even with the crutches as support, able-bodied Jean is also immobilized. Her inability to navigate the mud with Faye's crutches, or perhaps because of them, illuminates her internal stagnation and unarticulated desire for liberation. During colonization, Jamaica, Faye, and Jean are in need of independence in order to achieve voice, mobility, and maturation.

As foreshadowing of Jean's attempt at self-reclamation stands Jean and Faye's childhood preoccupation with rewriting a classic colonial depiction of island life, the narrative *Robinson Crusoe*. "They acted out scenes based on the titles of chapters: 'I See the Shore Spread with Bones' or 'We March Out Against the Cannibals.' . . . Jean felt there should be a female in the story, so they invented a native girl named Monday. Eventually the got rid of Crusoe altogether, although every now and then, they came upon his footprints and searched for him in vain."[38] Both of the specified chapters explicitly synthesize images of island landscapes with the iconographic subaltern brown body. Faye and Jean's rewriting of this text assuages for their nascent imaginations the brutalizing and inhumane representations of "natives" as compliant Fridays, savage cannibals, or eviscerated bones. With their creation of Monday, the girls reimagine an island paradise free of the colonist and his ever-defining gaze, although his footsteps continue to mark the terrain. They reclaim the landscape with a representation, a (re)presentation of themselves reintegrated in the narrative. They achieve psychological liberation from the racist and patriarchal definitions that hierarchically layer texts such as *Robinson Crusoe*.

Like Jamaica, Faye turns to England, to the colonizer, as the agent of her autonomy. In England, Faye has surgery and gains freedom from her crutches. Like the newly emancipated Jamaica, Faye experiences the liberation of relatively unencumbered progression, but is still marked by the lingering scars of her past. "She developed a long swift, but ungraceful stride, never looking where she was going, and forever bumping into things. . . . Having shed the restraints of painful disease, she began to revel in unruliness."[39] Faye's response to severance from her crutches functions as a cautionary tale for independent Jamaica. By the time of Jean and Faye's maturation in the 1970s the "unruliness" of the country becomes the catalyst for Jean's decision to flee from her home, chastened by voices from the past to "run through the burning gate" Jamaica has become.[40]

Faye's physical impairment both mirrors and parallels Jean's psychological disability. Jean's deep insecurity, as demonstrated by her theft of Faye's crutches, results in an inertia that defines most of her adult life. The narrative structure of *The True History of Paradise* alternates portraits of Jean's passivity, lack of agency, and vulnerability with her exodus from the island. This journey toward exile, textually interspersed between Jean's personal history and the first person narratives of her ancestors is the first act that moves Jean's life forward. Ironically, Jean's first significant exercise of autonomy is her decision to leave Jamaica. In order to remember and to recuperate her self and the multiplicity of past voices she hears, Jean believes she must depart her homeland.

"Love entered this part of the world centuries ago, not as truth, but as word. In the Great house, in the schoolhouse, and in church; by rape, and rod, and hymn. Who would tell us that we loved before? Jean wonders. Who would remind us that we loved once in our own tongue, in our own way, long before we crossed the water, we survivor, that there was love once originating in ourselves?"[41] Jean's departure indicates a willingness to survive and to love herself. Her exit from the island authorizes a redefinition of her body as the physical manifestation of Jamaican histories and of an ancestrally and self inscribed body worthy of salvation. Within her body is written, griot-like, the true(r) histories of paradise. "A woman saunters up to the street corner and stands there . . . she is practically naked. Her bare breasts hang almost to her waist. . . . [T]he soldiers, hearing the commotion, look across the road and see the half-naked woman waving her arms and cursing. They shout and move as a group toward her. I turn around to look, but it's too late—the blinding sun, the speed of the car. Panic and history are mine."[42] Jean's departing journey from Jamaica is an assimilation of the fragmented, misunderstood, and exposed parts of the woman's body— of Jamaica itself. Her flight, facilitated by her white male English lover, is a claim, a compromised claim perhaps, for corporeal authority and personal survival.

With their creation of the characters Clare Savage and Jean Landing, Michelle Cliff and Margaret Cezair-Thompson utilize the physical aspects of their characters in order to rewrite the histories those bodies traditionally signify. Countering claims of authority and authenticity made by early European writers such as Richard Ligon while documenting their interpretations of the Caribbean and its inhabitants, these novelists acknowledge the persistence of racialized and gendered markings but redefine the meanings of those signs by giving voice to the subjective realities of the women inhabiting those imprinted bodies. David Buuck has established that while "contemporary theorizations of postcolonialism have begun to focus on the formation of identity within a broad matrix of economic, cultural and political determinants, many constructions of these issues continue to rotate around the binarisms of 'center-periphery,' 'self-other,' and 'colonizer-colonized.' "[43] These novels eschew simplistic and traditional polarities by forcing their conflation—in the paired friendships of the protagonists with their doppelgängers. Ultimately, both Clare and Jean reach toward reclamation of their black and female bodies. Clare and Jean assert self-ownership as they, to the extent possible, become agents of their own histories—an agency made possible by the characters' subversive consummation and reformation of the narratives of their families, their nation, the Caribbean, and even the world—"terrestrial tales of the lost and found."[44]

As Clare learns at the end of *Abeng* "They are all gone now—the ones who did these things—gone to their reward, but the afterbirth is lodged in the woman's body and will not be expelled. All the waste of birth. Foul smelling and past its use."[45] Untold history—unremembered memory—the afterbirth of life, of lives, remains festering and poisonous within, but cyclical and fertilizing, albeit messy, if released—the past as prologue.

NOTES

1. Richard Ligon, *A True & Exact History of Barbadoes*
2. Ibid., 52.
3. Ibid., 47.
4. Phillis Wheatly, "On Being Brought from African to America," 171.
5. W. E. B. Du Bois, "The Conservation of Races," 73.
6. Margaret Cezair-Thompson, *The True History of Paradise*, 24.
7. Ibid., 25.
8. Alison Easton, "The Body as History, or Writing the Body: The Example of Grace Nichols," 59
9. Ibid., 59.
10. Although both Clare and Jean are descended from ancestors of many racial groups, both ultimately are perceived and self-define racially as black women.
11. Katherine McKittrick, " 'Who Do You Talk To, When a Body's in Trouble?"; M. Nourbese Philips' (Un) Silencing of Black Bodies in the Diaspora," 223.
12. Rachel Manley, "Thoughts on Writing from Exile," 201–2.
13. Michelle Cliff in Raiskin, "The Art of History: An Interview with Michelle Cliff," 72.
14. Easton, "The Body as History," 59.
15. Toni Morrison, *Beloved*, 38.
16. McKittrick, "Who Do You Talk To," 224.
17. Cliff, *Abeng*, 37.
18. Cezair-Thompson, *The True History of Paradise*, 32.
19. Ibid., 49.
20. Ibid., 9.

21. Cliff, *Abeng*, 96.

22. Cliff in Schwarz, "An Interview with Michelle Cliff," 615.

23. Ibid., 101. The word *buckra*, according to the glossary at the end of *Abeng* means "white person," specifically one representing the ruling class (also backra).

24. Ibid.

25. The original name of the island of Jamaica was Xaymaca/Hamaica. The name derives from the aboriginal inhabitants of the islands, probably the Taino or the Arawak, and means land of many rivers or land of wood and water.

26. Cliff, *Abeng*, 120.

27. Ibid., 122.

28. Cliff in Schwarz, 616.

29. Cliff, *Abeng*, 122.

30. "Somebody."

31. Cliff, *Abeng*, 124.

32. Ibid., 124.

33. Ibid., 166.

34. Cezair-Thompson, *A True History of Paradise*, 67.

35. Ibid., 17.

36. Ibid., 67.

37. Ibid., 70.

38. Ibid., 72.

39. Ibid., 73.

40. Ibid., 317.

41. Ibid., 235.

42. Ibid., 331

43. Buuck, "Doppelganger: Hybridity and Identity in the Work of Dembudzo Marechera," 121.

44. Cezair-Thompson, *A True History of Paradise*, 66.

45. Cliff, *Abeng*, 165.

BIBLIOGRAPHY

Barnes, Natasha. "Body Talk: Notes on Women and Spectacle in Contemporary Trinidad Carnival." *Small Axe: A Journal of Caribbean Criticism* 7 (March 2000): 93–105.

Buuck, David. "Doppelganger: Hybridity and Identity in the Work of Dembudzo Marechera." *Research in African Literatures* 28 (Summer 1997): 118–33.

Cezair-Thompson, Margaret. *The True History of Paradise*. New York: Plume, 2000.

Cliff, Michelle. *Abeng*. New York: Plume, 1995.

Dance, Daryl Cumber. "Matriarchs, Doves, and Nymphos: Prevalent Images of Black, Indian and White Women in Caribbean Literature." *Studies in the Literary Imagination* 26 (Fall 1993): 21–32.

Du Bois, W. E. B. 1897b. "The Conservation of Races." *American Negro Academy Occasional Papers* No. 2, reprinted in Philip Foner, ed. *W. E. B. Du Bois Speaks, Speeches and Addresses 1890–1919*. New York: Pathfinder Press, 1970. 73–85.

Easton, Alison. "The Body as History and 'Writing the Body': The Example of Grace Nichols." *Journal of Gender Studies* 3 (March 1994): 55–58.

Ligon, Richard. 1657b. *A True and Exact History of the Island of Barbadoes.* London: Frank Cass, 1970.

MacDonald-Smythe, Antonia. "Autobiography and the Reconstruction of Homeland: The Writings of Michelle Cliff and Jamaica Kincaid." *Caribbean Studies* 27 (July–December 1994): 422–27.

Manley, Rachel. "Thoughts on Writing from Exile." *Small Axe: A Journal of Caribbean Literary Criticism* 12 (September 2000): 201–8.

McKittrick, Katherine. " 'Who Do You Talk to, When a Body's in Trouble?': M. Nourbese Philips' (Un) Silencing of Black Bodies in the Diaspora." *Social and Cultural Geography* 1 (2000): 223–36.

Morrison, Toni. *Beloved.* New York: New American Library, 1987.

Scanlon, Mara. "The Divine Body in Grace Nichols's *The Fat Black Woman's Poems.*" *World Literature Today* 72 (Winter 1998): 59–67.

Schwartz, Meryl F. "An Interview with Michelle Cliff." *Contemporary Literature* 34 (1994): 595–619.

Raiskin, Judith. "The Art of History: An Interview with Michelle Cliff." *Kenyon Review* 15 (Winter 1993): 57–72.

Robinson, Tracy S. "Fictions of Citizenship, Bodies without Sex: The Production and Effacement of Gender in Law." *Small Axe: A Journal of Caribbean Criticism* 7 (March 2000): 1–27.

Wheatley, Phillis. "On Being Brought from Africa to America." In Henry Louis Gates and Nellie McKay, eds. *The Norton Anthology of African American Literature.* New York: W.W. Norton and Company, 1997: 171.

The Ground Beneath Our Feet:
Rastafari and the Construction(s) of Race

Sarah Daynes

... although it is imagined it is not imaginary.[1]

ONE STRIKING CHARACTERISTIC OF THE NOTION OF RACE IS ITS
ascription in a set of paradoxes, the stronger of which concerns its reality. Indeed, while from a biological point of view race does not exist—
since there is no biological fact allowing the distinction of races within
mankind—it also has a concrete reality: it is used by groups and individuals, and has, as history has shown, tremendous consequences in
everyday life. Thus, race becomes socially real, even if scientifically
unreal.[2] In a way, one could say that race is brought to life by the meanings associated with it, and this dependence on meaning attribution
makes it a socially and historically determined construct, dependent on
the context in which it emerges.[3] As Hoetink points out concerning the
variety of classifications found within the Caribbean area, "the same
word may have different meanings, and ... white, colored, or black do
not always mean what our own experience suggests they should."[4]

Various political as much as scholarly debates have originated in this
paradox. For instance, the "social reality" of race is often advanced as a
reason to work on race as well as to repel any sort of criticism concerning the perpetuation of race through the profusion of academic
works written and published about it.[5] Additionally, the difficulty in
defining and conceptualizing race might have stemmed from the simultaneously real and unreal quality of race: it always appears to be very
easy to define—after all, doesn't everybody know what race is?—and
still it is one of the trickiest concepts in social sciences: like religion, it
seems that the more one examines the concept of race, the more difficult its definition becomes.[6] The comparison with religion is not a
coincidence; in this field too there has been a long quest for definition,

161

and the production of too many definitions, which overwhelming number could be taken as a symptom of the difficulty at end, as Clifford Geertz pointed out. Moreover, sociologists of religion have stumbled on essentialism, just as sociologists of race have; and one way to solve this problem was to argue for a sociology of *believing* instead of *belief*. One of the overarching claims that I will make in this article greatly resembles the movement found within the sociology of religion and is precisely about seeing race *as a process*, informed by the meanings associated with (and imposed on) it.

The difficulties met in defining race become especially visible if one considers the conventional distinction social scientists make between race and ethnicity, which is neither clear nor obvious. For instance, it is quite commonly accepted that ethnicity has to do primarily with culture, and race with phenotype.[7] However, as Wade notes, the perception of phenotypical differences itself as well as the meanings associated with them, vary and are socially constructed, and are therefore culturally variable.[8] Additionally, the ethnic process is a social process, which uses culture, but as a marker, not as essential content: in other words, it is not about cultural difference, but about the use of culture within a process of social differentiation.[9] Therefore, by taking a closer look at the concepts, one might find ethnicity to be "more social," and race to be "more cultural," than commonly expected (although this is a very simplified way to put it).

Traditionally, ethnicity also implies a choice, an identification, while race has a fundamentally imposed character—which transforms ethnicity into a sort of "positive race," often claimed, and with which individuals actively identify. Because ethnicity is usually associated with identification (therefore with the individuals' active behavior) while race is connected to social categorization (therefore to a passive imposition, exerted by society onto individuals or groups), the term "race" is usually preferred by sociologists, and "ethnicity" by anthropologists.[10] Additionally, the concept of ethnicity was first theorized by anthropologists—notably by Fredrik Barth, 1969—who emphasized the fluid, dynamic and interactive character of group boundaries, although they actually took on the abandoned ground of sociologists like Max Weber and Everett Hughes.[11]

However, even if we accept the hypothesis that ethnicity is on the side of identification and race is on the side of categorization, we should keep in mind that identification and categorization are two elements of the same process of social group formation and social identity, and therefore cannot be analyzed in complete independence of each other. The

way in which individuals or groups self-identify, the way they categorize others (knowing that categorizing the other is also a way to categorize oneself), as well as the consequences of social categorization, are
all of equal importance. Moreover, it is futile to focus on one process
while excluding the other, since what matters is the dialectic between
self-identification and categorization of the self: race is not entirely chosen, nor is it entirely imposed, and the same holds true for ethnicity.

So where do we go from here? I will argue that race is a social construct that must be analyzed within its context of emergence. It could
be defined as the naturalization of physical differences—and the set of
meanings associated with them: the notion of race refers to *naturalized*
categories based on *ideas* about appearance and descent, which change
over time: therefore, race is socially and historically elaborated, as well
as culturally varying. The notion of ethnicity, while not necessarily
well-distinguished from race, nevertheless necessarily implies an identification process, whether individual or collective. Both are fundamentally relational processes: they are not the property of the group,
but exist only within the relationship between one or more groups. As
put by Eriksen (2001), they exist *in between* the groups and not *within*
them—which implies that we understand them as social processes that
engage the "cultural stuff," in the sense of Barth.[12]

Starting from these claims, a series of questions can be posed on the
relationship of ethnicity and race, as well as on the concept of race itself.
If race is one of the modalities taken by ethnicity, does it make the latter anything other than social identity? Furthermore, how far can the
social constructionist model of race and ethnicity go? How much can
we deconstruct the processes of identification and racialization before
seeing the concepts of race and ethnicity crumble before our eyes? Can
we analyze the ultimate unreality of race without losing sight of its hard
reality? I would argue that we can, by always sticking to the ground
beneath our feet. As Ien Ang points out, we have to articulate, in a
simultaneous way, the refusal of conceptual essentialism and the recognition that race *feels* natural and essential for the people.[13]

In this article, I will focus on the notion of race as implying both
categorization and identification processes. The contemporary Rastafari movement shows clear signs of the combination of these processes
with respect to black-white differences within the movement and the
question of religious identity.[14] My interpretive analysis of discussions
of religion and race on a Rastafari Internet club will show that Rastafarian women exhibit three ideal-typical orientations toward racial
categorization and identification in defining the meaning and reli-

gious boundaries of the Rastafari movement. However, because of the context out of which these discussions emerge within the Rastafari movement, a mixture of orientations has been adopted in practice in order to negotiate the current social dynamics involved in Rastafari. I will then conclude by looking at the links made by the women of the club between gender, sex, and race when discussing the question of conversion.

RACE AND THE EMERGENCE OF THE RASTAFARI MOVEMENT

Rastafari, today widely known through the success of reggae music, is a religious movement that appeared in Jamaica in the beginning of the 1930s. The first academic work on Rastafari was carried out by Simpson in the 1950s, followed by a report written by some scholars at the University of the West Indies in the 1960s. But it is only at the end of the 1970s, after Rastafari penetrated the international public space, that scholars really gained interest in this Jamaican religious cult.[15] Today, most scholars agree on considering Rastafari as a resistance movement[16] that has an equally religious and social-political character, and a strong potential for revolution, while intensively referring to tradition; besides, Rastafari must therefore be considered as a cultural movement implying a specific worldview and way of life.[17] Rastafari does not have any leader, institution, dogma, and religious hierarchy; if some organizations are found within the movement (like the *Nyabinghi Order,* the *Ethiopian World Federation* or the *Twelve Tribes of Israel*), most believers remain independent from any group. Due to this acephaleous character, individuals conserve an extremely high degree of independence, in their beliefs as well as in their practices—which is reflected in the variety found within the movement itself. But however fluid its boundaries can be in terms of beliefs and behaviors, Rastafari still shares a "common ground" that traces the limits of belonging. Its homogeneity is based on three main points. First, its *messianic and millenaristic character,* Rastafari being, in an essential way, a movement of *revelation,* the revelation concerning a truth that is simultaneously religious, social, political, etc. and being conjugated in three tenses: the past (revelation of the origin), the present (revelation of the current world), and the future (revelation of what is to come). Secondly, its claim for *Africaness* (what Homiak calls "an Africa-oriented ethos")[18] and the focus on a bipolarization between "Europeans" and "Africans," expressed through the categories of Good and Evil. Finally, the importance given to the principle of *resistance*, grounded in the history of slavery, and which rules most of Rastafari concepts, whether they are religious, political, social, or cultural. Rastafari presents itself as essentially being a movement of resistance that has to struggle in a world of adversity. Those three points can be considered as the nodal concepts of Rastafari, and determine its specificity; the multiplicity found within the movement concerns the modalities by which individuals develop and conjugate these nodal concepts. Another characteristic of Rastafari, as a consequence of its simultaneous multiplicity and unity, is the existence of essential tensions within it, which all play a crucial role in its evolution. These tensions can be coupled as follows: Individual autonomy / Community; Privatization of beliefs / Collective identity; Bricolage and (re)invention / Historical chain of memory; Revolution and revelation / Tradition.[19]

Since its emergence in the 1930s, the Rastafari movement has been organized around an essential distinction, both racial (blacks versus whites) and social (the rich versus the poor), while both categories were also coinciding in colonial Jamaica. Militating against the oppression of the poor and for the blackness of God, Rastafari has been ascribed in a racial problematic, associated with a colonial situation as well as to the past of slavery. Jamaica was colonized by the Spanish in 1509. In less than fifty years, the Indians were exterminated; if the Spanish imported slaves from Africa, the colonial exploitation of Jamaica really started with the English, who came into control in 1660 and massively settled, developed the sugar cane plantations, and intensified slavery. Jamaica has a long and rich history of rebellions (such as the Morant Bay rebellion) and runaways (the Maroons—from the Spanish *cimarrons* —established free communities, fought the English, and signed treaties that guaranteed their freedom and autonomy). The slave trade was abolished in 1808, and slavery in 1834; a cheap workforce was then imported to replace slavery, as in most other British colonies; in Jamaica, it included mostly East Indians but also Chinese, Syrians, and free Africans coming from other British colonies. The very strict hierarchy of color, which has existed since slavery, is also a social hierarchy: in simple words, the lighter the skin, the higher the social status. Waters concludes that "in summary, ethnicity and class are inextricably linked in the Jamaican social structure."[20]

Rastafari therefore emerged in this specific context: a colonial society organized on a strict hierarchy based on racial stigma, and in which the quasi-totality of the popular class is composed of slave descendants. The affirmation of "Blackness" as a positive identity was central in the emergence of Rastafari, which developed notions of the Good and the

Bad rooted in entangled factors: religious (God versus Satan), sociopolitical (in link with the colonial context, for instance the Queen being
seen as evil), socioeconomical (poor versus rich), and racial or ethnic
(blacks versus whites). The ultimate goal of the movement was not the
improvement of Jamaican society, considered as hell, but the repatriation of the slaves' descendants to Africa, the land of their fathers, considered as heaven. Until the 1960s, the situation was very simple for
Rastafari: Jamaican slaves and their descendants are Africans in temporary exile, not in diaspora, and they will soon go back home. Moreover,
the movement was using the racial terms of the global society: a clear
separation between two groups, blacks and whites, which determines
social status as well as economical, political and social opportunity, and
the access to power. In a way, the movement used a pre-existing racial
classification by reversing it; this "term-to-term reversal" is not specific
to Rastafari, but appears in numerous other colonial or post-colonial
religious movements; as Littlewood points out, "restoration of a world
now upside-down demands yet another turning around in which the
current relations between Black and White will be again reversed."[21]

This clear distinction between blacks/good versus whites/evil, articulated within the colonial context, was questioned during the 1970s,
when "non-blacks" gained interest in the Rastafari movement, and tried
to enter it. Until then, it had remained not only an exclusively Jamaican,
but also a lower class Afro-Jamaican movement, coinciding with its
context of emergence. But after the birth of reggae music in the 1960s
and its international success in the 1970s, the Rastafari movement faced
a major growth among the African-Jamaican population, and a sudden
interest from people of different ethnic, social, and cultural backgrounds. But how could a movement centered on the uplift of black
people accept white people within? Moreover, how could white people
associate and identify with a movement based on the blackness of God,
the struggle against European domination, and the goal of repatriation
of black people to Africa? The entry of white individuals into Rastafari
is an important event, for its black members as well as for its white
members, and a paradox that is still a source of conflicts today.

THE ISSUE OF WHITE RASTAS:
THE CASE OF AN INTERNET CLUB

On the Internet, the question of race is extremely interesting, because
no classification of people by their appearance is possible. Deductions

made from the language and content of the messages are the only means to "classify" people, but they are very unreliable—it is, for example, very easy to modify written language in order to "sound" different. Hence, Internet clubs and message boards raise a certain number of interesting issues that would be absent, or less marked, in the observation of a "face-to-face" group. First, they allow a vivid observation of the meaning associated with race, since what individuals say and how they say it form the only basis for others to infer their "race" or "ethnic belonging"; appearance, gestures, accent, are absent, and this gives way to a heavy use of language in order to "signal" one's ethnic or racial identity, or to "infer" it from other individuals' discourses.[22] Second, and hence, they allow for an observation of the possible conflicts found between the interpretation of individuals' racial or ethnic belonging and what they really are (or claim to be). Someone might "seem white" and therefore be treated, and interacted with, as such, until this comes into conflict with either a hint or a straightforward revelation that the person is not white. Third, and that is a consequence of the two preceding points, individuals cannot rely on ethnic or racial classifications as easily, and as safely, as in face-to-face interactions: they know that they have to be cautious in their interpretation of the discourses of other individuals, because a white person might "sound black" and a black person might "sound white." Hence, they use caution in siding with other members, for instance during collective discussions, before they actually have some certainty concerning the different individuals' identity. Finally, I want to note that my observations have shown that, on the Internet, people are both more tolerant and more intolerant than they would be in face-to-face interactions. They are more tolerant because they are not sure about who they are talking to (and therefore want to "keep doors open" until they are sure of their interlocutor's identity), and because they seem to be less sensitive to stereotypes as well as emotional reactions; but they are also more intolerant, or at least much more straightforward in their opinion, because they do not speak "to someone real." Oftentimes, some individuals would say things on the Internet that they would never dare say in a face-to-face interaction. This simultaneous tolerance and intolerance was well expressed in the club I observed, because people were at once more open to talk to everyone than they would be in "real life", but also quite obsessed by "finding out who each really was"; as if it was both feasible (and easy) to let go of physical appearance and the meaning associated with it and to just talk with people freely, but also difficult to really interact without it. Moreover, what is really interesting is the interaction between "reality" and "cyber-reality." One might think that the Internet, because of the absence of physical markers, allows for an observation of an ideal, strictly symbolic notion of race; as if the Internet could act as a laboratory in which interactions were not "tainted" by physical reality. But the interactions I observed showed otherwise; "the real" still irrupted within the discussions, in the sense that individuals made it significant in order to define the authenticity of the persons they were interacting with, as well as their own. Despite its lack of concreteness, physical appearance still mattered; and this was made very apparent in the way individuals reevaluated their siding with one member or the other in function of what they had revealed, later on, of their physical appearance.

I say "later on," because the question of race appeared quite late in my observation of the group. The discussion I have observed took place in 1999 in an Internet club that was created by a Rastafari woman with the specific purpose of providing Rastafari women with their own space of exchange, although men were not excluded from being members.[23] During several months, women addressed various topics, such as masculine domination, gender roles and statuses, food practices, and political commitment. Then, they started discussing the issue of the entry of white people into Rastafari, which immediately opened on the question of race. In fact, the "racial issue" had remained completely absent from the discussions during two months, until this message posted by Rachel.[24] "*I would like to know what the sistrens out there think about white people joining the faith. I am a Japhite sistren myself and have lived this livity for many years but still experience some negative vibes from some people although more people seem to accept the I these days*" (Rachel, June 1999).

This question represented a danger for the balance of the group and the consensus that had been established, because it called for a very clear positioning, not only concerning opinions but also, and above all, personal identity: who is black and who is white, and what each thinks of the other—Rachel starting herself, by clearly saying that she is white: "Japhite."[25] Numerous responses quickly followed; women started discussing race and, quickly after, focused on the question of religious conversion and relationships. "*Being White myself, my answer has to be wary . . . the more we can observe ourselves and understand how our thinking has contributed to the oppression of the world, and the better it will be for everyone*" (Brenda, June 1999).

This message clearly answers the question posed by Rachel: Brenda states her personal racial identity, and her opinion concerning the entry of white people into Rastafari, this issue being enlarged to "racial relations" in the world as a whole. This first answer to Rachel's message is a good example of the immediate extension of the discussion beyond Rastafari itself: all evoke the general topic of blacks/whites relations. Three main positions can be distinguished among the answers posted to Rachel's initial message: members who oppose the entry of whites into Rastafari, those who do not oppose it but have a mitigated position concerning individual reactions, and finally those who defend the complete universality of the movement. The following post is a good example of the first position: *"InI is a Nubian Rastafar-I woman . . . Mi a feel that the Nubian sistren need to deal with the Nubian brethren and sistren. Mi naw embrace the European"* (Carine, June 1999).

Carine positions herself personally—"Nubian"—and then gives her point of view on the issue: blacks and whites, here called "Nubians" and "Europeans," are clearly separated in two groups, and are not considered as having to live together. *"If there are white people who believe in Jah and call themselves Rasta who can really tell them that they don't? . . . InI can only decide how InI want to relate to these people and how much we really trust them . . . Respect to all white people who call themselves Rasta . . . But I don't trust you and I know you don't expect I to trust you. What is important though, is that InI can live in inity for peace to abound throughout the earth"* (Lisa, June 1999).

This message illustrates another position: Lisa supports the collective acceptance of white Rastas ("who can really tell them that they don't?"), but it does not necessarily mean that an individual acceptance ("InI can only decide how InI want to relate to these people"). In a way, she establishes a compromise between the respect due to white Rastas and the trust that can, or cannot, be given. In other words, she expresses a very common position within Rastafari, which does not contest anybody's faith but nonetheless lets each decide of one's own decisions and choices concerning one's own life. This point is very clear at the end of the message: she supports "peaceful collaboration and cohabitation," without implying intermixing. Because of the history that exists between the two groups, trust can not be given easily; moreover, she makes it clear that whites do not expect blacks to trust them. *"We are all one race, the human race. Even so I can overstand that white people have been the downpressors for much too long and many still are. I know that it makes it hard to trust conscious white people"* (Rachel, June 1999).

This message actually comes as a confirmation of what Lisa was saying about trust: as a white woman, Rachel says that she understands that black women might not trust her easily. She defends a very universalistic position, which considers that only one race (mankind, the "human race") exists on a biological level, but she also takes history into account, history as having progressively constructed different groups and divided them. The goal of Rachel is to live as one, but without ever forgetting the past and the history of domination and oppression. "*Many think that Rasta is knowledge only for blacks—but if so is the case Jah can't be the one true God*" (Ingrid, June 1999).

Ingrid, a European member,[26] supports a position that is very widely shared by Rastas who live in Western countries: Rastafari is a monotheist faith, and if it is not universal, then it does not hold "Revelation," but is just another (false) religious cult among others. In another words, she raises a point that actually became an essential issue within Rastafari as the movement was spreading internationally: how would it be possible to believe that Jah is the true, only God, if he does not address all human beings, without exclusivity? Here race is therefore viewed within a strictly religious context: universality is a necessary condition for the validation of the "truth" found within a religious movement of revelation.

Finally, a few members insisted on the fact that racial distinctions are a means of division and oppression used by "Babylon,"[27] and therefore should not be used by Rastafari, because it reproduces the wrongdoings of Babylon and therefore serves the cause of Evil. Mary for instance talked about the "skin game," and concluded: "Do not look for your brothers in flesh, look for your brothers in spirit! . . . Do you trust me? Another trick of Babylon" (Mary, June 1999).

Following this discussion, its instigator, Rachel, added that her question was necessary for her to decide whether she would participate in the club or not. There is no doubt that she was very sensitive to the issue of race, as she started opening up about her "isolation" and the troubles she faced because she was white. And this was the case for the other members as well: they all discussed the topic with passion, raising numerous different questions and stating diverse opinions. One of the most interesting topics that emerged following the issue of white Rastas concerns *the progressive construction of the notion of race:* members discussed the emergence and evolution of the different "races," using and mixing three different explanations.

The first, which one could call "the Lucy theory," emphasizes the idea of a common black African ancestor for all mankind. All members agree that the population of the earth spread from an original and unique point, which is Africa. They refer to the discovery of Lucy, in the Rift valley, as proving that the first human being was an African.

This is extremely important for them, because it means that even "mainstream" science (considered as possibly corrupted since it is an emanation of Western society) correlates the fact that, although Europeans have depreciated African history, the first human being was not European, but African.

The second explanation is a religious distinction of human races on the basis of the biblical story of Noah and his three sons. After the flood, the only survivors, who repopulated the earth, were Noah and his three sons and their wives: Ham is considered as the father of the black people (Africans), Shem of the Semitic people (Asians, Indians), and Japhet of the white people (Europeans). Therefore, from the same African root (Noah being considered as a "Black African man") appeared three distinct races from three different founding fathers: "I agree with Ellen when she says that civilization spread from Africa. We are all sons and daughters of Noah who was a black African man. Shem is the father of the Semitic peoples, Ham the father of the black race and Japhet the father of the white race—therefore we are all one race, the human race" (Rachel, June 1999). This religious distinction of three races has also been widely used by Europeans to justify slavery, citing the curse of Ham: in the book of Genesis, Ham was cursed for having seen his father Noah naked;[28] the fact that he is considered as the founder of the "Black race" was interpreted as a biblical justification for the enslavement of African people.

A third explanation, used less often, could be called a "mystico-religious theory of evolution." It concerns the progressive distinction of human races through their gradual evolution and the essential importance of melanin. Some members hence explain the existence of human races (here mainly seen as a polarized opposition between whites and blacks) as the result of a distinct evolution: in the beginning was the African people; some of them started migrating from Africa, moving through the Middle East to Europe and Asia. Facing a less warm and sunny environment, their production of melanin progressively decreased, which gave them their white skin: "Indeed all peoples originated in Africa and migrated to other parts of the world before the beginning of the last Ice age some 40,000 years ago. . . . This climate required less body pigment and is responsible for producing these lighter pigmented people who differed from their ancestors they had left behind when they migrated" (Lisa, June 1999). Then came the Ice Age, which forced the Northern people to go back South. They therefore settled back in Africa, where they mixed with the original African people and gave birth to the "other races": "White people came on the scene after the ice age when there was the movement from the North and the invasion of Africa. These people from the North lacked melanin in their skin and were of a different genetic make up to the original Nubian-Ethiopian people because of the conditions under which they lived. Invaded Africa resulted too in mixing of the burnt/black skin people and the white people, giving the yellow, brown, etc." (Lisa, June 1999). This theory emphasizes the African origin, and borrows from the Darwinian theory of evolution as well as from diverse mystical sources, in particular the ones linked to Ancient Egypt and its "secrets."[29] It emphasizes the superior quality of melanin and therefore the weakness of the white race, as well as the genetically inherited character of white violence and barbarism, explaining it by their cold and dark European environment and the harshness it implied for their life and very survival.

Those three explanations, although different in terms of content as well as context, are all monogenic theories of race: in all three cases, mankind has a single origin. The emergence of races within mankind is primarily explained by the influence of environment (as in the "Lucy" and "mystico-religious" theories) or by the desire of God to make mankind diverse, a posteriori a common origin found in Noah (as in the "religious" explanation). Indeed the members who emphasized the latter also kept saying that, if there were indeed three groups, they also came from the same father, which creates unity within diversity.

THE ISSUE OF CONVERSION: GENDER, RACE, AND GOD

From the original question about "white Rastas" asked by Rachel, women immediately turned to discussing race in a general way. But they also started to discuss the question of conversion, which led to a secondary thread in the discussion that focused on the links between gender, sex, and race. This secondary thread is actually of a crucial importance because it addresses the issue of conversion and thereby the boundaries of the religious movement and the modalities of passage of the new believers as much as the inclusive or exclusive mode of acceptance taken by the Rastafari movement and its members. Most interestingly, these religious issues were inextricably linked, in the discussion, with gender and race.

The first point raised in the discussion concerns the entry of women into Rastafari through their relationship with a Rastaman and, although focusing primarily on white women, addresses women in general. It is worth noting that the question of men themselves (and their racial identities) is never addressed: "the Rastaman" is always by implication black. All women criticize those who become Rasta because they have met a man: it is obvious for them that one does not convert for the love of a man, but for the love of God, the latter being considered as the only true, authentic faith. Dinah, for example, mentions that if a woman enters the faith for a man, then she "misses the tap." Beyond the issue of the motivations for religious faith, this discussion also refers to the secondary status of woman within the Rastafari movement. By criticizing the fact that women usually follow a man into the Rastafari movement, the women in the club actually support quite a "feminist" position, which considers that women must be independent from "their man," at least when it comes to their faith. The Rastafari movement, indeed, gives a limited spiritual and mystical importance to women, who are often excluded from religious ceremonies and "reasonings,"[30] and some Rastamen believe that a woman's only access to God is through a man, because of her impurity. Dinah refutes this conception and asserts that women not only can but also should have a direct access to God, for their faith to be authentic and "true." Elise therefore advises, "Don't follow Rastafari because you want to stay with your boyfriend." For most women in the club, religious faith and commitment are part of a personal quest for truth and of an engagement between God and one's self, and therefore cannot be based on another human being. Love of a man can only serve as a trigger, for example, as a way to meet the movement, but it cannot be the source for one's faith.

Even more problematic, for these women, is the case of white women who become Rasta for the love of a man, who is always assumed to be black. Carine, for example, asserts "Mi naw embrace [these white women] who only want the rastaman." Different levels are here intermingled: the wrongfulness of conversion motivated by love; the issue of white women entering the movement; the issue of white women having a relationship with black men; the fact that white women might be motivated solely by their sexual desire (they "only want the rastaman"); and finally the issue of interracial relationships. For many women in the club, the relationship between a white woman and a black man is a "sex thing," not a loving relationship, and some members mentioned that by choosing a black man, white women were stealing black men from black women. And if a black man chooses a white woman, it is because he is "tired of fighting the stubborn black woman" and because white women are "easy to control" (Anna).

This is where the second point makes its appearance: the relationship between racial identity and the choice of a partner. Men and women do not simply fall in love: their choices are considered as directly dependent on their social and racial identity. According to Anna, a black man will date a white woman because it is easier for him to deal with her than with a black woman, not because he likes her better or is in love with her. His choice is hence made by defect, since, of course, what is implied all along is that the "natural" choice of a partner is racially endogamous.[31] In other words, endogamy is considered as the natural order, which makes exogamy a transgression that can be explained only for reasons foreign to love. In the case of Anna, this reason is the docility of white women and the easier character of the relationship for the Rastaman. This is, of course, a paradox since, as shown by the opposition it met in the club, the transgressive choice of a white woman will also be a source of difficulties.

Another reason appears for this judgment in considering the weight of the past. Anna explains how the past of slavery still marks all relationships, whether in between or within the two groups. The plantation system, the sexual subjection of black women to white men, the "original rape," and the eviction of black men from their roles as husbands and fathers continues to have a strong influence on today's relationships. More than an influence, most women of the club consider that it actually structures the present, without leaving much space of choice and action to individuals. Many, for example, voice their difficulties in establishing a "normal" relationship with black men. Here appears a historical explanation that concerns both gender and race: the relationships between men and women and between blacks and whites are considered as being structured by the past, in such a way that individuals cannot escape it. A set of stereotypes is applied to relationships, using archetypical figures: the white woman is drawn to the black man for sex and the ultimate taboo their relationships have represented in the past; the black man dates the white woman because she is easier to control than the black woman; the black woman dates the white man because she is "deceived" by the black man; the white man dates the black woman because of the persistence of the master/slave fantasy, etc.[32] Note that for each of those sentences "the" could be replaced by "any": choice is not individual anymore, but rather it is necessarily collective and impersonal. Individual love is evicted from the relationship, to the profit of collective consequences of the past. Choosing one's partner outside of one's group necessarily implies not only a collective choice instead of an individual one, but also a collective refusal. Women do not date men anymore, they date categories, and dating one category necessarily implies that the other category is refused. This point reveals the weight of the consequences of racialization. Through the choice of a partner are expressed positions and meanings, from which individuals cannot escape. Relationships hold a collective meaning, which is imposed on them. The choice of a partner has heavy social consequences: when exogamous, it becomes a transgression expressed as the refusal of a collective group or category; when endogamous, it remains heavily charged with collective meaning, even though it is less visible, and often taken for granted, ignored, or denied. In other words, a racialized society necessarily accompanies the choice of a partner by the refusal of the group to which he or she does not belong to: for a black woman, choosing a white man means choosing all white men and refusing all black men; it also means the refusal of blackness as a collective identity and as a category. Simple difference, which makes one choose one partner rather than another, becomes a radical alterity that imposes the function of representing the collective to the individual, and this fully and permanently.

THE CONSTRUCTION(S) OF THE NOTION OF RACE: THE PARADOX OF RELIGIOUS MODERNITY

The elaboration of "racial theories" can be considered as an example of the paradox of modernity, which allows the coexistence of religious beliefs and scientific explanations. The club members all live in the West; they therefore live in societies dominated by the Western paradigm of science, but at the same time have a strong religious faith. In fact, they simultaneously take into account and use two worldviews, religious and scientific, and the theories that they develop can be considered as an adaptation to modernity, religion, and science being used not in a conflictual way, but as complementary sources of mutual confirmation. This permanent paradox between tradition and modernity results in the elaboration of "racial theories," which have to be considered as an always different and original resolution, drawn from the personal beliefs and experience of each individual. These racial theories are also the product of another important paradox: being white while believing in a black God, and being a "product" of Western culture while condemning it. For example, all the members of the club, whether black or white, totally agreed on two points: the first human being was black, and the foundations of Rastafari are black. Besides,

Haile Selassie, considered as the returned Messiah, is viewed as a black African man, and most members accept the idea of a black God, if God should have a color. However, members disagree on the current situation and on the position that should be adopted in everyday life: a continuum can be traced, from the total refusal of nonblack participants on one end, until the most universal conception and acceptance on the other end. Of course, most individuals take a position in between these two extremes. They also mix the two poles in varying ways—for example, a universalist conception on a theoretical, collective level, coexisting with a difficulty in accepting white people within the movement in everyday life.

For all the members of the club, the "racial issue" is important; however, it is lived and thought in different ways, depending on skin color, ethnic identification, cultural environment, country of origin or residence, personal experience and way of life. For example, the question of the difference between Europe and the United States concerning race and racism has been raised during the Internet discussion; and the experiences faced by people of African descent in the United States, in the Caribbean and in Europe appeared to be very different as well. Globally, the "racial issue" is more sensitive and essential for the American members, whatever their racial identification and categorization is. And beyond the individual level, it remains important for the Rastafari movement, because it emerged as a *black liberation movement*, centered on the opposition between blacks and whites in colonial Jamaica and grounded in the tradition of resistance to slavery. Until the 1960s, the movement was strictly black, and strongly opposed to whites. In the 1970s though, it faced both the interest of nonblack people interested in Rastafari and their eventual (attempt of) entry into the movement, and an international expansion linked to the massive success of reggae music. These two new events lead to a redefinition of the notion of race, the message of the movement being shaken by the question of *universality:* from this day on, the growth of Rastafari has depended on its ability to universalize, and to shift from an exclusive black liberation movement to an inclusive universal religion—or to make the black struggle universal, which in a way it succeeded in doing.[33] In other words, if Rastafari is the revelation of the truth and the word of God, it cannot address a specific group only, which closely links the universal character of the movement to the conception of race it develops, or more exactly its position toward exclusion or inclusion. The positions observed in the Internet club, often mixed at diverse degrees, allow the elaboration of an ideal-typical typology of three positions that concern the universality of Rastafari.

The first position *opposes the entry of white people into the movement.* The question of history is here essential: because of what happened in the past, and because of the current racism faced by black people, white people cannot be trusted. Besides, there is a strong emphasis on the strictly black character of the movement, on its emergence in a black, lower class context, and on its essential role in an exclusive mode of black liberation and resistance—therefore excluding white people. A typical discourse would be "Mi a feel that the Nubian sistren need to deal with the Nubian brethren and sistren. Mi naw embrace the European" (Carine, June 1999).

The second position emphasizes *the universality of the religious message.* God is the only God, the God of all and God for all. Therefore his message is meant for all people. The variation of skin color is considered as the result of a harmonious and balanced divine creation. The Rastafari movement, as a movement of revelation and truth, is the movement of all the believers. Emphasis is put on an opposition between Good and Evil which does not take physical criteria into account, and which therefore is not based on a black/white distinction: it becomes moral instead of racial. A typical discourse would be: "Many think that rasta is knowledge only for blacks—but if so is the case Jah can't be the one true God" (Ingrid, June 1999).

The third position emphasizes *the nonexistence of the notion of race.* The notion of race is an illusion, a tool created and used by "Babylon" in order to dominate, oppress, and divide, as well as to justify slavery and colonization. Using the notion of race, even turned upside down, would imply the collaboration to a system that Rastafari opposes: in order to fully fight Babylon's domination, one has to refuse the notion of race altogether. A typical discourse would be: "The European slave masters have used racial classifications to conquer and divide. Using the same classifications means becoming as evil as the devil" (Martha, June 1999).

Those three types are, in reality, found at diverse degrees within the Rastafari movement, but not in their pure form: because they are ideal-typical, they are mixed, superimposed, enriched, and used in an infinite possibility of combinations by groups and individuals.[34] For instance, one can believe that race was a tool of domination for colonial powers (position three), but still decide to use it for political reasons and claim that, due to the historical context and current situation, it is important to keep the Rastafari movement black (position one). The dichotomy that can exist between the theoretical, collective level (the "principles" level) and the practical, individual level (individuals' daily life) is another good illustration of how people actively mix ideal-typical positions in different ways: in theory, white people are accepted in the name of a universal God; in practice, each is free to adopt any suiting position (from full refusal to full acceptance) and to draw the limits of interaction at any place. In a way, this position mixes the perfectibility of God, hence allowing the movement to be universal, and the imperfectibility of mankind, individuals being in control of their own behavior.

Indeed this combination of two positions can also be considered as a solution to the paradox between the religious exigency of inclusion and the exclusive roots of the movement. The construction of the notion of race within the Rastafari movement is also a direct witness of the tensions that exist within it, tensions that, ironically, are direct consequences of its success—the latter raising, in particular, issues linked to its expansion, whether we talk in social, cultural, ethnic, or religious terms. Rastamen and Rastawomen around the world come from different societies, cultures, social classes, and political environments, and they also live under disparate conditions. Therefore, the meanings they associate with race are variable, the notion itself takes various modalities, and they accommodate in their own way to the essential tension that exists between the local emergence of Rastafari, its global expansion, and its universal exigency.

But independently of the places and people, Rastafari remains fundamentally organized around a distinction made between blacks and whites, based on the historical opposition between Africans and Europeans. At the turn of the century, seventy years after its birth, this opposition can indeed keep on being expressed in racial terms by those who oppose the adherence of whites to the movement, but it can also take place along a continuum that spreads from refusal to acceptance (or, in religious language, from exclusivity to inclusion, from one nation to all the nations of the earth, following an extension that is necessary for the validation of the religious message, without which it would not be the truth but just "some more words"). This continuum is built in a very complex manner, through an "intellectualization" of the original racial opposition: "race" becomes a "state of mind," which allows the integration of any individual who shares the beliefs and struggles of the group, independently of the color of his/her skin. This switch is in a way made from the biological toward the mental, from the outside toward the inside, and ultimately from a naturalized conception of the Good toward the centrality of individuals' choices independently of things they have no power on over, in this case the color of their skin: the distinction does not operate on the basis of physical traits anymore, but depends on intellectual consciousness and commitment—with all the residual conflicts that can result from the simultaneous coexistence of the "Africaness" of the movement with the universalization of its ideology and theology. Once again, its position toward "race" is an illustration of one of the great successes of the Rastafari movement: the association of collective homogeneity and strong sense of groupness with an almost complete individual independence and freedom of choice, as well as the ability to cherish the African roots of the movement while making its message universal.

CONCLUDING REMARKS

I stated in the introduction to this paper that the relationship between the concepts of race and ethnicity was not simple, that the concepts themselves were not easy to define nor to distinguish from each other, and finally that the main challenge rested in our sociological ability to revoke conceptual essentialism while recognizing the "essential feeling" that race can have for the people. The latter appeared strongly during the discussions I have observed, although the constructed character of race appeared as strongly: women showed various opinions about race, and they also displayed different explanations for the diversity of color found within mankind. By doing this, they built their own version of race, and also sometimes refused race completely. As I argued earlier, both race and ethnicity should be understood to involve categorization (which implies a process of imposition) and self-identification (which implies individual and/or collective choice), and these interwoven processes can be found in the discussions among the women of the Internet group. While most women took race for granted and used the black/white dichotomy, they also gave evidence of a choice between different "meanings" that were associated with these racial categories and the contextual situation of Rastafari itself. In fact, the different positions and explanations shown during the discussion I observed can precisely be analyzed as the result of the interrelationship that exists between external categorization and individual identification.

By observing Rastawomen discuss the issue of the entry of white individuals into the Rastafari movement, I was able to build three ideal-types concerning the dialectic of religious exclusion and inclusion in relationship to the notion of race, and the dialectic of categorization and self-identification. These types concern exclusion, inclusion, and refusal of race. Within the Rastafari movement, the specifically religious question of inclusion and exclusion has to address the issue of race, because of the specific context of emergence of Rastafari: the boundaries of the religious movement (which determine who can be a believer and who cannot, as well as who is a "true" believer and who is not) necessarily imply a discussion of race, even if it is to ultimately refuse race (as in the third type). It is worth noting, at this point, that the first two types—exclusion and inclusion—remain within a racialized conception of the world, while the third can be seen as an attempt to unracialize it. Still, in reality, both acceptance and refusal of race can coexist, for example, by denouncing the unreality of race as a biological fact while acknowledging its social consequences and asserting that it is politically necessary to keep on using it. The political necessity of race, in the case of the Rastafari movement, is usually grounded in the acceptance of how the world works today; in other words, racial categorization can be overwhelmingly important, and this is especially true of the society in which most members of the club live. Some of them therefore argue that what matters, in the end, is how society classifies you. Political necessity can also be justified by history; the refusal of white believers can become a political refusal of what white civilization has represented: slavery, imperialism, colonialism. *In other words, "race" can be refuted by individuals, while still being used by them in the social world.*

The multiple ways in which the ideal-types blend in reality, here illustrated by the case of Rastawomen discussing the entry of white people into Rastafari, show how the processes of categorization and identification come together in the making of race and in its use by individuals and groups. They also show how, in "the real world," the dismissal of race can team up with the use of racial categories, although it might seem paradoxical. In fact, it illustrates the simultaneously unreal and real character of race, and shows that the centrality of race within a given society matters, regardless of individuals' personal position toward race: however unreal race can be, it also has an acute and concrete reality for people as well as tremendous consequences on their lives—which of course is, for social scientists, nothing but the ground beneath our feet.

NOTES

The title of this essay borrows from Salman Rushdie's novel. I am most grateful to Terry Williams and Richard Jenkins for reviewing the first version of this paper, to

Orville Lee for our helpful collaboration, and finally to Linden Lewis for his insightful comments, in particular about the Rastafari movement.

1. Richard Jenkins, *Rethinking Ethnicity*, 169.

2. Charles Mills, *Blackness Visible*, 76–77.

3. The case of the United States has been widely studied; see Gossett 1997 and Smedley 1999. For a comparative analysis within the Caribbean area, see Hoetink 1985.

4. H. Hoetink, "Race and Color," 82.

5. See for instance the concluding sentences of Eduardo Bonilla-Silva's article "Race as an Essential Social Fact" (1999: 905), written in response to Mara Loveman's critique of his work in her book review "Is Race Essential?" (1999), both in the *American Sociological Review*.

6. The terms "race" and "ethnicity" are also often used without much precision or taken for granted. They are sometimes used interchangeably, without any clear definition of what the author means.

7. A common distinction, for instance, would be the one made between the "Italian ethnic group" and the "black racial group" – the first one referring primarily to culture, the second to skin color and other physical attributes.

8. Peter Wade, "Race, Nature and Culture," 21–22.

9. Jenkins, *Rethinking Ethnicity* ; Eriksen, "Ethnicity and Culture"; among others.

10. Ibid.

11. Max Weber defined ethnic groups as "those human groups that entertain a subjective belief in their common descent because of similarities of physical type or of customs or both, or because of memories of colonization or migration; this belief must be important for the propagation of group formation; conversely, it does not matter whether or not an objective blood relationship exists" (1978: 389).

12. Fredrik Barth, "Introduction."

13. Ien Ang, "Identity Blues."

14. I am fully aware that the use of terms like "black" and "white" itself entails an implicit recognition of race as a "natural thing." However, when using them in this article, I will always refer to their use by the people, and will therefore not imply the existence of those groups as such, but only within a discursive system. Therefore the "black" and "white" groups are here understood as social constructions in a specific context, not as fixed, real, and essential entities. In other words, "black" means "who is thought to be black within a specific context."

15. Before 1970, very few academic articles focused specifically on the Rastafari movement: Simpson (1955a, 1955b, 1962), Kitzinger (1966, 1969), Hogg and Brown (1966).

16. Horace C. Campbell, *Rasta and Resistance*.

17. Ernest Cashmore, "The De-labeling Process"; Laënnec Hurbon, *Le Phénomène Religieux* ; P. D. M. Taylor, "Perspectives on History"; Barry Chevannes, *Rastafari* ; S. D. Glazier, "New Religious Movements."

18. Homiak, 494.

19. "Bricolage" is here used in the sense of Roger Bastide (1970), and "chain of memory" in the sense of Danièle Hervieu-Léger (2000).

20. Anita Waters, *Race, Class, and Political Symbols*, 42.

21. Richard Littlewood, "History, Memory, and Appropriation," 234.

22. Some "white" members would actually use some Jamaican-English terms, or grammatical constructions that are typical of, for instance, African-American or Jamaican English (such as "ain't" or "irie", etc). On the other hand, a lot of members

use plain English, thereby making it impossible for others to know, from written language only, what their ethnicity, racial identity, or citizenship are.

23. Most members of the club, and all those who participated in the discussions, were women. When not specified, they were American.

24. All names have been changed to protect privacy. The quotations are original, including misspellings.

25. "Japhite," in relation to the biblical story of Noah and his three sons, Ham, Shem, and Japhet, considered as the fathers of the three peoples who resettled the earth after the flood, respectively the African, Semite, and European peoples. Concerning racial classifications made on the basis of the biblical text, see McKee Evans 1976 and Gossett 1997.

26. Here "European" refers to citizenship. Ingrid states elsewhere in the discussion that she is "white."

27. Within Rastafari, "Babylon" is a metaphoric category that refers to "the bad" as opposed to "Zion," the category of "the good"; both are also religious (Satan versus God). Babylon refers to Western, industrial, capitalist societies, while Zion refers to the original creation of God. These two categories cover a wide range of oppositions, which are essential in organizing Rastafari worldview as well as defining the boundaries between the "inside" and the "outside": Good vs. Bad, God vs. Satan, Nature vs. Unnature, Pure vs. Impure, etc.

28. Or more exactly his son Canaan, and with him his descendants, since the curses and blessings of the Patriarchs, in the Bible, apply to lineage and not only individuals. "Cursed be Canaan: a servant of servants shall he be unto his brethren," Genesis 9:25.

29. There is a connection with the "Melanin scholars" current that emerged in the U.S. recently.

30. Concerning "reasonings" and their role within the Rastafari movement see J. Homiak, *The Ancient of Days Seated Black: Eldership, Oral Tradition and Ritual in Rastafari Culture* (PhD dissertation, Brandeis University, 1985), pages 262–359.

31. The term "racially endogamous" refers of course to the boundaries set by the individuals between groups that they consider as being racial. In other words, it refers to individual conceptions, which are historically contextualized and variable, not to an objective, conceptual, and universal "racial" system.

32. Here we also find possible references to Frantz Fanon's *Black Skin, White Masks* (New York: Grove Press, 1967 [1952]), although I was unable to determine whether the women of the club had read it or not.

33. Another important event that occurred in the mid-1970s is the death of Haile Selassie, considered the Messiah by the Rastafari movement. This event put Rastafari in a situation of "failed messianism" (Desroche 1969) but, instead of weakening the movement, it seems it has revitalized it. It also played a major role in the redefinition of the movement's theology and ideology, especially concerning the conceptions linked to the essential categories of redemption and hope.

34. Weber clearly stated on numerous occasions that ideal-types are not to be found in reality in a "pure" form, and about his types of authority he said: "the idea that the whole of concrete historical reality can be exhausted in the conceptual scheme . . . is as far from the author's thoughts as anything could be" (1947:329). He also talked of ideal-types as being "utopias" that never exhaust the infinite possibilities of reality: "in its conceptual purity, this mental construct . . . cannot be found empirically anywhere in reality. It is a utopia" (1949: 90).

BIBLIOGRAPHY

Ang, Ien. "Identity Blues." In *Without Guarantee: In Honour of Stuart Hall*, edited by Paul Gilroy, Larry Grossberg and Angela McRobbie. London: Verso, 2000, 1–13.

Barth, Fredrik. "Introduction." In *Ethnic Groups and Boundaries*. London: Allen & Unwin, 1969.

Bastide, Roger. "Mémoire collective et sociologie du bricolage." *L'Année Sociologique*: 3ème série, 21 (1970): 65–108.

Bonilla-Silva, Eduardo. "The Essential Social Fact of Race: Response to Loveman." *American Sociological Review* 64, no. 6 (1999): 899–906.

———. "Rethinking Racism: Toward a Structural Intepretation." *American Sociological Review* 62, no. 3 (1997): 465–480.

Campbell, Horace C. *Rasta and Resistance: from Marcus Garvey to Walter Rodney*. London: Hansib, 1985.

Cashmore, Ernest. "The De-labelling Process: from Lost Tribe to Ethnic Group." In *Rastafari and other African-Caribbean World-views*, edited by Barry Chevannes. The Hague: ISS, 1995, 182–195.

Chevannes, Barry. *Rastafari. Roots and Ideology*. Syracuse, NY: Syracuse University Press, 1994.

Daynes, Sarah. "*Le mouvement Rastafari: mémoire, musique et religion.*" Thèse de Doctorat en Sociologie, Paris: Ecole des Hautes Etudes en Sciences Sociales, 2001.

Eriksen, Thomas Hylland. "Ethnicity and Culture—a Second Look." Plenary lecture, 6th SIEF conference, Amsterdam, April 21, 1998.

Glazier, S. D. "New Religious Movements in the Caribbean: Identity and Resistance." In *Born Out of Resistance: on Caribbean Cultural Creativity*, edited by Wim Hoggbergen. Utrecht: Isor Publications, 1995, 253–262.

Goldberg, David Theo. *Racist Culture: Philosophy and the Politics of Meaning*. Oxford: Blackwell, 1993.

Gossett, Thomas. *Race. The History of an Idea in America*. 1963. New York: New York University Press, 1997.

Hervieu-Léger, Danièle. *Religion as a Chain of Memory*. 1993. New Brunswick, NJ: Rutgers University Press, 2000.

Hoetink, H. "Race and Color in the Caribbean." In *Caribbean Contours*, edited by Sidney Mintz and Sally Price. Baltimore: Johns Hopkins University Press, 1985, 55–84.

Hogg, Donald, and Samuel Elisha Brown. "Statement of a Ras Tafari Leader." *Caribbean Studies* 6, no. 1 (1966): 37–38.

Hurbon, Laënnec. *Le phénomène religieux dans la Caraibe*. Montréal: Editions du Cidhica, 1989.

Jenkins, Richard. *Rethinking Ethnicity: Arguments and Explorations*. London: Sage, 1997.

Kitzinger, Sheila. "Protest and Mysticism: the Rastafari Cult in Jamaica." *Journal for the Scientific Study of Religion* 8, no. 2 (1969): 241–62.

———. "The Rastafarian Brethren of Jamaica." *Comparative Studies in Society and History* 9 (1966): 33–39.

Littlewood, Richard. "History, Memory and Appropriation: Some Problems in the

Analysis of Origin." In *Rastafari and other African-Caribbean World-Views*, edited by Barry Chevannes The Hague: ISS, 1995, 233–56..

Loveman, Mara. "Is Race Essential? Comment on Bonilla-Silva." *American Sociological Review* 64, no. 6 (1999): 891–98.

McKee Evans, W. "From the Land of Canaan to the Land of Guinea: The Strange Odyssey of the Sons of Ham." *The American Historical Review* 85, no. 1 (1976): 15–43.

Mills, Charles. *Blackness Visible: Essays on Philosophy and Race.* Ithaca: Cornell University Press, 1998.

Simpson, George Eaton. "Political Cultism in Western Kingston, Jamaica." *Social and Economic Studies* 4 (1955b): 133–49.

———. "The Ras Tafari Movement in Jamaica: A Study of Race and Class Conflict." *Social Forces* 34 (1955a): 167–71.

———. "The Ras Tafari Movement in Jamaica in Its Millenial Aspect." *Comparative Studies in Society and History* supplement II (1962): 160–65.

Smedley, Audrey. *Race in North America: Origin and Evolution of a Worldview.* Oxford: Westview, 1999.

Taylor, p.d.m. "Perspectives on History in Rastafari Thought." *Studies in Religion* 19, no. 2 (1990): 191–205.

Wade, Peter. "Race, Nature and Culture." *Man* 28, no. 1 (1993): 17–34.

Waters, Anita. *Race, Class and Political Symbols: Rastafari and Reggae in Jamaican Politics.* New Brunswick/ London: Transaction Publishers, 1989.

Weber, Max. *Economy and Society.* 2 vols. Berkeley: University of California Press, 1978.

———. *The Methodology of the Social Sciences.* 1904. New York: Free Press, 1949.

———. *The Theory of Social and Economic Organization.* New York: Oxford University Press, 1947.

Living "in the Shade of the White Metropolis": Class Dynamics in Chester Himes's Harlem

Norlisha F. Crawford

CHESTER HIMES'S HARLEM DETECTIVE SERIES, WRITTEN OVER THE period between the mid-1950s and the late 1960s, is in many ways simply traditional hard-boiled detective fiction as it had taken shape from the 1920s until the early 1950s. The narratives in the series feature a closed community setting, a murder leading to an investigation, a violent detective team that attempts to restore order to the community by identifying the murderer; over the course of the investigation the community is found to be riddled with corruption, and several characters are found to have had motives for wanting the murdered character eliminated. With the exception of a police detective team rather than one private detective, all of those conventions are in keeping with the traditions established over the genre's first three decades of evolution. Over that period, black characters were never the central characters in traditional hard-boiled detective fiction, but readers got a glimpse of them in many works in the genre. They are maids, janitors, street thugs, or buffoonish figures that step onto the stage of the stories in a brief sentence or two, performing servant duties for the white characters, or acting as walking metaphors for the authors' encoding that the urban landscape is a place of dark menace and social decline, or as comic relief for the white characters and reading audience. Poor black urban neighborhoods also sometimes appeared in traditional hard-boiled detective fiction. When the white detective, for instance, goes into a black community he usually is looking for information from a white criminal who is either in exceptional poverty and therefore living among blacks or is involved in exceptionally heinous activities that must be conducted from the place that is the least likely to receive police attention. "Blacks had moved in," Frankie Bailey says of the settings in several of Raymond Chandler's hard-boiled detective stories of the 1930s and 1940s, "whites had moved out, and the old neighborhoods were sliding downward into slums—neglected slums."[1]

Himes' Harlem series challenged the assumptions of the early main-stream hard-boiled genre texts by bringing black characters and their concerns to the forefront of the novels in his detective fiction series. In an interview given in 1964 Himes describes Harlem as a racialized enclave community in relation to its opulent borough home, Manhattan: "[Harlem] is a city of shadow in the shade of the white metropolis, where half a million Negroes exist on the crumbs of plenty, while they dream of an escape."[2] Wanting to escape Harlem would then seem to be a logical priority for any enterprising African American seeking to have more than a crumb of the national pie. But that is not the case Himes makes. They dream of escape from poverty, not from the company of other black citizens. Economic depravity and institutional neglect, Himes's works suggest, are the chief causes for the behavioral responses that so often are attributed to pathology as an inherent racial trait, and for the seeming inevitability of "sliding downward into slums." The precision of Himes's focus on causal effects is an important distinction to note because historically images have been used in popular culture forms to suggest that blacks are themselves depraved, abnormal, negligible beings, thereby justifying first their enslavement, then, following a series of de jure and legislative adjustments, the establishment of political, social, and economic policies to ensure their de facto oppression in U.S. society. Himes introduced with his Harlem series a whole new set of questions about and perspectives on the African-American experience in black urban communities in the United States, including, as this essay will show, among those citizens who choose to be involved with criminal activities as a method to economic opportunity as well as the effects of those choices on the social structure of his Harlem community.

When viewed in comparison to hard-boiled detective fiction's traditional depictions of black characters, reading the Harlem detective novels one feels as if after their workday among whites finished, Himes got on the bus, in the car, or walked the streets with some of the black characters he found in the traditional books and left not only the metropolis but those shifting border communities Bailey describes as of uncertain social status and even less respect. Himes and we, the readers, go with the black characters back to their home turf. And there in a community where the individual characters or their families have lived for tens of decades but own little, where they have created a culture out of joy as much as adversity, where their value systems have been honed on the anvil of despair, and yet where theirs are the dominant voices, where they can garner respect as well as derision, Himes's working-class and poor people have established their socioeconomic place. It is a dirty, dangerous place of precarious existence, on one hand, but on the other hand, it is a place of hope, vivacity, and ingenuity. It is not a place that houses simply a mass of undifferentiated humanity. There is a diverse and complex socioeconomic mix among Himes's Harlemites. And yet, with the exceptions of earlier detective fiction works by Pauline Hopkins and Rudolph Fisher, it is only in Himes's Harlem detective fiction series that a truly multivariant depiction of socioeconomic class issues is explicitly and intricately entwined with the construction of black characters in the genre.[3]

In this discussion I will focus on socioeconomic stratification within Himes's fictional Harlem. Himes writes about black gangsters and killers, "addicts, bums, crooks, pimps, prostitutes, [and] suckers." In this essay, I will follow Himes's lead and write about some of those characters, too. I think a detailed critical examination of a few emblematic Himes characters and their fit in a finely tuned stratification of socioeconomic classes in his Harlem detective fiction will allow for a more nuanced understanding of the characters themselves and will suggest why despite *and* because of its origins as a formulaic popular literary genre the Himes Harlem series was, and remains, an important explicative addition to the bodies of both African-American and American literature.

Speaking in 1964, when already expatriated ten years in France, Chester Himes declared, "Harlem is located in Manhattan . . . Manhattan symbolizes wealth. Manhattan is automobiles, television sets, fully-equipped kitchens, overfed children, clean streets, and houses that don't stink of urine and sex like the lousy hallways of Harlem."[4] Creating a setting that would produce characters that are often "bitter, hungry, and violent," Himes's Harlem is also a place where the characters share with white characters in traditional hard-boiled detective fiction a strong belief in idealized national values concerning economic success. They believe in what Bernard Bell terms "the myth of the American Dream." And while I disagree with the narrowness of his argument that regards Himes's criminal characters as "pathological," I agree with Bell that "myths are a kind of behavioral charter that leads to both negative and positive responses."[5] That is certainly the case of the influence of the myth of the American Dream in Himes's Harlem characters' lives. The black detective team looks out of their car windows at a group of Harlem citizens en route to church; in third-person omniscient voice Himes suggests the ways that socioeconomic standing factors in the characters' thinking about themselves as subjects with agency in the conduct of their lives, "on a typical Sunday morning . . . come sun or come rain."

> Old white-haired sisters bundled up like bales of cotton against the bitter cold; their equally white-haired men, stumbling along in oversize galoshes like the last herd of Uncle Toms, toddling in the last mile toward salvation on half-frozen feet.
>
> Middle-aged couples and their broods, products of the post-war generation, the prosperous generation, looking sanctimonious in their good warm clothes, going to praise the Lord for the white folks' blessings.
>
> Young men who hadn't yet made it, dressed in lightweight suits and top coats sold by color instead of quality or weight in the credit stores, with enough brown wrapping paper underneath their pastel shirts to keep them warm, laughing at the strange words of God and making like Solomon at the pretty brownskin girls.
>
> Young women who are sure as hell going to make it or drop dead in the attempt, ashy with cold, clad in the unbelievable colors of cheap American dyes, some at the very moment catching the pneumonia which would take them before that God they were on their way to worship.[6]

Himes picks a churchgoing scene to show his citizens on the move all across Harlem and even into the metropolis. He chooses the scene to detail the hopes and aspirations of his Harlem citizens across intra-racial economic divides. He offers in the scene a multigenerational picture that seems to match chronologically the historical, social, and economic movement of African America from the beginning of the twentieth century into its mid-century decade—struggling out of poverty after the failed reconstruction in the South, the land of bales of cotton; striving in the fledgling middle class of the urban North, where legislative maneuvers have managed to loosen the strangleholds of law and tradition to give some hearty souls access to some limited economic opportunities in the mainstream economy; and the hopeful young men and women who imagine that they too will have a chance to continue the march for progress into the comfortable middle-class. Himes does not seem to offer the young people much hope, though, because God's words are incomprehensible to the men and pneumonia awaits the women. Religion is in effect ruled out as a source of more than simple blind movement; it may foster aspiration but offers no practical route to the means of change. Himes is indifferent to the fates of characters following that path. They are not the characters that his novels chronicle. Even if they are depicted as Harlem's normative citizens, they are at the periphery of the action, not the community's key economic players.

Class ranking is dictated by money, social and political power, and access to those who have one and/or the other. There are upper-, middle- and lower-class rankings established by those within the community. There are tiers of subtle difference within the three overall rankings. While the terminology is shared with mainstream America, the upper, middle and lower classes in Himes's Harlem do not, nor can they be expected to, correspond one-for-one with classing grouping of the same name in mainstream communities. Characters within the Harlem novels as well as readers of the Harlem novels accept the meanings for the terms imposed by Himes for this literary community. Within the Harlem community the characters on the lowest rung of the economic ladder choose various approaches to survival. Some seek relief from the sweltering heat of their apartments by sitting "half-nude" in the open tenement windows. Others "crawl out on the fire escapes, [shuffle] up and down the sidewalks, [prowl] up and down the streets in dilapidated cars."[7] In the winter, still others among this class, "[dress] in light-weight suits and topcoats sold by color instead of quality or weight in the credit stores, with enough brown wrapping paper underneath . . . to keep them warm."[8] As was discussed earlier in this essay, these citizens are a large segment of "the good colored people of Harlem" in Himes's series. They are seen going to church on Sundays, walking down the streets carrying bags of groceries, escorting their children to school, and going to work as gardeners, milkmen, garbage collectors, truck drivers, maids, elevator operators, and other service workers in and around Harlem and metropolitan New York. These characters are in all the novels in the series, but they are not memorable. And yet, they may in many ways share the perspectives of most mainstream readers, who are peering in on the raucous activities of the Harlem criminal characters in the same spirit as ordinary Harlem citizens within the novels are peering out of their windows or doorways and gingerly stepping out into the streets to view with open mouths and excitement the spectacles of violence and bizarre activity that regularly take place in their community. They also quickly disappear behind locked doors and lowered eyelids when the police arrive on the scene to investigate crimes. They do not want to tangle with their ruthless neighbors or get involved with the police who regularly ignore their needs and disrespect them as citizens. These characters are peripheral to the main story, but even they are shown to be influenced by the culture of poverty and its attendant correlate resourcefulness when negotiating their circumstances. A wheel being stolen from a car is placed on the curb in a way that allows it to go rolling rapidly down the street. A normal respectable Harlem citizen will become the wheel's new owner. "A heavy-set, middle-aged man wearing a felt skull cap, old mended sweater, corduroy pants and felt slippers, was emerging from the back apartment when the wheel crashed into the back wall of the hallway. He gave it a look, then did a double take. He looked about quickly, and, seeing no one, grabbed it, ducked back into his apartment and locked the door. It wasn't every day manna fell from heaven."[9] The man's reaction is typical of the normal Harlem citizenry. No one will judge the man's actions as wrong—unethical or immoral, if indeed the matter is ever discovered and discussed. The receipt of the tire is a simple act of God; the man was in the right place, at the right time, with the right presence of mind to accept that generosity. But some characters are more ambitious. They choose to rise above their socioeconomic circumstances by creating a more self-generated and regular delivery of earthly manna, thereby also creating class stratification within the Harlem community.

Those characters that compose the middle classes in the fictional Harlem community are mainly of two groups: legitimate small business people—owners of restaurants, bars, funeral homes, barber shops, beauty salons, and landlords who rent rooms in their homes—and those who cater to vice markets and money scams—madams who own or manage whorehouses, people running religious or spiritualist scams, drug dealers, those who provide places for gambling, and numbers runners primarily compose the second group. Some of Himes's middle-class Harlemites have professional positions, such as policemen, politicians, and members of the clergy, but these positions frequently serve only as covers for the "real" work in vice markets. As Edward Margolies says of these characters, "the difference between legitimate authority and crooks is not so much morality as power."[10] As might be expected, these "professionals" all live under markedly better circumstances than do their poor neighbors. Himes describes one turn-of-the-century building on 149th Street as one of the "better-class residences for the colored people of Harlem."[11] Groups of middle-class "colored boys and girls" are seen by the black detectives at the skating rink in Central Park "in ski ensembles and ballet skirts . . . skating the light fantastic."[12] In another middle-class neighborhood, a character notes "a red brick building with a fluted façade . . . [and] Big new cars lined the curb."[13] Many within the middle class, however, are at the low end of the group, just one scam away from poverty, but secure for the moment. In *Blind Man with a Pistol*, three Harlem married couples are being interrogated by the black detective team and a white officer about what they saw and heard the night a murder was committed in their building's basement. The tenants' employment situations are instructive for understanding how the citizens in this portion of Himes's Harlem middle class support themselves. In the first apartment, Mr. Tola Onan Ramsey says he is a presser at the local dry-cleaners where his wife irons shirts. In the next apartment, Mr. Socrates X. Hoover says he parks cars at Yankee Stadium, while his wife says she keeps "appointments." When questioned for details about the appointments, she says they are "just appointments" of no "special kind."[14] In the last apartment, Mr. Booker T. Washington says he is the manager of a pool hall and his wife is a housewife who sometimes tells fortunes from her home. When the detectives discuss the tenants and the interviews after leaving the building, the white detective is especially exasperated by what he sees as a lack of information they have received: "I mean that shit about their occupations," he says.[15] "Well, it's half-true, like everything else, replies Grave Digger." The black detective then interprets more fully to his white colleague the tenants' Harlemized occupations: "Washington hangs around the . . . poolroom where he earns a little scratch racking balls when he hasn't snatched a purse that paid . . . Hoover watches parked cars at night . . . around Yankee Stadium to keep them from being robbed of anything he can rob himself. . . . And what else can two big yellow whores do but hustle? That's why those sports [their husbands] make themselves scarce at night. . . . Ramsey and his wife do just what they say . . . all you got to do is look at all those suits and shirts [hanging on a rack] which don't fit him."[16] These characters live above the very poor, who work only legitimate, but menial and low-paying jobs. Everyone in the Harlem community knows why so many citizens are confined to those jobs, but they accord them no particular respect for doing the work. The three couples in the apartment, by contrast, are accorded some degree of added respect because they have shown initiative and created hustles which mean that none of them have to take what is considered the lowest level of employment: "work in white folks' kitchens."[17] Subjectivity as working men and women is claimed on their on terms, even if the ethics of their choices are contested and contextualized within parameters set by restrictions imposed by the larger society. The savvy, if embittered detective, Grave Digger, pointedly asks the white detective three questions that when answered reveal the politics of race that cause and maintain the kind of life and living environment they have found in the apartment building: "Why would anyone live here who was honest? Or how could anyone stay honest who lived here? What do you want?"[18] Grave Digger then explains what for him and his African-American partner, Coffin Ed, is obvious: "This place was built for vice, for whores to hustle in and thieves to hide out in. And somebody got a building permit, because it's been built after the ghetto got here."[19] In other words, given the kinds of wages the typical Harlem citizen can earn legitimately, how can anyone, but especially those who in official metropolitan government help to firmly seal closed the doors to employment accessibility, expect to fill any building they permit to be constructed in Harlem without implicitly condoning and supporting the health and welfare of underground economy activities among potential tenants. There probably are even bribes involved in the dealings between white permit processors and white owners of the construction companies that build the Harlem apartments, Grave Digger suggests. The black detectives, like their creator, Chester Himes, will not let whites and others have what they want: the freedom to feign ignorance about the mechanics of Jim Crow oppression and thereby elude responsibility for their own collusion in maintaining the status quo. If black Harlem characters have learned to bend and twist to make the best of their bent and twisted circumstances, Himes declares, then so be it. But those who participated to bend and twist the circumstances are not allowed to then suggest that there is somehow something inherently immoral or unethical about those in Harlem who manage to succeed, despite their circumstances. Following that logic, Himes creates in his upper echelon characters his most spirited presentations of the class divide.

In *Blind Man with a Pistol* (1969) two upper-class Harlem characters are featured in the plot. Guided strictly by the community's standards of conduct, both have assessed their community's needs and found creative ways to address those needs and make money. For this essay's purposes we will look closely at one of the characters, General Ham, who is the leader of a religious group that worships in the Temple of Black Jesus. He is first described to the reader as he is arriving at his church: "A short, fat, black man with a harelip. His face was running with sweat as though his skin was leaking. His short black hair grew so thick on his round inflated head it looked artificial, like drip-dry hair. His body looked blown up like that of a rubber man. The sky-blue silk suit he wore . . . glinted with a blue light. He looked inflammable. But he was cool."[20] His physical appearance is somewhat comical and less than dignified, in the conventional sense. But the last sentence uses a vernacular expression, "cool," that suggests he actually is a man in control of himself, and controlling things in his environment. He is a henchman for one of Harlem's most successful crime bosses, Doctor Moore. The description the narrator gives of the General's boss as he later collects money offers a sharp contrast in appearances between Ham and Moore, suggesting as well the "cool" beauty of deep-pocketed underground economy wealth in this community: "[His] black velvety skin . . . looked recently massaged. Despite his hair . . . his light-brown eyes beneath thick glossy black eyebrows were startlingly clear and youthful. Long black lashes gave him a sexy look. But there was nothing lush about his appearance, still less about his demeanor. He was dressed in dark gray summer worsted, black shoes, dark tie, white shirt, and wore no jewelry of any sort, not even a watch. His manner was calm, authoritative, his eyes twinkled with good humor but his mouth was firm and his face grave."[21] Not simply contradictory, this description suggests characters that are like chameleons. General Ham is a larger than life figure; the man he works for adopts a much quieter and yet more commanding demeanor. Like Rinehart in Ralph Ellison's *Invisible Man* (1953), they adapt as is appropriate for their roles in their environment. Doctor Moore can read that environment like a book. His employee, General Ham, among his flock can afford to look less crisp, less sophisticated by conventional standards because he wants his working-class church members to receive him as one of them. When Doctor Moore is out collecting money, he has to appear to be a no-nonsense operator who will brook no interference with the smooth operations of his enterprises. In both instances, he knows the power of his players' positions within his community and he directs each one accordingly. He does not have to impress anyone with a false "lush" appearance. He is already "velvety . . . glossy . . . clear . . . youthful . . . and sexy," among other attributes. He does not need a watch; he is surrounded at all times by a small cadre of helpers who know he is an authority figure. Adding to his personal persona of wealth, power, and leadership, the small dark man is flanked by two silent black male assistants, who dress in white collars as clerics when with him in public and "white cotton jackets and cooks' caps" when serving in his home. He also has two "dangerous-looking black men clad in black leather and caps" serving as his driver and personal security team. Known simply as Doctor Moore to everyone, the powerful underground kingpin's apartment in one of Harlem's most upscale buildings reflects in part the money General Ham's church has gained from its parishioners, and that his boss therefore has at his personal disposal: "The entrance hall was sumptuously furnished. A wall-to-wall carpet of a dark purple color covered the floor." His apartment contains other furnishings associated with comfortable living, including "straight-backed chairs of some dark exotic wood with overstuffed needlepoint seats . . . translucent curtains and purple silk drapes."[22] But because Doctor Moore spends little time in his apartment, and has no interest in aesthetics (as his plain, if expensive, clothes and lack of jewelry attest), the apartment is almost bare.

Doctor Moore has several sources of money at his disposal, but he has one business that most supports his comfortable lifestyle. He is a pimp. The prostitutes who work for him are beautiful and cultured enough to fit in with high society white and black men on the Manhattan interracial "cocktail circuit." This is how the Doctor's real money is made. When his cook has to buy butter for the evening meal's cornbread, Doctor Moore instructs him to "tap the trunk" where the daily collections are stored. When one of his prostitutes fails to bring him money on the same evening, however, she is admonished harshly and told by the Doctor, "I mean business. The rent isn't paid and I am behind with my Caddy."[23] The "Caddy" is a black Cadillac limousine, so well cared for it shines "in the sun like polished jet." Its status as a luxury vehicle of the top order is suggested when the narrator says it "whispers" when driven. Doctor Moore's upper-class status, despite his words to the prostitute, is also evident when he goes on rounds to collect money donated to his people making speeches for Black Power on the streets. His driver routinely pulls up to the curb in no-parking zones. The Doctor is a powerful man in the Harlem community, meaning among other things that he has connections with and support (well paid for) from white people in authority in public institutions. No patrolman will dare give him a ticket or tell him to move the Cadillac for fear of having to answer to their white superiors.

The nature of economic power in Himes's Harlem is understood by community members as both complexly interconnected within Harlem and beyond the pale of mainstream society's professed norms. The reader is never told whether or not his church parishioners know about General Ham's connections with Doctor Moore or his other business. In any event, that knowledge would be irrelevant to his parishioners. The attraction of General Ham's religious guidance involves his impassioned exhortations to his poor and working-class congregation to rise up against racial oppression. Mixing traditional black religious practices, with racial politics and personal greed, his church's most sacred religious icon is "a gigantic black plaster of paris . . . Jesus Christ, hanging by his neck from a rotting white ceiling. . . . There was an expression of teeth-bared rage on Christ's black face. His arms are spread, his fists balled, his toes curled. Black blood dripped from red nail holes. The legend underneath read: 'THEY LYNCHED ME.' "[24] The parishioners in the Temple of Black Jesus are proud that their leader, General Ham, and his approach to Christianity are unorthodox, by white religious standards. That heterodoxy is for them a deliberate stance against racial oppression and the societal status quo, which dictates that all blacks stay subservient, docile, and above all else, accepting of their socioeconomic and political positions in the United States. The obvious rage, pain, degradation, defiance, and resistance that their Christ figure depicts is what they want to hear talked about by their religious leader. The General says to his enthusiastic followers, "Don't call me Prophet. . . . A prophet is a misfit who has visions. . . . Neither am I a latterday Moses. . . . Moses was a square. Instead of leading his people out of Egypt he should have taken over Egypt, then their problems would have been solved. . . . I ain't' a race leader neither . . . the only place to race whitey is on the cinder track. . . . I'm a soldier . . . I'm a plain and simple soldier in this fight for right. Just call me General Ham. I'm your commander. We got to fight not race."[25] And with that, his followers are satisfied, even if he also is working for a pimp. That seemingly contradictory business would likely be explained, if parishioners were to question him, as yet another way to outwit hypocritical whites because the men Doctor Moore's prostitutes serve are generally whites, or prominent blacks who collude with whites to oppress poor blacks. General Ham and Doctor Moore, then, in their own convoluted and self-serving ways bring back into circulation in Harlem some of the money kept away by others. So, as the narrator flatly states, "They believed in a Prophet named Ham. They welcomed the Black Jesus to their neighborhood."[26] And why should they not believe? Himes's narrative asks. "The white Jesus hadn't done anything for them," while in the black Jesus they at least could see a reflection of themselves, their own historical situation, and be roused to resist the legacy of that history in their own lives.[27] With enterprise one of the community's own rank and file, General Ham, has successfully risen in class status because he has combined racial pride, indignation, street smarts, and a devil-may-care attitude, with hope for increased prosperity despite an unjust and hostile world.

In Himes's Harlem detective fiction class formation is an intricate and particular process that adds a crucial layer of significance to Himes's overall presentation in the series of his characters and the culture he creates among them. He focuses on the perspectives of poor and working-class criminal characters that are ruthlessly ambitious. They reject mainstream ethics because they understand the constructed nature of many middle-class rules of conduct, while embracing enthusiastically middle-class drive for material wealth and social status. Because Himes's characters are rebellious, unruly, and have no respect for many of the so-called middle-class values, their unconventional actions may be deemed ridiculous, unreasonable, immoral, or even illogical. But close critical examination of the circumstances of Himes's Harlem criminal citizens, from the characters' perspectives, reveals a particular logic that makes their actions decidedly rational in their socio-economic context. Rachel Adams explains the concept of the disruptive "wild" slave that informs much of Morrison's character construction in *Beloved*, and offers incisive commentary for applying to our understanding of the symbiotic historical relationship between Himes's "criminals" and those in the larger U.S. society: "The wildness exhibited by these slaves cannot be seen as the antithesis of the slave owner's civility but as a mirror that reflects the way that slavery has contaminated everything, threatening to dissolve moral categories and meaning itself."[28] Substitute the words "Himes's Harlem criminal citizens" for "slaves," in the quote, and "the idealized national community's civility" rather than "the slave owner's civility," and one is forced to see the whole enterprise of "crime" as much more an historic and systemic quagmire—slavery and its legacies—and much less the purview of racialized individual actors—individual will, not withstanding.

Himes's black Harlem characters simply cannot be understood from any one perspective, and certainly not from any one negative perspective. In other words, despite the critical tendency to define the criminals of Himes's Harlem monolithically, no one term, like pathological, or critical stance, like nihilism, can encompass all that they are or suggest as literary subjects. Even as they seem to wholeheartedly embrace idealized notions of economic success bred of individual will and drive, they also contextualize and temper their adherence to the myths of idealized ethics and morality that are posed as the guiding lights for one's conduct when achieving economic success in the United States—and by extension in the literature produced from within the culture, including hard-boiled detective fiction. Gangsterism and graft haunt all American lives because the very systems that support the national society are rigged so that some citizens enjoy unfair advantage for economic opportunity while others automatically are denied access, according to Himes. So, unless willful ignorance is the goal, there is no point in fantasizing that anyone escapes unscathed, including the reader of the novels. The specific situations and attitudes of Himes's characters are informed by the characters' status as *black* poor and working-class male and female citizens, already a complicated nexus of subjectivities. Their economic status is directly influenced by under-employment resulting from racism, racist practices and traditions. According to Himes, with arguably some hyperbole, the crime rate was the highest in the world in Harlem because "the only employment young Negroes could find were jobs as street sweepers and porters."[29] Under such dire constrictions for employment opportunities, Himes's ambitious black characters feel that they are left with only criminal enterprises—theft, fencing of stolen goods, religious scams, gambling, prostitution, drug-dealing, loan-sharking, and various management arrangements for all of those activities—if they want to succeed economically. When white detectives question why so many Harlem citizens get involved with scams and so few play by mainstream rules of ethical and moral conduct, Himes's black characters bristle with indignation at the hypocrisy. They respond that the very question suggests yet another ploy by those in the mainstream to rationalize blocking them as black citizens from avenues to economic success. Even the black detectives, who live in Queens and are cruelly brutal in many aspects of their policing duties in Harlem, remark that there is a vicious racial double-standard at play in the community: "If you white people insist on coming up to Harlem where you force colored people to live in vice-and-crime-ridden slums, it's my job to see that you are safe."[30] The bitter irony of whites being the subject of institutional protection by black cops even in Harlem, when whites go there expressly to satisfy illicit vices, creating more market demand for the very criminal activities that mark black citizens as unworthy of institutional protection is an explicit critique of that hypocrisy. Most of Himes's characters do not feel they can afford the rules of ethics and morality professed by mainstream society because with few exceptions they do not have access to the legitimate enterprises where ethical and moral behavior are assets. The disconnect between idealized national values of ethics and morality and their practical application for economic success is also a common refrain in traditional hard-boiled fiction. Rather than issues of race and racism, however, class differences are posed as the sole source for narrowly constricted accessibility. The fight for full access to opportunity is, in other words, naturalized as the domain of white men. Examining briefly that process of naturalization for who is worthy of citizenship rights and how Himes's character make sense of the differences in expectations as citizens in the shadow of the metropolis will help to further show why Himes's manipulation of the genre provides a magnifying glass-like view for understanding his Harlem citizens' economic decisions.

White working class men in traditional detective fiction, like mild-mannered gangster Ned Beaumont in Dashiell Hammett's hard-boiled classic *The Glass Key* (1931), often identify with each other based on their shared sense that the economic playing field has been made unequal because other white men do not play by "the rules." They make comments that clearly show the disdain and distrust they feel for those in the upper classes, that they see as unfairly gaining socio-economic advantage from the labors of white working men. When Beaumont's boss tells him that he intends to marry the daughter of a wealthy state Senator, Beaumont's response is to offer a warning. The Senator is "one of the few aristocrats left in America. . . . [S]ew your shirt on when you go to see them, or you'll come away without it, because to them you're a lower form of animal life and none of the rules apply."[31] Beaumont's comment is biting and shows his bitterness about class-related hypocrisy. The Senator, he says, is an "aristocrat," but the sarcastic tone suggests that what Beaumont means to convey is that the Senator thinks of himself as better than the other man, who is a busi-nessman and a known underworld figure. The Senator, himself corrupt but operating under the cloak of professional and upper-class status, feels no ethical, moral, or perhaps even legal, obligation to treat the man fairly. He would steal the very shirt off the back of the other man because "none of the rules apply" for civil or moral conduct in rela-tionships with those the Senator considers socioeconomically beneath him. The black maids and janitors, as well as the black thugs and even the comic characters that fill-in the backgrounds of traditional hard-boiled detective texts could all have voiced the same sentiment, if not the same words, but in the connected contexts of class *and* race. In tra-ditional mainstream hard-boiled detective fiction the texts concede no class connections across race but they also suggest no way to ease the tensions between whites divided by class privilege.[32] The barriers between white working-class characters and those in the upper classes by and large remain intact in the genre.

Himes situates his narratives in a community of black characters. His depictions of the class dynamics there offer readers a perspective on issues related to class that is very different from that found in traditional hard-boiled genre narratives. Rather than the unresolved and bitter divisions that one finds in traditional hard-boiled detective fiction, class stratification and formation in Himes's detective series suggests some-thing positive and robust about the fictional Harlem community and its citizens. That black Harlem citizens are able to generate enough funds to create distinct economic stratum is a feat that in and of itself is constructed in the series as a sign of their inventiveness and resilience. Himes looked beyond hard-boiled detective fiction's traditions to models that would allow him to show his characters' triumphs. Like Br'er Rabbit characters, traditional in African-American oral stories, Himes's ambitious black Harlem citizens have to outfox the fox, that is, find ways to get around racist restrictions. Like legendary badman Stagolee, also a character from early African American oral traditions, Himes's criminal Harlem characters have to be smart, driven and daring in their pursuit of upward mobility and economic success (Fry, Roberts). With those cultural forerunners in mind, Himes constructs a setting of absurdist realism in his Harlem series to suggest the precarious nature of the environment and the desperate lengths his characters with upwardly mobile aspirations will go to try to rise above their imposed socioeconomic circumstances. And yet, Himes is careful to show that the characters do not think of themselves as absurd or desperate.

Sister Heavenly, in *The Heat's On* (1966), is typical of Himes's black characters. She returns home one evening to find that she has lost everything. Her home, out of which she ran a heroin and cocaine den disguised as a place for receiving special blessings and spiritual guidance, has been burned to the ground. With it went her cache of money used for bribes (and possibly her retirement) and all of her treasured mementos from past liaisons with various male lovers. Her response to her loss is "Well, I'm back on my bare ass where I started, but I ain't flat on my back."[33] As she walks away from the charred remains of her old life, she begins immediately to plan a new business/scam to support a new life. Sister Heavenly lives the blues ethos: she may be down but she's not out. From the perspective of a class critique, Sister is important because she is a poor woman who refuses to accept the role assigned to her class. She is defiant and will make money so that she can live well on her own terms, taking whatever avenues of opportunity are available to her. She does not whine, look for excuses, fall into self-pity, or even blame herself when she suffers misfortune. Without rancor she pays a white police detective a weekly bribe to keep her business safe from raids, so she knows her socioeconomic situation is not strictly of her own making but rather a consequence of a larger structure of economic corruption that in a variety of ways affects all citizens. Because Sister Heavenly is not political, she does not call out, as such, the politics of race or capitalism. But because she is practical—a realist about the terms of her socioeconomic position—and a staunch believer in what literary and cultural studies scholar bell hooks aptly terms the "ethic of liberal individualism," Sister Heavenly will find a way to recover economically within her Harlem community.[34]

The Harlem—and its citizens—that Himes has created is a community governed by a worldview not unlike the one Russian scholar and theorist Mikhail Bakhtin describes as the "carnivalesque" in his landmark work, *Rabelais and His World* (1968). In Michael Holquist's introduction to the work, he says Bakhtin's study "explores . . . the interface between a stasis imposed from above and a desire for change from below, between old and new, official and unofficial."[35] Himes read and talked about Rabelais' sixteenth-century stories concerning French political life and culture, even having his characters on three occasions mention Gargantua. The convoluted and fantastical tales as well as the narrative form of the Gargantua stories and the later travels of Gargantua's son, Pantagruel, and his manservant, Panurge, are too numerous and various to summarize here. The three most important things to note for this discussion are that, one, the stories' narrative perspectives are greatly influenced by Gargantua's and Pantagruel's giant size—they experience the world from perspectives that are completely alien to the smaller peoples and other cultures they encounter. Two, their travels and experiences take them to places where the social norms found would be deemed alien by Rabelais's readers, then and now. And, three, the scenes of excessive eating, drinking, lovemaking, joking, roasting, singing, and masquerading are both joyous and spontaneous *and* filled with the potential for social upheaval.

When, for example, human-sized Panurge falls by accident into giant Pantagruel's mouth, he finds a whole civilization of human-sized people who live there. The inhabitants inside of Pantagruel's mouth experience a world similar to that of those who live outside with Pantagruel. Those who live within Pantagruel's mouth, for instance, see his teeth not as teeth but as large boulders bordering their fertile landscape. It is never made clear to the reader if the people even know they are living in someone's mouth because they never discuss their circumstances from that point of view. A farmer Panurge questions about all this is apparently uninterested in exploring the outside world, but he briefly notes what he has heard about it: "[I]t is commonly reported, that without this there is an earth, whereof the inhabitants enjoy the light of a Sunne and a Moone, and that it is full of, and replenished with very good commodities."[36] The farmer explains that all he knows about his world is what he sees and has experienced all of his life—it is a thriving place, with country hamlets and large cities and an active commercial environment that supports the citizens living there. Further, Rabelais makes up words and mixes them (along with Greek, Latin, and other languages) without translation or explanation into the Gargantua and Pantagruel texts. Readers are forced to make sense of the new words in the narratives' contexts, understanding them as standardized terms. Rabelais, the author and narrative authority, thereby allows the reader to experience the power relationship he is suggesting about both the constructed natures of societies and the imposition of meanings. Terrence Cave says that Rabelais' works "should . . . be read as a challenge to the reader: be ready to be disconcerted . . . [and] shocked out of your habits and prejudices."[37] Which world can claim to be the norm? Rabelais asks in his works.

Himes asks the same question in the Harlem series: Who is unnatural? Who establishes what it the norm? Unlike white characters in traditional hard-boiled fiction, black characters in Himes's Harlem accept the symbiotic nature of their class standings. They are not threatened by those who are above them or superior to those who below them; they do not feel restricted to their current status when opportunities to move upward present themselves. Most of Himes's Harlemites seize or create opportunities in scams *and* legitimate local businesses. The deconstructive nature of Rabelais's work with regard to social norms is what, I think, Chester Himes understood in the Gargantua and Pantagruel's stories and chose to replicate in his own work, the Harlem novels.[38]

Peter Stallybrass and Allon White have argued that in the United States, because of historic evolution out of racial and economic binary opposition, the two peoples posited as most opposite—blacks and whites—developed cultural rituals and forms that necessarily were symbiotic to some degree.[39] The concept of Whiteness required an opposite concept of Blackness in order to exist. Accordingly, in order to insure the survival of the "inferior" group and, by extension, the survival of the "superior" group, the development of African-American cultural forms had to be encouraged by whites—even as they also were vigorously denounced. Bakhtin is quoted by Fiske as saying, "Carnival is not a spectacle seen by the people: they live in it, and everyone participates because its very idea embraces all the people."[40] Himes understood this complicated reality. That is why it was paramount to him that the symbiotic social spectacle he staged in his detective series occurred in a centralized domestic space, not on the margins, on a site that engaged all of the players. That place was Himes's Harlem.

Himes was especially interested in notions of leveling, places where blacks and whites meet on equal ground. He explicitly notes the influence of Rabelais's work on his in *The Primitive* (1957). In one instance, Himes's protagonist tries to refute the charge that his fictional work is too angry, too much in the style of unmitigated "vulgar" racial protest: "Then what about Rabelais? The education of Gargantua? What's more vulgar than that?"[41] Himes uses the term "vulgar" to refer, on one hand, to the explicit emphasis on lower bodily functions in Rabelais's work—including belching, spitting and yelling, giving birth, oversized genitalia, and having sex—and to the explicit sexuality and objectification of the body in his own work. Beyond that, Himes's characters connect with Bakhtin's reading of Rabelais's presentation of vulgar carnival behavior as political. Holquist says that Bakhtin's vision of Rabelaisian carnival is "about freedom, the courage needed to establish it, the cunning required to maintain it, and—above all—the horrific ease with which it can be lost."[42] The work suggests that socially disruptive behavior, no matter how seemingly benign, serves the marginalized and the powerless by giving them collectively a hidden force of resistance against social oppression and repression. The oppressed reject the status quo and redefine what are "acceptable" norms of behavior. In the riotous excess, or spectacle, of sixteenth-century French carnival scenes, Rabelais saw the potential for at least easing, if not entirely slipping the yoke of social control.

In a similar vein, Himes's scenes of grotesque realism in carnival-like celebrations capture not just moments of short-term physical release for the folk from social restrictions, rather, they suggest that his ordinary Harlem characters also have a profound understanding of socioeconomic and political structures. Because they understand the politics of race, in relation to their socioeconomic status, they are released, at least in their minds, from the burden of acceptance of social devaluation based on any inherent inferiority. With the Harlem detective fiction series Himes creates "an anti-illusionistic style that remains physical, carnal, material, [while telling] social truths."[43] Unlike deterministic naturalism, grotesque realism does not presume that the individual or group is helpless before the forces of Fate or institutional hierarchy. In *Blind Man with a Pistol* (1969), for example, there are three actual carnival scenes (the presence of the carnivalesque spirit permeates all of the texts in the series). In all three, the participants are both black and white, young and old, traditional citizens by mainstream standards and Himes's "usuals," that is, "many prostitutes, pederasts, pickpockets, sneak thieves, confidence men, steerers, and pimps."[44] The specifics of one of the carnival scenes is instructive for understanding the connection between Rabelais's and Himes's concepts of the potential for sociopolitical and economic transformation through the deconstruction of societal norms and understanding the multiple nature of subjectivity.

The instigator in the following carnival scene is a young African-American man named Marcus Mackenzie. He is an ex-soldier, who has returned from Europe with a rich Swedish wife and a grand idea for how to end racism in the United States: he is going to teach the religion of Brotherhood. The people in Harlem soon pronounce Brother Marcus naïve—after all, he came up with his idea when he was in Europe, surrounded by white European Negrophiles. From the Harlemites' view—and Himes's—only one who is isolated from the reality of U.S. Negro life could believe that a peaceful solution like the concept of brotherly love would solve the "Negro problem." Still, because they are moved by MacKenzie's sincerity, they agree to support his March of Brotherhood: "Black people walking down the street grinned, then laughed, then shouted encouragement . . . [because] no one doubted him. The intensity of his emotion left no doubt."[45] Sexual overtones, and the sense of intense carnal attraction between the black and white participants, although their march was originally conceived as a political rally, quickly overshadow the march itself:

> The black youth driving the old Dodge car slipped in the clutch. The white youth sitting at his side raised his arms with his hands clasped in the sign of brotherhood. The old command car shuddered and moved off. The forty-eight integrated black and white marchers stepped forward, their black and white legs flashing in the amber lights. . . . Their bare black and white arms shone. Their silky and kinky heads glistened. . . . Somehow the black against the white and the white against the black gave the illusion of nakedness. The forty-eight orderly young marchers gave the illusion of an orgy. The black and white naked flesh in the amber light filled the black and white onlookers with a strange excitement."[46]

From the beginning of the passage, when the driver "slipped in the clutch," to the "naked flesh" and "excitement" of the frankly sexual end of the passage, the concept of a profound, elemental attraction uniting these two apparently opposing peoples grows as the scene progresses. In addition, the complementary nature of the relationship between the black and white participants is shown when their white and black skins appear most stark, most clearly defined, most "naked" next to each other. Then, "an unseen band" strikes up "a Dixieland march" and the scene instantly changes to merriment, and a pure Rabelaisian carnival scene:

The colored people on both sides of the street began locomotioning and boogalooing as though gone mad. White women in the passing automobiles screamed and waved frantically. Their male companions turned red like a race of boiled lobsters. The police cars opened their sirens to clear the traffic. But it served to call the attention of more people from the sidelines . . . a long straggling tail of laughing, dancing, hysterical black and white people had attached itself to the original forty-eight. Black and white people came from the station waiting room . . . from nearby bars, from the dim stinking doorways . . . the flea-bag hotels, the cafeterias, the greasy spoons . . . the shoe-shine parlors, the poolrooms—pansies and prostitutes, ordinary bar drinkers and strangers in the area who had stopped to get a bit[e] to eat, Johns and squares looking for excitement, muggers and sneak thieves looking for victims. . . . They [all] joined the *carnival* group thinking maybe they were headed for a revival meeting, a sex orgy, a pansy ball, a beer festival, a baseball game. The white people attracted by the black. The black people attracted by the white.[47]

On one hand, this appears to be a scene of chaos; on the other hand, it is a scene where the social barrier between whites and blacks is broken down, where social hierarchy is dissolved. The potential for the moment to transform into an opportunity for meaningful change is there. And yet, no revolutionary awakening occurs. The outbreak of carnival activities remains superficial, at the level of the sexual and sensual. On one hand, that physical and carnal attraction is important because the personal is political, so racial barriers and social taboos are breached. Beyond that, the fact that the police move immediately to quell the commotion when it grows beyond its original confinable scope suggests that the authorities recognize the revolutionary potential inherent in spontaneous popular movements. But a key element for profound political transformation is missing here: the word. No one steps up to give purposeful direction to the crowd—to give form, substance and political meaning to the force of the crowd. And so, the outbreak remains in many respects on the level of the senses. And yet, it is also in those unguarded moments when blacks see whites and whites see blacks for what they are, merely other human beings. The veneer of racial superiority and any other differences are shown to be as superficial as any other costume covering. Human beings are equals at the level of the senses—that they all are capable of love, hate, joy, and sexual desire is made apparent. It is in moments such as this carnival scene when Himes's Harlem characters actually experience life on the same level as white characters. The experience reinforces what many Harlemites already know: that they are equally capable for succeeding socioeconomically, despite white peoples' long-term scams to shut blacks out of the economic mainstream and given only the tools available within their own community.

Chester Himes was a product of the black middle class, having been born and reared in midwestern America with his university professor father and schoolteacher mother. And yet, he found himself, at age nineteen, in jail serving a twenty-five year sentence for armed robbery. Between the two extremes of life experience, Himes was made personally aware of the effects of class difference. In the Harlem detective series he created a multilayered presentation of poor, working-, middle-, and upper-class black characters that is made even more incisive because he focuses on a subset of the larger community—the criminal class. It is a small but influential group in his fictional community group. These are slippery characters, in that, one may be drawn to them because they are wickedly comic, genuinely exuberant in their enjoyment of the rich African-American cultural milieu of blues, jazz, and dancing in local clubs, drinking and eating with relish and outrageous abandon from the menus of Southern soul food restaurants, cleverly beguiling with their language play, and inventive in the colorful schemes and scams they concoct. And yet, they are also merciless in their zeal to make money, drawing no lines of distinction between whites or blacks when playing their con games or even in choosing to murder to protect themselves or the material goods or money they have gained. Himes does not offer excuses. Himes does offer characters that attest to a specific shared historical memory of deprivation and long deferred desires for access to the rewards of full U.S. citizenship. He does offer a communal context that is the culmination of hundreds of years of multigenerational hurt and psychic damage. A context in which, "extreme rage," as Lisa Adams notes, "engendered by prolonged psychological and physical cruelty may erupt in many ways, including violent aggression between one injured party and another."[48] Himes's Harlem series helps perceptive readers to find ways to empathize with these characters' predicaments, and therefore understand their choices of action. And yet, to understand is not to condone. The novels simply suggest fuller critical perspectives. Each reader of Himes's Harlem series has an opportunity to examine her or his own presumptions about who is a normative citizen and how that subject position is defined, recognizing that even among this group of "outlaw" characters the ultimate goal of their unruly activity is to find ways to the material comforts and respect accorded those who have full citizenship, which the characters see as related to financial success. In the shade of the white metropolis, "neat categorical oppositions between the past and the present, madness and sanity," moral and immoral, even normal and abnormal, "threaten to become unmoored, as wildness bursts forth at the heart of civilization."[49] For better or worse, Himes's ambitious Harlem characters are shaped in part by the same myths traditionally taught to those living in what is posed as the heart of U.S. civilization. Himes's ambitious Harlem characters are guided by the same ethic of liberal individualism as their white Manhattan counterparts in legitimate, for-profit businesses. In fact, it is the very notion of what is legitimate that is under contestation in Himes's presentation of the various classes that have evolved in his Harlem. If necessity is the true mother of invention, as the adage supposes, than most of the absurdist businesses/scams devised by Himes's Harlem characters are logical market-driven enterprises that are in their own right and context, legitimate. The politics of race, racism, and racist practices and traditions that date back to the earliest days of the seventeenth-century colonial past of what would become the United States of America have forced Himes's mid-twentieth-century Harlem entrepreneurs into the underground economy. And there, because they are as skilled, imaginative, and capable as the next white woman or man, they succeed. Himes argues, through his presentation, which assumes the point of view of the Harlem characters, that their success is no more or less than the achievement of the American Dream, under the absurdist terms of racial segregation in the United States.

NOTES

1. Frankie Bailey, *Out of the Woodpile*, 48.
2. Michel Fabre and Robert E. Skinner, eds., *Conversations*, 16.
3. Pauline Hopkins's serialized novel, *Hagar's Daughter*, was published in the *Colored American* magazine, over a period of months in 1900–1901. Written in the Romance literary style most popular for general reading audiences in the United States at the time, Hopkins created a tale of miscegenation that aimed to denounce racism and to show both the fallibility of notions of racial purity and impurity, and the tragic results of assigning values to the lives of human beings based solely on racial categorization. In the course of the investigations of the murder of an upper class and despicable white man as well as the disappearance of a black female domestic servant, who may be the key witness to the murder, a young black servant girl is enlisted to assist the white detective who has been brought in to solve the cases. The girl, Venus, proves to be smart, resourceful, fearless, and ultimately not only uncovers the whereabouts of the key witness, but rescues her. Accordingly, Venus becomes the first black detective in the genre. While class stratification among African Americans is not her narrative's focus, Hop-

kins's work does show blacks of differing classes. Rudolph Fisher, while publishing in the genre after both Hopkins's contemporary John Edward Bruce and later George Schuyler, was the first African American author to fully incorporate issues of class stratification as a deliberate and significant marker of diversity and complexity among African American characters in detective fiction. In *The Blues Detective: A Study of African American Detective Fiction* (1996), Stephen Soitos identifies Fisher's novel *The Conjure Man Dies* (1932) as "the first black detective novel to use all black characters and to place [them] in the black environment of Harlem" (222). Soitos goes on to say that "Fisher also showed that the black detective novel could show issues of race and class. He was not afraid to critique all levels of class in black Harlem while generally presenting an urban landscape infused with elements of black pride and community" (222).

4. Fabre and Skinner, *Conversations*, 12.

5. Marjorie Pryse and Hortense Spillers, eds., *Conjuring*, 106.

6. Chester Himes, *All Shot Up*, 97.

7. *The Heat's On*, 23.

8. See note 5.

9. Himes, *All Shot Up*, 9.

10. Edward Margolies, *Studies in Black Literature*, 4.

11. Himes, *All Shot Up*, 56.

12. Ibid., 107.

13. Ibid., 57.

14. Himes, *Blind Man with a Pistol*, 81.

15. Ibid., 84.

16. See note 14 above.

17. Ibid.

18. Ibid.

19. Ibid.

20. Himes,, *Blind Man with a Pistol*, 73.

21. Ibid., 48.

22. Ibid., 52.

23. Ibid., 55–56.

24. See note 20 above.

25. Himes, *Blind Man with a Pistol*, 76.

26. ibid., 75.

27. See note 26 above.

28. Kimberly Wallace-Sanders, ed., *Skin Deep Spirit Strong*, 165.

29. Fabre and Skinner, *Conversations*, 14.

30. Himes, *The Real Cool Killers*, 65.

31. Hammet, *The Glass Key*, 9.

32. For more detailed discussions of the decisive ideological battles waged between working-class white males, often native-born and immigrant skilled craftsmen and artisans, and the powerful, rich white males, usually Anglo-Saxon Protestants and native-born, who owned American plants and factories or held professional managerial positions related to industrialization in the post–World War I period, when the hard-boiled genre arose, see Sean McCann's *Gumshoe America: Hard-boiled Crime Fiction and the Rise and Fall of the New Deal Liberalism*, David Cochran's *American Noir: Underground Writers and Filmmakers in the Postwar Era*, and Erin Smith's *Hard-boiled: Working-class Readers and Pulp Magazines*.

33. Himes, *The Heat's On*, 96.

34. bell hooks, *Killing Rage*, 165.

35. Holquist in Bahktin's *Rabelais and His World*, xvi.

36. Rabelais, *Gargantua and Pantagruea* translated by Sir Thomas Urquhart and Pierre LeMotteux; with an introduction by Terrance Cave. New York: Knopf: distributed by Random House, © 1994, 282.

37. Rabelais, *Gargantua and Pantagruea* translated by Sir Thomas Urquhart and Pierre LeMotteux; with an introduction by Terrance Cave. New York: Knopf: distributed by Random House, © 1994, xv.

38. Some discussion of Rabelais's carnivalesque theories of politically disruptive play may be helpful here because understanding how his stories worked will show how they informed much of the disruptive nature Himes created in the Harlem detective fiction narratives. In Rabelais's time, end-of-the-harvest folk celebrations both reinforced the socio-economic and political status quo *and* served as a site for transgression of that status quo. Bakhtin says Rabelais's goal was to "destroy the official [meaning] of [popular] events" (439). From the king's, landed gentry's, and Catholic Church's points of view, festivals were a way for peasants and laborers to release tension, energize (for work to come), and let go of animosities that may have built up against those who would gain the most from their labor. In other words, their interest in the promotion of these events was economic—they wanted to keep peasant laborers happy, relaxed, and apolitical, so that agricultural production, and therefore profits, would continue as usual. From the laborers' points of view, however, these celebrations were an opportunity to break down barriers of hierarchy and to explicitly expose the constructed nature of their social and economic status. Public acknowledgment of economic exploitation may have been dangerous under everyday circumstances—deemed seditious—but in masks, costumes, and festival play the people could express their understanding of and opposition to the political and economic structures of their society. Robert Stam says of Bahktin's conception of carnivals, "[They] . . . shattered at least on a symbolic plane, all oppressive hierarchies, redistributing social roles according to the logic of the 'world upside down' " (134). Rabelais's public celebrations were, according to Bakhtin, utopian festivals favoring free and familiar contact and the intermingling of bodies. Wine, food, song, sexual activities—all the elements deemed necessary for a joyous abandoning of constrictions—were in abundance, and kept everyone equally occupied, thereby undermining standardized constructs of social hierarchy. On a level field, where hierarchy-dependent controlling systems break down and their agents become indistinguishable from the general populace, everything and everyone then becomes available for interrogation. Ideally, the carnival site becomes a place of freedom, of liberation, of deconstruction of social class, for the oppressed. With no presupposed value for either of the opposing entities, the carnivalesque embraces binary opposites to mediate supposed differences.

39. Peter Stallybrass and Allon White, *The Politics and Poetics of Transgression*, 17.

40. Bahktin in Fiske, "Offensive Bodies and Carnival Pleasures," 86.

41. Himes, *The Primitive*, 94.

42. Holquist in Bakhtin's *Rabelais and His World*, xxi.

43. Robert Stam, "Mikhail Bakhtin and Left Cultural Critique", 142.

44. Himes, *Blind Man with a Pistol*, 22.

45. Ibid., 23, 27.

46. Ibid., 27.

47. Ibid., 28.

48. Wallace-Sanders, ed., *Skin Deep Spirit Strong*, 167. Rachel Adams is discussing the tradition of some African-American literary characters that despite their own hurt or marginalized positions in society cannot empathize with one another and other marginalized human beings.

49. Adams, "The Black Look and 'the Spectacle of Whitefolks': Wildness in Toni Morrison's *Beloved*," in *Skin Deep Spirit Strong*, ed. by Kimberly Wallace-Sanders, 176.

BIBLIOGRAPHY

Bailey, Frankie. *Out of the Woodpile: Black Characters in Crime and Detective Fiction*. New York: Greenwood Press, 1991.

Bakhtin, Mikhail. *Rabelais and His World*. Translated by Helene Iswolsky. Bloomington: University of Indiana Press, 1984.

Ellison, Ralph. *Invisible Man*. New York: Random House, 1952.

Fabre, Michel, and Robert E. Skinner, ed. *Conversations with Chester Himes*. Jackson: University of Mississippi Press, 1995.

Fiske, John. "Offensive Bodies and Carnival Pleasure," *Understanding Popular Culture*. Boston: Unwin Hyman, 1989.

Fry, Gladys-Marie. *Night Riders in Black Folk History*. Chapel Hill: University of North Carolina Press, 2001.

Hammett, Dashiell. *The Glass Key*. New York: Vintage Crime/Black Lizard [1931] 1984.

Himes, Chester. *All Shot Up*. New York: Signet Books, 1960.

———. *Blind Man With a Pistol*. New York: Vintage Books, [1969] 1989.

———. *The Heat's On*. New York: Vintage Books, [1966] 1988.

———. *The Real Cool Killers*. New York: Vintage Books, [1959] 1988.

hooks, bell. *Killing Rage: Ending Racism*. New York: H. Holt and Co., 1995.

Margolies, Edward. "The Thrillers of Chester Himes." *Studies in Black Literature* 1, no. 2 (1970): 1–11.

Pryse, Marjorie, and Hortense Spillers, eds. *Conjuring: Black Women, Fiction, and Literary Tradition*. Bloomington: Indiana University Press, 1985.

Roberts, John W. *From Trickster to Badman: The Black Folk Hero in Slavery and Freedom*. Philadelphia: University of Pennsylvania Press, 1990.

Stallybrass, Peter, and Allon White. *The Politics and Poetics of Transgression*. Ithaca: Cornell University Press, 1986.

Stam, Robert. "Mikhail Bakhtin and Left Cultural Critique," in E. Ann Kaplan, Ed. *Postmodernism and Its Discontents: Theories and Practices*. New York: Verso, 1988.

Wallace-Sanders, Kimberly, ed. *Skin Deep Spirit Strong: The Black Female Body in American Culture*. Ann Arbor: University of Michigan Press, 2002.

An Affirmation of Cultural Consciousness in August Wilson's *Joe Turner's Come and Gone*

Theda Wrede

He would not bleach his Negro soul in a flood of white Americanism, for he knows that Negro blood has a message for the world.

—W. E. B. Du Bois

AUGUST WILSON'S *JOE TURNER'S COME AND GONE*, THOUGH PLAY-ful and humorous in tone, strikes a disconcerting note in dealing with the double consciousness that affects the African American psyche. A phrase coined by W. E. B. Du Bois, double consciousness describes the condition of assessing one's worth through a socially predominant value system that is determined by the racial group in power.[1] An insecure identity and a constrained autonomy are the consequences of this state. It is, therefore, necessary for African Americans to remember and revalue who they are culturally, independent of and different from the white American majority.

Wilson presents a setting, Pittsburgh, complete with a value system and a cast full of hopes and fears pertaining to the place. A migration has led the play's characters from the post-Reconstruction South to this great city of the North where, attracted by the melting-pot promise, they hope to create a new identity for themselves. Contrary to their expectations, however, in the North, in particular, the spiritual conflict of double consciousness emerges with renewed force, as the migrants are separated from homes, families, and rural culture, and the ghost of slavery continues to haunt their minds.

The critical debate of *Joe Turner's Come and Gone* has centered on the issues of identity loss and identity recovery as they relate to social and geographical displacements. Mary Bogumil, in " 'Tomorrow Never Comes': Songs of Cultural Identity in August Wilson's *Joe Turner's Come and Gone*," argues that the characters, feeling geographically and socially "displaced" after Reconstruction, have to choose between, on the one hand, inventing a future and, on the other, reverting to a collective identity with cultural ties that have sprung from a shared past. Yet, the choice is never equitable since all the characters have to come to terms with the meaning of the memories inscribed in their community.[2] Kim Pareira, in turn, in "*Joe Turner's Come and Gone:* Seek and You Shall Find," discusses separation, migration, and reunion in African-American culture as essential for rediscovering a collective sense of self. The move from conflict to resolution as a cultural odyssey, Pareira holds, becomes "central to Wilson's exploration of the search by blacks for cultural identity and self-affirmation."[3] Migration is origin, expression, and consequence of the search for identity and "continue[s] to shape the lives of the [individual] characters."[4]

Both Bogumil and Pareira's arguments provide significant insights into the effects of migration onto a cultural identity. I perceive, however, in the protagonist Herald Loomis an additional psychic conflict— where the individual and the collective self confront one another. Situating the individual's identity crisis within the larger dialectic of consciousness that Du Bois famously describes, I will trace the effects of displacement on the individual's autonomy. Specifically, I claim, the journey to the North, though initially configured as an escape, can turn into an internal journey toward self-realization as cultural differences confront each other and personal experience is integrated into a larger cultural memory. Self-realization, in this sense, means to acknowledge the disparate elements that constitute African-American identity, a diasporic identity, that insists on being authenticated even when there are no roots to connect a people to the soil on which they live.[5]

Wilson aptly chooses the post-Reconstruction era and the enormous demographic changes it brought about to review the consequences of migration on a cultural sense of identity. Although Emancipation promised equality, racism and economic hardship continued in the South and led southern African Americans north in search of better conditions. In the post-Reconstruction South paramilitary organizations such as the Ku Klux Klan sought to reestablish white rule as they carried out lynchings and other violent crime. In Tennessee, the Jim Crow laws were instituted as soon as 1881, initiating a gradual reintroduction of statutory discrimination throughout the South.[6] Lacking government support further aggravated conditions for African Americans by failing to provide both financial means for survival and an education for the "poor ignorant field hands,"[7] as Du Bois states, who sought to gain autonomy and improve their condition.[8] Sharecropping represented merely a disguised form of enslavement since sharecroppers not only often worked under former slave drivers (presently gang foremen) but also were frequently not paid for their work.[9] With practically the only jobs available to African Americans in menial labor (men usually worked in farming[10] while women also found employment as servants and washerwomen) and child labor being very common, schooling had very minor importance. Du Bois laments this lack of education as a serious kind of racism: "Looking now at the county black population as a whole," he writes in 1903, "it is fair to characterize it as poor and ignorant. . . . They are ignorant of the world about them, of modern economic organization, of the function of government, of individual worth and possibilities,—of nearly all those things which slavery in self-defense had to keep them from learning."[11] Thus subject to physical and financial exploitation, crop failure and educational discrimination, impoverished African-American farmers and sharecroppers escaped, along with the unemployed, to the cities in search of the "Promised Land."

The first mass urbanization occurred between 1880 and 1910 and was followed by the Great Migration between 1914 and 1940. Desiring greater autonomy, financial safety, and education for themselves and their children, African Americans moved to large cities—located predominantly in the North: Chicago, New York, Philadelphia, Baltimore, Pittsburgh—and many smaller towns. That the migrants were driven by hope that originated in despair becomes manifest in what they left behind and the risks they took:[12]

> [To make the journey] was not necessarily an easy decision, given the risks of a long-distance move. To many black southerners, northward migration meant abandoning the dreams of independence through land ownership that had been central to southern black culture since emancipation. Communal and familial ties would have to be stretched or transplanted, if not severed entirely. Many migrants had to surmount legal and extralegal obstacles devised by southern whites dependent on black labor. In the end, those who left tended to be motivated by a combination of factors, which they often summarized as "bettering my condition," a phrase that embodied a broad comparison of conditions and possibilities in the South with images of the North.[13]

Specifically, life in the North promised self-reliance, including the right to vote, to choose where to live and work, and, significantly, freedom from fears, humiliations, and shame. African Americans longed, Carole C. Marks states, "to achieve their version of the American dream."[14]

Upon arrival in the North, nevertheless, the migrants again faced decisions, this time concerning their new identity as free citizens in a new and more liberal environment. Thus driven by the "longing to attain self-conscious manhood," Du Bois explains, "to merge [t]his double self into a better and truer self," they realized that a "merger" was not possible in a society that, albeit not officially racist, condoned racism all the same.[15] Discriminations involved restrictions on African-American political participation, on professional advancement opportunities, and was manifest in job competition, layoff policies, and racial violence.[16] As a result, the migrants felt two contradictory urges—of either joining by rejecting their own culture or refusing to participate in Northern mainstream society.

Wilson establishes this psychosocial background in his description of the play's geographical setting. Pittsburgh in 1911 equals a "melting pot" in both the literal and figurative senses. It is a city full of creative energy with its "fires of the steel mill rag[ing] with a combined sense of industry and progress" and barges departing with coal and iron ore and returning with steel, suggestive of ample employment in the industry.[17] Promethean-like, the personified city—"flexing its muscles"—epitomizes the ingenuity and control of creation by enabling combinations and amalgamations of raw natural materials literally converting these into the "fresh, hard, gleaming" and refined amalgam steel. But symbolically, Pittsburgh means hope to the newly arrived to be absorbed and assimilated in the great melting pot.[18] The migrants are prepared to lose their separateness to a collective American identity that promises to be just as hard, polished, and superior as steel.

By the same token, Wilson suggests that a forced absorption into the mainstream entails great dangers to an African-American sense of self, both as an individual and as a collective since in order to create a future, the past must be forgotten. Indeed, the imagery implies that the newcomers experience ambivalence:

> From the deep and near South the sons and daughters of newly freed African slaves wander into the city. Isolated, cut off from memory, having forgotten the names of the gods and only guessing at their faces, they arrive dazed and stunned, their heart kicking in their chest with a song worth singing. They arrive carrying Bibles and guitars, their pockets lined with dust and fresh hope, marked men and women seeking to scrape from the narrow, crooked cobbles and the fiery blasts of the coke furnace a way of bludgeoning and shaping the malleable parts of themselves into a new identity as free men of definite and sincere worth.[19] (Wilson)

Wilson opposes two central notions—"markedness" and "memory"—that cause a profound ambivalence towards the new life and tamper the migrants' hope that they may give voice to "a song worth singing." Implying the experiences of enslavement, indentureship, and racism through the trope of "markedness," Wilson insists on the psychological depth of slavery that a mere displacement is unable to erase. At the same time, phrases like "isolation" and being "cut off from memory, having forgotten the names of the gods and only guessing at their faces," which refer to those ethnic recollections preceding enslavement, alert the audience to that kind of memory that is seemingly forgotten. The trauma of enslavement thus persists while cultural memory appears inaccessible. Given this predisposition, the migrants, it seems, must violently create their own: "Scrap[ing] from the narrow, crooked cobbles and the fiery blasts of the coke furnace," they seek "a way of bludgeoning and shaping the malleable parts of themselves into a new identity."[20] Thus foreshadowing those psychological issues that will be central to the plot at the beginning of his play, Wilson raises a few key questions: if a future is only possible through repression of a past trauma that nonetheless has led to the present situation and continues to inform the migrants' sense of self, where should the individual situate him or herself socially and culturally? And while the "Bibles and guitars" and the "hearts kicking in their chest with a song worth singing" indicate hope and joy, these metaphors also refer to cultural peculiarities that may remind of life in the South. If that is so, would an association with the African American community further enhance trauma in the quest for autonomy, or could a new relationship with the ethnic group perhaps even help overcome it?

The conflict between the self and the collective is exemplified in the play's protagonist Herald Loomis. In particular, his longing for autonomy is emblematic of the newcomers' desire for self-affirmation, and his rejection of his culture mirrors their struggle in choosing between inventing an individual identity, which the North—as an escape from memories in the South and a move toward assimilation into the mainstream—seems to offer, and recovering an identity through remembering a shared African-American past. Recently arrived in Pittsburgh and in search of his wife from whom he has been separated for eleven years, Loomis at first believes to find total autonomy in severing all ties with the African-American community. "Possessed," he is traumatized by the experience of seven years of indentured labor in the Joe Turner crew.[21] He deeply distrusts white Southern culture yet cannot value his own. He feels that Christianity has betrayed him, as he was a wandering preacher when captured, and now social gatherings and their rituals, reminding him of his former faith, repulse him.

Burdened with this emotional baggage, Loomis does not seem fit for a new start. Though in search of "a world that speaks to something about himself," he is "unable to harmonize the forces that swirl around him."[22] Communal celebrations and their rituals especially disgust him as they remind him of Joe Turner and the effects the experience has had on his belief system. During the juba dance ceremony, he exclaims: "Stop it! Stop it! You all sitting up here singing about the Holy Ghost. What's so holy about the Holy Ghost?"[23] Loomis blasphemes Christianity and condemns his community's celebrations. He does not recognize the African roots of the dance and songs, which the stage directions describe as "reminiscent of the Ring Shouts of the African slaves. . . . It should be as African as possible, with the performers working themselves up into a near frenzy."[24] Loomis is aware only of the Christian aspects of the dance; hence, it is the Holy Ghost that stands between him and his understanding of the ritual.

Loomis's healing occurs through an "initiation" into his culture and its common past in two phases that are both marked by a vision. The first vision, although apparently alluding to Christian myth, goes back to the experiences of the Middle Passage: "I done seen bones rise up out the water. Rise up and walk across the water. Bones walking on top of the water."[25] The bones "march in a line" before they fall back into the ocean and sink. When reemerging, washed to the shore, they "got flesh on them" and are black.[26] Here, Christian and African myth conflate, reminding the audience of the biblical story of "The Valley of Dry Bones" and, at the same time, of an "African recast" of this myth, one in which the bones turn into black bodies.[27]

The vision denotes a subversive moment and the beginning of a healing process: by evoking the experience of the Middle Passage and the arrival of African slaves on the shores of the American continent, Loomis unknowingly undercuts that kind of Christianity that supports the powerful landowners. In retrieving, in his vision, a time before being "cut off from memory" and before "forgetting the names of the gods,"[28] he reestablishes a link to his ancestors, which identifies him as a member of his culture, an ancient culture with its own rites and myths and a past dating back to the time before the arrival of African slaves in America.[29] The vision shows that despite centuries of oppression and forgetting, African spirituality transcends a superimposed Christian faith. This recognition of the subversive potential of African American Christianity marks an initial personal autonomy.[30]

Although revealing his multiple identities as an American with roots both in Africa and the South, the vision does not enable Loomis to "rise." Instead, he still perceives himself as lying and waiting "on the breath to get into my body."[31] He must wait for the second vision that will allow him to stand up as an independent and free man. This vision, disclosing a surviving "African-ness," is preceded by a recollection of his experiences in the Joe Turner Crew. Bringing to consciousness these memories will help Loomis find himself.

Loomis is fundamentally assisted by Bynum Walker, a conjure man who is in tune with his African heritage and the world around him. At the beginning of the play, the audience encounters Bynum as he performs ancient rites that involve marking circles with pigeon blood, then burying the birds and praying over them.[32] Bynum makes "the impression of always being in control of everything."[33] His great stability and self-assurance spring from his "grand design"[34] and his knowing his "song"—the "Binding Song."[35] Thus, his mission is to bring people together; he states, "I'm a Binder of What Clings."[36] Because he understands the psychological conflict of the African-American community as rooted in their "carrying other people's songs and not having one of [their] own,"[37] he attempts to help those who suffer: the boarding house provides a gamut of representative characters—seekers of lost partners, of love, of a future, and ultimately of an honorable identity. Bynum counsels Jeremy, for example, on attaining love through respecting a woman: "But it's a blessing when you learn to look at a woman and see in maybe just a few strands of her hair, the way her cheek curves . . . to see in that everything there is out of life to be gotten,"[38] and he helps Mattie overcome her mourning over a lost husband: "He ain't bound to you if the babies died. . . . Ain't nothing to be done. . . . There's somebody searching for your doorstep right now."[39] When he senses Loomis's disorientation and recognizes in Loomis the "shiny man" for whom he has been searching—the man who has revealed to him the "Secret of Life"[40]—Bynum helps Loomis articulate this past and hence ascertain his identity in the present.

Employing the blues song as a means to remember and help others remember, Bynum mediates between Loomis's disrupted identities and thus catalyzes his spiritual growth, encoded in the phrase "to sing one's song."[41] Bynum sings in the traditional call and response pattern of the blues:

> They tell me Joe Turner's come and gone
> Ohhh Lordy
> They tell me Joe Turner's come and gone
> Ohhh Lordy
> Got my man and gone
>
> Come with forty links of chain
> Ohhh Lordy
> Come with forty links of chain
> Ohhh Lordy
> Got my man and gone[42]

The song narrates how Joe Turner, the brother of the governor of Tennessee, captured people in the street and put them in chain gangs. Joe Turner represents the oppressive and arbitrarily violent system that has shaped Loomis's personal experience, a system that objectifies its victims and generates their distrust of anything white.[43] Consequently, Bynum's singing makes Loomis tremendously uncomfortable: "Why you singing that song? Why you singing about Joe Turner? . . . I don't like you singing that song, mister!"[44] Despite these objections, Bynum gradually uncovers Loomis's repressed trauma and helps him come to terms with his experiences: "Mr. Loomis done picked some cotton. Ain't you, Herald Loomis? You done picked a bunch of cotton."[45] Bynum also understands that the Joe Turner experience is the origin of Loomis's erratic behavior because it caused his forgetting "how to sing [his song]," he states, "A fellow forget that and he forget who he is."[46]

Songs occupy an important position within African-American culture generally, functioning not only to express mood or to narrate a story, but also to affirm identity—as songs come from, Wilson says, "way deep inside."[47] The blues, in particular, represents an African-American struggle in relating personal experience to collective memory that is expressed in an "increasing personalization of musical expression," Waldo F. Martin Jr. observes, paradigmatic of "the postemancipation quest to arrive at a more satisfactory representation of African-American perspective on the modern existential condition. The blues has most effectively turned inward and explored the complexities of lived experience."[48] Mirroring Loomis's conflict when asserting his individual identity within a larger cultural context, Bynum's song about Joe Turner exemplifies this exploration of lived experience. Although the blues' concern with the African American experience may suggest a tragic undertone, its mood is essentially hopeful. The blues is, Martin says, "a music of hope and affirmation building upon diverse African-dominated roots."[49] Thus, in spite of telling of a traumatic individual experience, the song functions essentially as a source of inspiration for Loomis because it reviews the events within a larger cultural framework. The singing about the past communicates memories that shape the self in the present; in a coherent narrative, it brings together the fragments of Loomis's past to regenerate and affirm his identity— as a member of the Joe Turner chain gang in the past, as an individual with a distinct personality in the present, and as a constituent part of a collective memory.

Through its songs, African-American culture has sustained a sense of belonging. The blues expresses the twofold experience of peoples who were forcibly removed from their native soil and, living on the American continent, have constructed a new identity. Its African origin, a number of secular influences—"minstrel, vaudeville, and ragtime tunes as well as ballads and work music"[50]—and religious roots, such as spirituals, gospels, and hymns, make up the blues' distinctly African-American character. Wilson states in an interview, "Contained in the blues is information about how to live your life within this world view. . . . The blues contains a social view, and also a religious view. It also encompasses mythology, history, social organization."[51] Songs help the culture recall its African heritage, the Middle Passage, the sufferings and joys of life in the South and the migration north, which all became absorbed in a collective sense of cultural belonging. Cultural memory permits the play's characters to perceive themselves as members of their own separate community. To acknowledge these various ties means to recognize the self: Loomis needs to reconnect completely with his ancestry, to "stand up and sing his song," as Bynum says, in order to overcome his double consciousness and be free.[52]

Involving a type of bloodletting rite that enables him to "stand,"[53] Loomis's second vision reveals to him his mission in life and reconnects him with his African ancestors on a more fundamental level than the first vision was able to do. Again, this vision is at first informed by an aversion to Christianity, an aversion that compels Loomis to talk about a white Jesus brandishing a whip while overseeing African slaves. The image identifies a number of crucial problems the Christian faith posed on the African slaves, who were forced to forget their gods and accept a white Christ as their spiritual guidance.[54] Worse, silently consenting to their subjugation, Christianity, as interpreted by the plantation owners, conspired in quieting the slaves with hopes for a better afterlife. Loomis explains ironically: "And Jeremiah go back and lay up there on his half rations and talk about what a nice man Mr. Jesus Christ is 'cause he give him salvation after he die."[55] Refuting the Christian belief in salvation and in a separate afterlife, Loomis instead affirms an Africa-rooted perception of a continuum between the ancestors and their descendants through which collective memory is retained. He says: "I been wading in the water. I been walking all over the River Jordan. But what it get me, huh? I done been baptized with blood of the lamb and the fire of the Holy Ghost. But what I got, huh? I got salvation? My enemies all around me picking the flesh from my bones. I'm choking on my own blood and all you got to give me is salvation?"[56] His ancestors, after surviving the ordeals of the Middle Passage and subjected to a Christian baptism, have been suffering through their descendants ever since, despite the promise of salvation. Consequently, "drowning" in his own, his ancestors, and in Jesus' blood that supposedly takes away his sins, Loomis cannot accept the belief that bloodletting has a cleansing effect. To demonstrate his antagonism, he "slashes himself across the chest. He rubs the blood over his face and comes to a realization," but exclaims suddenly: "I'm standing! I'm standing. My legs stood up! I'm standing now!"[57] At this moment Loomis completely and consciously connects with his ancestors, recognizes and accepts his heritage, and continues the chain of remembering. He now understands the bloodletting rite—which reminds of Bynum's rituals involving pigeon blood—as pertaining to his African-American self and not to the religious concepts of the dominant race. Thus, having been unable to stand up after his first vision, he is ready to walk and determine his itinerary autonomously.[58]

As a result of the spiritual cleansing that has put him in touch with his ancestry, Loomis remembers his "forgotten song": he comprehends his identity as an individual, as well as a member of his racial and ethnic group. The stage directions make clear his newly found independence, again embedding it in the trope of song: "Having found his song, the song of self-sufficiency, fully resurrected, cleansed and given breath, free from any encumbrance other than the workings of his own heart and the bonds of the flesh, having accepted the responsibility for his own presence in the world, he is free to soar above the environs that weighed and pushed his spirit into terrifying contractions."[59] Physical and spiritual freedoms coincide: in overcoming the double consciousness that compelled him to conform to the dictates of the Northern setting, Loomis moves from object to subject position and hence becomes "free to soar." His experiences in Pittsburgh thus yield unexpected insights: Loomis validates his personal experiences by integrating them into a larger cultural memory, which also helps him overcome his trauma. He learns to esteem his as a distinctive American culture that originates in Africa, has been shaped by life in the South, and continues to change in the North—a diasporic culture that has been able to persist despite oppression and forced conversion attempts.[60] Wilson shows, through Loomis, that an alternative to double consciousness rests in validating an African-American diasporic identity.

In *Joe Turner's Come and Gone*, August Wilson thus unravels the complex problems of an African-American self-definition. Loomis's experience is paradigmatic of the fate of African Americans, especially after Reconstruction, when racial discrimination and poverty made life in the South for many unbearable. In spite of their hopes, the migration to the larger cities in the North confronted African Americans with new forms of racism and a feeling of displacement that thwarted their assimilation into the great American melting pot. Loomis's reconnecting to his ancestry and his cultural heritage offers a way out of his dilemma by affirming what is truly African American. By retrieving and accepting his link to the African-American community, Loomis attains autonomy and the psychological freedom that the abolition of slavery could not provide. At the end of the play, he "heralds," as his name suggests, the empowerment of his race through bonding with its ancestry. Wilson states, "Black culture is a distinctly American culture—it was developed in America, not Africa. But because the people were originally African, it's an African culture. So we share commonalities as Americans, but there are differences. . . . That doesn't mean we can't get along with one another. We can recognize each other's cultural differences and accept them."[61] The play thus opens the view for difference, the difference in values and perceptions that provide alternatives to the dominant culture. Over the centuries, African-American culture has proven its capacity to survive. August Wilson, in his play *Joe Turner's Come and Gone*, gives us a brief and powerful glimpse of African-American persistence and creativity.

NOTES

1. In *The Souls of Black Folk*, W. E. B. Du Bois specifies double consciousness as "a peculiar sensation . . . this sense of always looking at one's self through the eyes of others, of measuring one's soul by the tape of a world that looks on in amused contempt and pity. One ever feels his two-ness,—an American, a Negro; two souls, two thoughts, two unreconciled strivings; two warring ideals in one dark body" (5).

2. Mary I. Bogumil centers her argument on the juba dance ceremony, which offers

the individuals a means to recover a sense of belonging to the community thus helping them to "find their song that will lead them down the 'right road' " (469).

3. Kim Pareira, "Joe Turner's Come and Gone."

4. These two critics, as well as August Wilson criticism more generally, also share a close examination of African-American customs and traditions, evident in the blues and spiritual rituals, which provide a sense of identity for many of Wilson's characters. Pareira discusses the notion of "song" as referring to identity *and* music—identity expressed through a culture's music. Analyzing the trope of song in her book-length study *An In-Depth Study of the Major Plays of African American Playwright August Wilson: Vernaculizing the Blues on Stage*, Qun Wang perceives songs as a means both to retain and express cultural identity. Through the blues, in addition to certain religious practices, she argues, the community manages to sustain a sense of unity. Betty McEady views African-American creativity as playing a "mystical role" in offering inspiration to its listeners: "one should see the blues theme as the vehicle to inform and educate the larger, even global, society about black experiences in the United States. Wilson's blues vernacular represents his spiritual, social and political messages about the purposes of black theater" (vii). Likewise, Jay Plum in "Blues, History, and the Dramaturgy of August Wilson" explains the significance of the blues as portraying, in Wilson's play, the experiences of an entire culture by linking the past with the present, and the present with the future, thus reflecting the "complexities of African-American culture" (566). Plum holds that the blues song is a method of reclaiming an identity and of demarcating a difference decisive for an escape from a marginal existence.

5. In my use of the term "diasporic identity," I specifically have Paul Gilroy's concept from "Identity, Belonging, and the Critique of Pure Sameness" in mind. Gilroy states, "Diaspora is a useful means to reassess the idea of essential and absolute identity precisely because it is incompatible with that type of nationalist and raciological thinking. . . . It demands that we attempt to evaluate the significance of the scattering process against the supposed uniformity of that which has been scattered. Diaspora posits important tensions between here and there, then and now, between seed in the bag, the packet, or the pocket and seed in the ground, the fruit, or the body. By focusing attention equally on the sameness within differentiation and the differentiation within sameness, diaspora disturbs the suggestion that political and cultural identity might be understood via the analogy of indistinguishable peas lodged in the protective pods of closed kinship and subspecies being" (125). Gilroy introduces the concept of hybridization into his discussion of African-American identity since the hybrid's, he states, "recombinant form is indebted to its 'parent' cultures but remains assertively and insubordinately a bastard. It reproduces neither of the supposedly anterior purities that gave rise to it in anything like unmodified form. Here, as least, identity must be divorced from purity" (117).

6. Armstead L. Robinson writes, "In slow but decisive steps during the 1880s the Radical policies of integration were replaced by racial segregation, which was eventually written into southern constitutions and civil law during the 1890s" (142).

7. Du Bois, *The Souls of Black Folk*, 132.

8. Describing the poverty in Dougherty County, Georgia, Du Bois observes that houses were frequently "dirty and dilapidated" as well as "crowded" (114).

9. In "Blacks in the Economy from Reconstruction to World War I," Gerald D. Jaynes explains that "the majority of laborers on tobacco and cotton plantations worked in gangs for a sharewage, usually one-third to one-half of the net proceeds of the crop

that was divided between anywhere from ten to fifty workers after the crop was harvested and sold by the planter. Moreover, for most sharecroppers the contracted payments were due in a lump sum at the end of the crop year. In either case, during the year, laborers obtained their subsistence food and clothing, usually on credit, from either plantation stores or independent merchants" (168–69). When in 1866 and again in 1868, crops failed due to weather conditions, planters could not pay their creditors and laborers.

10. Robinson states, "in the immediate postwar period, the absence of ready access to 'free' land meant that most former slaves had few economic choices open to them. Circumstance compelled them to seek waged-labor positions on land owned by whites, many of whom were bitter former slaveholders still enraged over the defeat of the Confederacy and impoverished by the failure of their crusade for national independence" (145).

11. Du Bois, *The Souls of Black Folk*, 117–18.

12. The migrants were not entirely unprepared for the new life, however. Carole C. Marks points out that institutions already in place in the South moved north and created a social network, such as self-help organizations, benevolent and mutual aid societies, lodges and literary associations (185).

13. James R. Grossman, *Land of Hope*, 6.

14. Carole C. Marks, "In Search of the Promised Land," 189.

15. Du Bois, *The Souls of Black Folk*, 5.

16. Grossman explains that despite these racial barriers, exceptions also existed: "Frustrations and conflicts at the workplace, racial violence, and various forms of exclusion and discrimination did indeed mark visible boundaries of Chicago as a Promised Land during and immediately after the Great Migration, but the barriers seemed neither as systematic nor as unbreachable as they had in the South. Because protocols were neither enshrined in law nor absolute, enough exceptions existed . . . to provide hope" (260).

17. Wilson, *Joe Turner's Come and Gone*, xi.

18. Ibid.

19. Ibid.

20. Ibid.

21. Ibid., 13.

22. Ibid., 14.

23. Ibid., 52.

24. Ibid.,

25. Ibid., 53.

26. Ibid., 54.

27. "Thus saith the Lord God unto these bones; Behold, I will cause breath to enter into you, and ye shall live: And I will lay sinews upon you, and will bring flesh upon you, and cover you with skin, and put breath in you, and ye shall live; and ye shall know that I am the Lord . . . as I prophesied, there was a noise and behold a shaking, and the bones came together . . . and the flesh came upon them . . . and the breath came into them, and they lived, and stood up upon their feet, and exceeding great army" (Ezek. 37:1–10).

28. Wilson, *Joe Turner's Come and Gone*, xi.

29. At the same time, Loomis becomes the mouthpiece of, as Sandra G. Shannon states, "the pain and sufferings of his ancestors—indeed the entire African-American race" (37).

30. Discussing the social functions of the African-American church throughout history in "Black Religious Traditions: Sacred and Secular Themes," Gayraud S. Wilmore identifies subversive potential in the church's mingling of Western Christian and African elements: the church fulfilled a number of functions simultaneously. Wilmore designates these paradigms as "survival," "educational, moral, and cultural elevation," and "liberation—direct action on the part of churches to free the slaves, combat racial discrimination, and garner black political, economic, and moral power" (285–86). The African slaves drew no clear boundaries between the spiritual and the secular, between the Christian and their African religions: the "survival" strategies thus entailed a mingling of African religion with Christian precepts so that, Wilmore states, "the African conjurer and medicine man, the manipulation of charms and talismans, and the use of drums and dancing were present in the slaves' quarters as survival strategies, even after conversion to orthodox Christianity" (290). And despite the civilizing objectives of "elevation" in which Northern white missionaries preached to former slaves following Emancipation and, in the early twentieth century, in urban "institutional churches," a reversion could be observed to "the same patterns of emotionalism and other African forms of religiosity that helped the slaves survive the brutality of plantation life in the eighteenth century" (285–86).

31. Wilson, *Joe Turner's Come and Gone*, 55.

32. Ibid., 2–3.

33. Ibid., 4.

34. Ibid.

35. Ibid., 10.

36. Ibid.

37. Ibid., 9–10.

38. Ibid., 46.

39. Ibid., 23.

40. Ibid., 9.

41. Ibid., 71.

42. Ibid., 67.

43. Qun Wang notes that the play is imbued with the system's oppressive character so that Joe Turner's "shadow is constantly felt by the characters and audience alike" (83).

44. Wilson, *Joe Turner's Come and Gone*, 69.

45. Ibid., 70.

46. Ibid., 71.

47. Ibid.

48. Waldo F. Martin, *"The Sounds of Blackness,"* 261.

49. Ibid.

50. Ibid.

51. In an interview with DiGaetani, Wilson uses the trope of song to represent, he says, "the foundation on which all my plays are based. . . . It is a cultural response that teaches you how to live your life. . . . It is grounded in an oral culture." It is this oral culture that survived against the assimilatory forces that negate the value of a distinctly African American culture. Therefore, the blues is, as Wilson points out, "more of a world view" (279–80).

52. Wilson, *Joe Turner's Come and Gone*, 91.

53. Ibid., 93.

54. Wilson explains, "The fact that Africans, when they came to America, their religion was stripped from them, everything; their language, culture, ideas. And when you look in the mirror, you should see your God. So in fact, what we do is, we worship an image of God which is white, right? Which is the image of the very same people—we're talking about image now—the very same people who have oppressed you, who have put you on the slave ships, who have beaten you and who have forced you to work, etc. The image was a white man" (quoted in Wang 87–88).

55. Wilson, *Joe Turner's Come and Gone*, 93.

56. Ibid.

57. Ibid.

58. To critic Dana A. Williams, the vision symbolizes the "true song of redemption and liberation" that is "inside the spiritual dynamism of the ancestors—perceived and made useful in the present as opposed to being arrested in the past" (316). Kim Pareira considers Loomis's vision, first and foremost, a return to the beginning: Loomis, "having already endured slavery . . . now returns to the moment when his people arrived at these shores, for his spirit must make the journey from the beginning" (74).

59. Wilson, *Joe Turner's Come and Gone*, 94.

60. Examining the play's allusions to African spirituality in "Yoruba Gods on the American Stage," Sandra Richards asserts that cultural diaspora, indeed, qualified life back in Africa, where migration and hybridity were common: "Wilson has fashioned a diaspora text that, given its specific reference to Yoruba belief systems, posits migrancy as the norm and implies an African that is always-already hybrid" (95).

61. See DiGaetani, "August Wilson," 279–80.

BIBLIOGRAPHY

Bogumil, Mary L. " 'Tomorrow Never Comes': Songs of Cultural Identity in August Wilson's *Joe Turner's Come and Gone*." *Theater Journal* 46:4 (1994): 463–76.

DiGaetani, John L. "August Wilson." In *A Search for a Postmodern Theater: Interviews with Contemporary Playwrights*. New York: Greenwood Press, 1991, 275–85.

Du Bois, W. E. B. *The Souls of Black Folk*. New York: Penguin Books, 1996.

Gilroy, Paul. "Identity, Belonging, and the Critique of Pure Sameness." In *Beyond the Color Line: New Perspectives on Race and Ethnicity in America*, edited by Abigail Thernstrom and Stephan Thernstrom. Stanford: Hoover Institution Press, 2002, 97–133.

Grossman, James R. *Land of Hope: Chicago, Black Southerners, and the Great Migration*. Chicago: University of Chicago Press, 1989.

Jaynes, Gerald D. "Blacks in the Economy from Reconstruction to World War I." In Scott and Shade, *Upon These Shores*, 167–81.

Marks, Carole C. "In Search of the Promised Land: Black Migration and Urbanization, 1900–1940." In Scott and Shade, *Upon These Shores*, 182–97.

Martin Jr., Waldo F. "The Sounds of Blackness: African-American Music." In Scott and Shade, *Upon These Shores*, 251–69.

McEady, Betty. "Preface." *An In-Depth Study of the Major Plays of African American Playwright August Wilson: Vernacularizing the Blues on Stage*. Lewiston, NY: Edwin Mellen Press, 1999, V–VIII.

Pareira, Kim. "Introduction." *August Wilson and the African-American Odyssey.* Urbana: University of Illinois Press, 1995, 1–12.

———. "*Joe Turner's Come and Gone:* Seek and You Shall Find." *August Wilson and the African-American Odyssey.* Urbana: University of Illinois Press, 1995, 55–84.

Plum, Jay. "Blues, History, and the Dramaturgy of August Wilson." *African American Review* 27:4 (1993): 561–67.

Richards, Sandra. "Yoruba Gods on the American Stage: August Wilson's *Joe Turner's Come and Gone.*" In *African Drama and Performance,* edited by John Conteh-Morgan and Tejumola Olaniyan. Bloomington: Indiana University Press, 2004, 94–106.

Robinson, Armstead L. "Full of Faith, Full of Hope: The African-American Experience from Emancipation to Segregation." In Scott and Shade *Upon These Shores,* 141–66.

Scott, William R., and William G. Shade, eds. *Upon These Shores: Themes in the African-American Experience 1600 to the Present,* New York: Routledge, 2000.

Shannon, Sandra G. "Conversing with the Past: *Joe Turner's Come and Gone* and *The Piano Lesson.*" *A Journal of the College English Association, Middle Atlantic Group* 4:1 (1991): 33–42.

Wang, Qun. *An In-Depth Study of the Major Plays of African American Playwright August Wilson: Vernacularizing the Blues on Stage,* Lewiston, NY: Edwin Mellen Press, 1999.

Williams, Dana A. "Making the Bones Live Again: A Look at the 'Bones People' in August Wilson's *Joe Turner's Come and Gone* and Henry Dumas's 'Ark of Bones.'" *College Language Association Journal* 42:3 (March 1999): 309–19.

Wilmore, Gayraud S. "Black Religious Traditions: Sacred and Secular Themes." In Scott and Shade, *Upon These Shores,* 285–302.

Wilson, August. *Joe Turner's Come and Gone.* New York: Penguin Books, 1988.

From the Pulpit to the Podium:
Marginality and the Discourses of Race

Andrea O'Reilly Herrera

The relationship between rhetoric and racism has for too long remained in the shadow of the word, and contemporary transformations taking place in rhetorical theory suggest the need for new insights into old dilemmas.
—Mark Lawrence McPhail, *The Rhetoric of Racism Revisited*

To think oneself free simply because one can claim—can utter—the negation of an assertion is not to think deep enough.
—Henry Louis Gates, *Black Literature and Literary Theory*

However unfeasible and inefficient it may sound, I see no way to avoid insisting that there has to be a simultaneous other focus . . .
—Gayatri Spivak, *In Other Worlds: Essays in Cultural Politics*

MARK LAWRENCE MCPHAIL, IN HIS INVESTIGATION OF THE THEOretical dynamics of racism (*The Rhetoric of Racism Revisited*), suggests that language has always functioned as the primary locus and facilitator of racist ideology in the United States.[1] Race rhetoric, however, has also formed the basis of liberation theories that aim to dismantle racist practices, which continue to manifest themselves at the social and institutional levels. The underlying conundrum is that in order to deploy any antiracist initiative, civil rights advocates or race workers have had to adopt the very practices and work within the very institutions that have cultivated and sustained their oppression and marginalization. The purpose of this paper is to examine the manner in which race rhetoric functions in U.S. religious and academic institutions, and, consequently consider the implications of dismantling racist apparatuses from these sites.

Generally speaking, race rhetoric in the United States has undergone several overlapping stages. Originally it had religious sanction, emanating from the pulpit as well as from scientific and academic institutions, and was dominated by white supremacist ideology.

A complex of historical factors (such as the gigantic global enterprise of the African slave trade) and mythic grounding (such as stories from the Old Testament) influenced the construction of modern racial categories. Christianity was hardly the sole or even primary force in this process. Yet religious myth, originating from interpretations of biblical stories such as the curse on Canaan, son of Ham, as well as speculations about God's Providence, played an important role in the formation, revision, and reconstruction of racial categories in the modern world.

Although Christianity necessarily was central to the process of *racializing* peoples, Judeo-Christian stories were not immediately or inherently amenable to providing a religious basis for modern racial slavery. Once slavery took root in the Americas, it was easy enough for religious authorities simply to decree that if slavery existed, God must have a reason for it——and that reason must be in the Bible. But theologians confronted another problem. Slavery in the Americas was specifically a racial form of bondage—Europeans and Euro-Americans enslaving Africans and African-Americans. This stood in distinct contrast to traditional forms of slavery found throughout the world, ones involving prisoners of war, captives, and subordinated castes of permanent workers (like the Israelites in the Hebrew Scriptures) within a kingdom or empire. These forms of traditional slavery sometimes involved ethnic distinctions (especially in the Islamic world), but were not conceived of as "racial" in the modern sense. This was the kind of slavery addressed in the Bible. In the modern world, however, the religious justification of slavery would have to clarify God's providence particularly in having one "race" of people from one continent enslave another people from a different part of the world in a situation centrally involving economic servitude. In theologizing about this quandary, Euro-Americans worked out some of the meanings of "race" itself in the modern sense. They began to define what constituted whiteness and blackness, hierarchical, social categories that would long outlive slavery itself.[2]

In the South, antislavery sentiments stood no chance against the grim reality that slavery was profitable and gave even poor white men a chance at wealth. Here, the major proselytizers were not the famous preachers such as Whitefield, but instead relatively anonymous plainfolk evangelicals who changed the region from its backwoods indifference to its status as the Bible Belt, the land of conservative Christianity. Early colonial efforts at proselytization, led by the Anglican Society for the Propagation of the Gospel in Foreign Parts, experienced limited success with whites and virtually none among slaves. Virginia Anglicans struggled through the eighteenth century, attracting colonial elites but few others. Later in the century, the Baptists in Jefferson's Virginia shocked their world neighbors. They refused to pay taxes to the Anglican church, condemned horse-racing and its attendant gambling as sinful, and met in biracial groupings to celebrate their salvation from eternal damnation, sometimes hearing black or female exhorters in such meetings. Those under conviction—often women, sometimes black, generally younger and often of modest wealth—narrated their quests for glory. Though couching their stories in the expected self-abasing idiom—"a wretch like me," as the phrase from the first lines of "Amazing Grace" goes—salvation for these seekers meant that their private turmoil assumed cosmic significance. Initially, the southern elites scorned the evangelicals. Yet by the 1830s, and even more so by the Civil War, wealthy men and women filled the pews of the same incipient denominations whose forebears they had disdained as zealous ranters. As spired steeples replaced log churches and unlettered exhorters gave way (at least in cities) to gentleman theologians, southern clergymen propounded their own social vision of God, country, family, and slavery. In other words, they sold out.

Pro-slavery theologians worked feverishly through the antebellum era (1800–1860) to enunciate a Christian apologetic that would preserve the boundaries of whiteness/blackness while also supporting their efforts to Christianize the slaves. By the nineteenth century, white southern clergymen insisted, time and time again, that Christianization would make blacks more secure in their blackness—their enslavedness—because it would make them obedient and content in that obedience. With such reasoning at hand, white southerners supported a substantial missionary enterprise to the slaves. Contrary to views maintained during the seventeenth and eighteenth centuries, which often set in dichotomous relief whiteness and Christian freedom versus blackness and un-Christian unfreedom, in the antebellum era the missions to the slaves proved successful enough to convert a significant percentage of the enslaved population.

Escaped slaves such as Frederick Douglass and abolitionists such as William Lloyd Garrison, of course, commented frequently, and with all the acidity they could muster, on the gross hypocrisy of the campaign for Christianization. In the 1840s and 1850s, while residing in Rochester and publishing the black abolitionist organ the *North Star*, Douglass rhetorically devastated the slave system and the so-called revivalism that accompanied the spread of the iniquitous institution. As

Douglass told one gathering, "Revivals in religion, and revivals in the slave trade, go hand in hand together. The church and the slave prison stand next to each other, the groans and cries of the heartbroken slave are often drowned in the pious devotions of his religious master . . . while the blood-stained gold goes to support the pulpit, the pulpit covers the infernal business with the garb of Christianity."[3] Equally effective in the antislavery ministry was Sojourner Truth, the black abolitionist who once publicly bared her breast in front of detractors who doubted that she was a woman (at the same time offering to suckle those skeptics with the same breast that had nursed many white babies). "This unlearned African woman, with her deeply religious and trustful nature burning in her soul like fire, has a magnetic power over an audience perfectly astounding," wrote one admirer.[4]

The abolitionists blanketed the North with powerful visuals, including the famous image of the chained slave kneeling before a standing white man, the former asking, "Am I not a man and a brother?" Most important for this strategy of sentimentalism, however, was Harriet Beecher Stowe's melodramatic masterpiece *Uncle Tom's Cabin*, the best-selling book in America (save for the Bible) in the nineteenth century. Stowe's work exposed slavery's inevitable degradation of both slave and master. Stowe's angelic heroine, Little Eva, daughter of a dissolute but sympathetically portrayed slaveholder in New Orleans, communicates the moral: slavery is wrong because it is cruel and heartless. Stowe clinched the tale with the evil Yankee slavedriver Simon Legree presiding over the horrific beating of Uncle Tom, the pious slave. In the story's epilogue, the major black characters who have managed to escape North (including Eliza, after her famous tiptoeing across the ice floes of the Ohio River to the shores of freedom, carrying her child in her arms) set sail for Africa, where they proselytize for the Christian faith among their benighted African brothers.

Enslaved Americans certainly assimilated Christian belief within the framework of their synthesis of European- and African-based belief systems, but on the surface, at least, slave religion was reassuringly orthodox in its professed Christian sentiments (especially in comparison to trends of theological modernism then arriving in the United States from German scholars such as David Friedrich Strauss, author of the epochal text *The Life of Jesus, Critically Examined*). White southerners, once suspicious of the Christian message of freedom for all—*neither Jew nor Greek, neither slave nor free, neither male nor female*—eventually were persuaded that Christianity would ensure divine order. What only a few of them saw (and, indeed, only a few white northerners could see as well) was the way in which enslaved people would find in Christianity the route to freedom both in soul and in body. Mostly denied the written Word, slave preachers mastered the arts of oral religious expression. Sometimes it was in public, in separately organized black churches that remained under close white monitoring. In public their message was carefully contained. In private, however, when slaves spread the gospel among themselves, the preaching took flight. One black Texas minister, told by the master to preach obedience, subverted that message when he could: "I knew there was something better for them but I darsn't tell them so lest I done it on the sly. That I did lots." He told the slaves, "but not so Master could hear it, if they kept praying that the Lord would hear their prayers and set them free." Antebellum slave preachers thus became agents of covert proselytization. The mass exodus of slaves during the Civil War—called by historian Steven Hahn the largest slave revolt in American history—and the religious understandings of the war itself, exposed the underground world and culture of African–American Christianity.[5]

The place of evangelical religion in the struggle of African Americans remained equally central after the war. Black churches experienced a remarkably rapid growth after the Civil War. Black missionaries fanned out across the country; prominent churches in major cities erected impressive edifices; and black religious entrepreneurs established presses and publishing houses to provide edifying material for their own people. Baptist and Methodist churches claimed over 90 percent of black churchgoers, no accident since these two denominations took the lead in converting slaves and free blacks, and because these populist evangelicals required no education or the formal training of preachers or converts. Few matched the tireless organizing for African-American rights in church and state of Henry McNeal Turner. Known mostly for his advocacy (later in his life) of black American emigration to Africa, Turner's major achievement lay in the establishment of the African Methodist Episcopal Church (AME) in the South after the Civil War. Born free in South Carolina, Turner established residence and began to make his name and career in Georgia in the 1850s. Stunned by the erudition Turner displayed in the Methodist pulpit, some claimed that he was a "white man galvanized." After service as a Union Army chaplain, Turner set about organizing the African Methodist Episcopal church in Georgia, a black denomination banned from the South in the 1820s when black Methodists in Charleston were implicated in an aborted slave rebellion. When southern-style racism swept the country in the 1890s, Turner made his name as a progenitor of black theology, advocate of black American emigration to Africa, and organizer of AME missions work in South Africa.[6]

Meanwhile, however, white southerners after the war created their own civil religion, featuring its own theology, myths, rituals, and saints. Evangelists for the Lost Cause, notably the elite Virginia minister and historian John William Jones, propounded a mythical interpretation of the past that exalted the deeds of the fallen confederate heroes. According to the tenets of Lost Cause theology, God's chosen people (white southerners) had been baptized in the blood of suffering, and thus had been chastened and purified. In justifying the reimposition of white supremacist regimes in the southern states, religious proselytization compelled political activism.

In the era of Jim Crow, as well, many self-proclaimed race theologians and scientists challenged older religious notions of the unity of races by fantasizing instead about the separately created origins of races. Putting forth elaborately constructed rhetorical arguments, they reread African Americans back out of the category of "humanity," just as many of their seventeenth-century forebears had done. By mixing biblical and scientific reasoning, they took "scientific" studies of Negro inferiority (including those from phrenology, the pseudo-science of measuring the brain skeleton and inferring intelligence from such measurements) and found in scripture explanations (such as fables in Genesis) that allegedly supported the science. Many of these writers tinkered with the curse of Ham legend, struggling to fit the Genesis myths with the findings of the racially biased science of that era.

During the mid- to latter half of the nineteenth century, white progressives and African Americans rhetorically challenged white racist ideology and gradually reversed the effects of racism by mounting a kind of counterdiscourse that identified and thereby deconstructed the interpretive and representational distortions of blacks, especially in regard to biblical exegesis. In a parallel effort, abolitionists such as Lydia Maria Child facilitated and oversaw the construction and publication of slave narratives, which imitated popular literary forms in an attempt to appeal to a white audience's moral sensibilities and (to borrow Houston Baker's words) attempted through language to "humanize an oftentimes brutal and dehumanizing existence through the power of the word."[7]

The pulpit increasingly became a central site of resistance, and eventually played a pivotal role in African Americans' bid to gain civil rights. In the nineteenth century, particularly, when a small but significant set of educated black Americans encountered the romantic and racialist ideas of their era, many of them responded by trying to rhetorically reconfigure the black man *into* the reigning mythologies and categories. It was the destiny of black Americans, some of them believed, to bring civilization back to their home continent. It was biblically prophesied that it should be so. George Wilson Brent, a black Methodist minister, took the biblical stories as evidence of the black man's indispensable role in furthering human history.[8] Other black commentators also produced "race histories" that explained the origins and destiny of black people to African-American readers. They employed the standard variety of rhetorical arguments and biblical stories. These race writers, usually theologians and ministers themselves, often diverged on specific points, but they all agreed on disputing the racist notions of inferiority inherent in the Western idea of "blackness." Whether to accept the biblical mythologies but to invert the stories (as did George Wilson Brent), or to put on display entirely new mythological constructs (as did the black leader Marcus Garvey in Harlem in the 1920s), or to insist that blackness and whiteness were simply not biblical categories because "of one blood hath God made all nations," black Americans responded vigorously to the creation of blackness as a category of inferiority and shame.

The Christian mythic grounding for ideas of whiteness and blackness was powerful but unstable, subject to constant argument and revision. In the twentieth century, this grounding was radically overturned in part through a reimagination of the same Christian thought that was part of creating it in the first place. Black Christians who formed the rank-and-file of the Civil Rights Movement demolished the political structures of segregation. Key to their work was a transformation of Protestant thought in ways that deftly combined the social gospel and black church traditions, infused with Gandhian notions of active resistance and "soul force," as well as secular ideas of hardheaded political organizing and the kinds of legal maneuverings that led to *Brown v. Board of Education* and *Loving et ux v. Virginia* (the latter declaring laws prohibiting interracial marriages unconstitutional).

"You sing the songs which symbolize transformation, which make that revolution of courage inside you," a civil rights activist said of the singing that was an integral part of the Civil Rights Movement. The ordinary citizens who made up the rank-and-file of the black freedom struggle empowered themselves through religious song in a way exceeding that of any protest movement in American history. It was their sacred songs—an alternative and vernacular rhetorical form—that translated the theoretical ideas behind the movement (such as *satya-graha*) into the language that resonated deeply with a people's history.

The Civil Rights Movement had legislative aims; it was, to that extent, a political movement. But it was more than that as well. It was a religious movement sustained by the deeply Protestant religious imagery and fervor of southern black churches. As one female share-cropper and civil rights activist in Mississippi explained in regard to her conversion to the movement, "Something hit me like a new religion." The religion of the southern folk appeared to be apolitical. Critics called it "otherworldy." or "compensatory," and to some extent doubt-less it was. But W. E. B. Du Bois pointed out that while religion might be seen as "mere symbolism," to the freed people "God was real. They knew him. They had met Him personally in many a wild orgy of reli-gious frenzy, or in the black stillness of the night."⁹ As a scholar and social scientist, Du Bois was often critical of the black church as an insti-tution for its increasing insularity, its focus in the twentieth century on internal growth and power politicking, and its inability (before the Civil Rights Movement) to utilize its enormous resources effectively on behalf of African-American people. At the same time, however, Du Bois —as a poet and sensitive essayist—understood the kind of powerful work going on in the rituals and the ostensibly "otherworldly" preach-ing emanating from black pulpits.¹⁰

As Du Bois's work suggests, the implicit potential of southern folk religion—what contemporary scholars might call the "hidden tran-script" contained in religious behavior—bears close scrutiny. The his-torian Robin D. G. Kelley has argued that:

> we need to recognize that the sacred and the spirit world were also often understood and invoked by African Americans as weapons to protect them-selves or to attack others. . . . Can a sign from above, a conversation with a ghost, a spell cast by an enemy, or talking in tongues unveil the hidden tran-script?¹¹

To which one might add, can one's private and communal prayer when facing down racist sheriffs, voting registrars, or snakes thrown on one's front porch embolden resistance, and serve as the antidote to the opiate of the people fed by Jim Crow's spokesmen? In Mississippi and Alabama and other places during the 1950s and 1960s, the "hidden transcript" came to the surface. The assassins who bombed the Sixteenth Street Baptist Church in Birmingham and numerous other ecclesiastical build-ings through these years recognized this as clearly as anyone.¹²

The religion of the movement, of course, employed the same evangelical language that historically had oppressed African Americans in the South. Many critics saw—with considerable justification—that the black church was so deeply implicated in the Jim Crow system that it had helped to inure a people to the repressive apparatus of the apartheid-era South. Leaders of the freedom struggle knew firsthand of the numerous congregations that closed their doors to movement meetings. "The preachers, number one, they didn't have nothing to do with it," two local activists recalled of the movement in Mississippi. "Teachers number two, they didn't have nothing to do with it. Until things got when they could tell they wasn't gon' kill 'em, and then they went to comin' in." In Holmes County, a Mississippi civil rights worker reported, "We got turned down a lot of times from the black minister. . . . He mostly was afraid because they [whites] whooped a few of 'em and bombed a few churches. The preacher didn't want his church burned down, and them old members was right along in his corner."[13] There was good reason, of course, for this fear. In the early summer of 1964, forty-one black churches in Mississippi, of various denominations and geographic locations, went up in flames. Violence targeting civil rights centers continued well beyond Freedom Summer and the congressional civil rights acts of the mid-1960s. Mississippi segregationists employed indiscriminate violence against African Americans in numerous locales, fraying the movement's faith in the creation of a "beloved community." A worker from the Student Non–Violent Coordinating Committee (SNCC) surveyed the damage to both buildings and spirit:

> Who now? My mother, father, sister, brother. God damn, how much blood do they want. They got the church—Society Hill—the movement church. Its doors were closed this summer, but it has always been the center of the movement in South McComb. All the Freedom School kids belong to Society Hill. It's Bryant's church. The NAACP holds its meetings there. I spoke there this summer. SNCC workers were there the past Sunday and the Sunday before. . . . The church is demolished. It was a terrible blast. The police are here, certain again to see that all clues are removed and destroyed.[14]

In the face of the violence of the 1960s, activists pondered painful questions. Could the sacrifice be justified? "We had told a lot of people to put down their guns and not be violent in Mississippi," SNCC organizer Dave Dennis later recalled, "and I wasn't so sure that the nonviolent approach was the right approach anymore. And I had to do a lot of soul searching about that." For many in the movement, the beatings administered the next year to John Lewis and scores of others attempting to march across the Edmund Pettis bridge in Selma, Alabama, marked the nadir for the philosophy of nonviolence and soul force.[15]

As the Civil Rights Movement entered the later 1960s, moreover, the kind of southern evangelical rhetoric that had been so instrumental to its success—in the hands of accomplished rhetoricians such as Martin Luther King Jr., Fannie Lou Hamer, and others—increasingly seemed tamed and subdued by the larger forces of deep structural and economic inequalities it encountered in Watts, Detroit, Chicago, and other places. The system in which movement language operated eventually was no longer able to envision the deepest transformations that it sought to effect.

Despite their disillusion, black activists gradually took center stage in converting the struggle for civil rights into an intellectual mission at the level of the university in what would culminate in a larger social movement that came to be known as the ethnic studies movement.[16] Building on a deep-rooted rhetorical tradition established by scholars such as W. E. B. Du Bois, George Washington Williams, C. L. R. James and literary figures such as Langston Hughes, Ralph Ellison, and Zora Neale Hurston (whose "reverence" for and use of the black vernacular became a touchstone for later theorists such as Henry Louis Gates), they lay the groundwork for what evolved into the formal theorization of race. The establishment of ethnic studies programs in the late 1960s and early 1970s (primarily on the West Coast) represented a collective attempt on the part of activists of color to transform an educational system that was racist and sexist. "Calling for unity among peoples of color," Bob Wing observes, a grassroots movement, which involved both students and professors, "demanded an education relevant to struggles for racial justice at home and abroad and for programs that would serve as powerful bases for launching and supporting student and community organizing."[17]

A host of contemporary scholars who have begun to assess the current state and impact of Ethnic Studies, such as Evelyn Hu-DeHart, Marable Manning, and Bob Wing among others, bemoan the fact that subject to "corporate multiculturalism" and (as the latter observes) "lodged within [primarily] white universities and bereft of powerful social movements," ethnic studies programs have "increasingly submitted to academia's elitist rules, rewards, and punishments" and in the process have been "stripped of their original mission": that is, to radically transform the curriculum and bridge the gap between two apparently disconnected constituencies—society and the classroom. In other words, success and support are not without "political and ideological costs."[18]

Although language has always played a central role in social movements and revolutionary projects of all kinds, and ethnic studies programs have undoubtedly had a tremendous impact, the mainstreaming of race rhetoric into institutional centers of higher learning has raised its own related sets of problems in that oftentimes there is a disconnect between theory, social reality, and practice. Citing Celeste Condit and John Louis Lucaites' analysis of African-American racial discourse, McPhail observes that African American rhetorical interventions emanating primarily from the pulpit, "prompt[ed] an evolution from the fallacy of 'separate but equal,' to an integrated equality' infused with a rhetoric of black identity, to the sociopolitical space in which we find ourselves, a space giving birth to 'new equalities.' "[19] In other words, black religious institutions (as pointed out above) have facilitated social action and offered the methodological means for change. The academy, on the other hand, has been a less propitious site for social transformation. As Manning has observed, some thirty years after the establishment of the first ethnic studies programs, there exists "a chasm between the most influential scholarship produced [within the academy] and the social movements and ethnic constituencies which gave rise to such Programs."[20] The question at hand is thus, What can race workers in the academy do to resist assimilation and, thereby, continue their "radical" intellectual work in the classroom in particular, and in the educational system in general?

This question can be addressed in several ways. On the one hand, centers of education—not unlike religious institutions—have provided intellectuals with powerful platforms for challenging dominant ideology. If racism (like sexism and homophobia) is a product of socialization, then mounting a public argument for democratizing knowledge and advocating social justice from a location such as the podium can theoretically challenge students' racist attitudes and potentially evoke individual transformation and eventually effect social and political change at the level of the institution. The great irony, however, is that the only means by which race scholars can accomplish these goals is to attain at least some measure of sanctioned authority from an institution that is increasingly corporate in nature and grounded upon a Eurocentric model, which in many quarters continues to generate and perpetuate racist and sexist ideology and practices.

Though we may never be able to circumvent entirely the need for institutional legitimation, many of us operate, nevertheless, as though we are somehow beyond the pale of the ideology upon which the academy is founded. Over the years, moreover, many ethnic studies programs have, as Glenn Omatsu observes, "increasingly narrowed [their] agenda to surviving at elite [institutions], as opposed to focusing on transforming the curriculum, empowering students to engage in social activism, and connecting with the community."[21] As a result of this struggle to survive at the institutional level, coupled with our inability to be self-critical, we chance losing not only our autonomy but also our focus. In the process we avoid the more pressing and operative question: How do race scholars maintain solidarity with the groups to which they purportedly ally themselves, and simultaneously, avoid being implicated to the point of impotence in such a system? More simply put, what happens when those who represent or speak on behalf of the periphery suddenly become part of the center? Is it possible to be insiders and outsiders at the same time?

Though the purpose of this analysis is not to dispute the liberatory potential of religious and academic rhetoric, or what bell hooks characterizes as the "generative power" of discourse and dialogue, it does, however, intend to problematize the notion that oppositional or counterdiscourses, which are initiated, housed within, and subject to elitist and exclusionary institutional hierarchies, sometimes tend to reify the very systems they seek to challenge or subvert.[22] In his preface to *The Signifying Monkey*, Henry Louis Gates struggles with this issue. Though he expresses his concern regarding the lack of "sophisticated" scholarly attention to "the black tradition," he is conscious also of the need to "return to the relationship between black vernacular and formal traditions."[23] Building upon the work of race critics such as Sterling A. Brown and Zora Neale Hurston, as well as Ralph Ellison, Gates attempts to write a critical work that reveals "how the black tradition has inscribed its own theories of its nature and function without elaborate hermeneutical and rhetorical systems," a book, he adds, which he hopes even his parents can understand.[24]

Consciousness of one's own problematic positioning both within the academy and to the object/subject of study is, however, only the first step. A parallel concern arises when racial discourse and theory—the "critical strategies of intervention" we employ in the classroom—become reproductions of the master narratives they seek to repudiate. For the appropriation of race rhetoric and the vocabulary of high theory necessarily implicates race theorists in a complicitous relationship with the very system and apparatus they are rejecting. As a result, race theory can easily misalign with our activities and goals in the classroom, and even divorce itself from the interests and concerns of the very sector of the population it can most potentially impact and affect: our students and by extension, the community at large. After years of watching competent undergraduate students in ethnic studies, humanities, and history courses struggling to see the relationship between what for some are off-putting and impenetrable theoretical texts and social activism, one cannot help but wonder if race theory sometimes becomes so dense and opaque that it has divorced itself from the very context in which it was originally generated and thereby undermines its potential for transformation and for equipping students with pragmatic strategies to survive and combat racism and sexism. As Audre Lorde wryly comments, "survival is not an academic skill."[25]

To date, only a handful of contemporary theorists have managed to circumvent what McPhail characterizes as the "estranging abstractions" and elitist rhetoric that distances us not only from our students, but also from our communities and from the social realities of privilege and oppression.[26] Contemporary feminist scholars such as Alice Walker, bell hooks, and Gloria Anzaldua, for example, have consciously rejected the sometimes mazelike, high language of theory.[27] In *Borderlands/La Frontera*, Anzaldua defies established norms by freely crossing generic boundaries and elevating the personal account or experience. She accomplishes this without apology by forging what she refers to as a "new language" that resides at the crossroads of language, culture, and genre. "The switching of 'codes' in this book," she announces in the preface,

> from English to Castillian Spanish to the North Mexican dialect to Tex-Mex to a sprinkling of Nahuatl to a mixture of all of these, reflects my language, a new language—the language of the Borderlands. There, at the juncture of cultures, languages cross-pollinate and are revitalized; they die and are born. Presently this infant language, this bastard language, Chicano Spanish, is not approved by any society. But we Chicanos no longer feel that we need to beg entrance, that we need always to make the first overture—to translate to Anglos, Mexicans and Latinos, apologies blurting out of our mouths with every step.[28]

Others have taken up the call to challenge all forms of what Cornel West refers to as "racial reasoning" (conclusions and assumptions that are founded upon racial essentialism and terminate in simplistic binarisms).[29]

The collective investment in what I refer to as *the thickly layered cloud bank of theoretical jargon* ultimately recreates yet another version of the center/periphery binary in that it separates the place of theorization—

the ivory tower as it were—from the practice of everyday life. This reality alone engenders the need for scholars of Ethnic Studies to construct an alternative narrative, which validates and speaks more directly to the experiences of our students; poses practical strategies for confronting and transforming their social and political realities; and presents opportunities to initiate or become involved in community organizing projects. In addition to calling for a more practical or hands-on component to Ethnic Studies programs (in the form of community service and internships), I are alluding more specifically to the need to establish a more inclusive rhetorical climate within the classroom—a new discursive space that allows previously unheard or marginalized voices to be heard. In so doing we begin to devise a pedagogy that invites a more inclusive "interpretive community" (to borrow Stanley Fish's words) and thereby acknowledges and addresses the uneven and oftentimes troubling relations between race theory and race practice. Rather than perpetuating or maintaining the notion that there is a clear boundary between what we do in the classroom and what happens just outside the classroom walls, such an approach bridges the gap between theory and practice by allowing simultaneously for theoretical and academic discourse, as well as alternative discourses and modes of inquiry and critical exchange.

Perhaps the most effective way to offset the potentially negative consequences of institutionalizing race discourse in the academy is to keep in the forefront the consciousness that all discursive positions are inherently hegemonic. As Arjun Appadurai reminds us, in the act of deterritorializing, we are ultimately reterritorializing.[30] In our effort to create a new system, we must be ever conscious of the paradoxical notion that all systems are bound and constrained by their own biases and orthodoxies. Only this level of vigilance and awareness will prevent institutionalized racial discourse from undermining its own efficacy and "reduce struggle," as one of the editors of this volume has observed, "to the page, the text, or the classroom."

Notes

1. Mark Lawrence McPhail, *The Rhetoric of Racism Revisited, Reparations or Separation* (Lanham, MD: Rowman & Littlefield, 2002).
2. Well before the full rise of proslavery thought in the mid-nineteenth-century South, proslavery ideologues in the North fleshed out many of the themes that would define the American defense of slavery and solidify the category of blackness. Still, the ambiguity of slave Christianization remained troubling. If blackness was (by definition)

un-freedom, and Christianity was (by natural law) freedom, then how could the two be commingled? Christianity and whiteness were both states of freedom, making it easy for many to essentially equate the two: white = free and Christian; black/Indian/other = unfree and unchristian. Would not the ultimate freedom promised by Christianity infect the minds of the not-free, such that they would begin to question their status or doubt the validity of Christianity? Yet the inescapable fact remained that white Christians somehow had to fit black people into God's Providence. Passages from the Old Testament, especially Gen. 9:18–27 (which outlined the curse on Canaan, son of Ham, who had originally espied Noah's naked drunkenness)—once exegeted properly—provided at least a start at a religio-mythical grounding for modern racial meanings, and a long-lived one. According to the historian Winthrop Jordan, the "curse" on Canaan, son of Ham—with Ham as a figure considered to represent black people, Shem standing in variously sometimes for Indians, other times for Jews, and Japheth supposedly being the progenitor of white people—first arose as a mode of biblical interpretation during the modern age of exploration, from the sixteenth century forward. It persisted through centuries in spite of "incessant refutation," and was "probably sustained by a feeling that blackness could scarcely be anything *but* a curse and by the common need to confirm the facts of nature by specific reference to Scripture." Respectable theologians often skirted the son of Ham story, as it smacked more of folklore than "high" theology. The fable nevertheless deeply penetrated the consciousness of religious southerners, who were for the most part biblical literalists. The son of Ham thesis served well in the sense that it seemed to explain how black people could be free Christians and unfree slaves at the same time. But the curse on Ham was at best a shaky foundation for religioracial mythologizing, for the passage invoked was simply too short, sexually lewd, and fable-like to bear up under the full weight of the interpretations imposed upon it. Once again, the Bible proved a powerful but somewhat troubling and unreliable guide in the formation of mythoracial ideologies.

3. Edwin S. Gausted, *A Documentary History of Religion*, 486.

4. Ibid., 488.

5. George Rawick, ed. *The American Slave*. Hahn's assertion is developed in Steven Hahn, *A Nation Under Our Feet: Black Political Struggles in the Rural South from Slavery through the Great Migration*.

6. For more on Turner, see Stephen Angell, *Henry McNeal Turner and African-American Religion in the South*.

7. Houston Baker, *The Long Journey Back*, 167.

8. In Brent's words: "Africa, our fatherland, the home of the Hamitic race, is the only country on earth whose past, present, and future so concerned the Lord." Even the son of Ham himself, Canaan, was blessed, for he "invested and built up a country and settled a nation bearing his name, whose glory . . . remains today the typical ensign of the Christian's hope, concerning Africa's future glory prophecy says 'Ethiopia shall soon stretch forth her hand to God.'"

9. Du Bois, *Black Reconstruction*, 124.

10. Ibid.

11. Robin D. G. Kelley, "'We Are Not What We Seem,'" 88.

12. Ibid. For more on freedom songs, see Kerran Sanger, *"When the Spirit Says Sing": The Role of Freedom Songs in the Civil Rights Movement* (New York: Garland Press, 1995).

13. Youth of the Rural Organizing and Cultural Center, *Minds Stayed on Freedom*, 54.

14. Mendy Samstein, "The Murder of a Community," September 23, 1964.

15. John Dittmer, *Local People*, 305–7.

16. See Bob Wing, "Educate to Liberate," 1–7.

17. Ibid., 2.

18. Ibid., 2–4.

19. Mark Lawrence McPhail, *The Rhetoric of Racism Revisited*, 138–39. See also Celeste Condit and John Louis Lucaites' *Crafting Equality, America's Anglo-African Word* (Chicago: University of Chicago Press, 1991), 128.

20. Quoted in Wing, "Educate to Liberate," 5.

21. Quoted in Wing, "Educate to Liberate," 5.

22. For more on this subject see hooks's *Teaching to Transgress: Education as the Practice of Freedom* (New York: Routledge, 1994).

23. Henry Louis Gates, *The Signifying Monkey*, ix–xv.

24. Ibid., xiv.

25. Audre Lorde, "The Master's Tools," 110–13.

26. McPhail, *The Rhetoric of Racism*, 237.

27. In addition to her writing, hooks's resistance to established rhetorical norms and linguistic standards is signaled by her insistence on using lowercase letters in her name.

28. Gloria Anzaldua, *Borderlands/La Frontera*.

29. See Cornel West's *Race Matters*, in which he coined the phrase "racial reasoning."

30. See *Modernity at Large, Cultural Dimensions of Globalizatio* (Minneapolis and London: University of Minnesota Press, 1996).

BIBLIOGRAPHY

Anzaldua, Gloria. *Borderlands/La Frontera*. San Francisco: Aunt Lute, 1987.

Appadurai, Arjun. *Modernity at Large: Cultural Dimensions of Globalization*. Minneapolis: The University of Minnesota Press, 1996.

Baker, Houston. *The Long Journey Back: Issues in Black Literature and Criticism*. Chicago: University of Chicago Press, 1980.

Dittmer, John. *Local People: The Struggle for Civil Rights in Mississippi*. Urbana: University of Illinois Press, 1994.

Du Bois, W. E. B. *Black Reconstruction: An Essay Toward a History of the Part Which Black Folk Played in the Attempt to Reconstruct Democracy in America, 1860–1880*. New York: The Free Press [1935], 1992.

Gates, Henry Louis. *The Signifying Monkey*. New York: Oxford, 1988.

Gaustad, Edwin S. and Mark A. Noll eds. *A Documentary History of Religion in America to 1877*, 3rd ed. Grand Rapids: Eerdmans, 2003.

Hahn, Steven. *A Nation Under Our Feet: Black Political Struggles in the Rural South from Slavery through the Great Migration*. Cambridge: Harvard University Press, 2003.

Kelley, Robin D. G. " 'We Are Not What We Seem': Rethinking Black Working-Class Opposition in the Jim Crow South," *Journal of American History* 80 (June 1993): 88.

Lorde, Audre. "The Master's Tools Will Never Dismantle the Master's House." In *Sister Outsider*. Trumansberg, NY: Crossing Press, 1984, 110–13.

McPhail, Mark Lawrence. *The Rhetoric of Racism Revisited, Reparations or Separation.* Lanham, MD: Rowman & Littlefield, 2002.

Rawick, George, ed. *The American Slave: A Composite Autobiography.* Westport, CT: Greenwood Press, 1972–79.

Samstein, Mendy. "The Murder of a Community," *Student Voice,* September 23, 1964.

West, Cornel. *Race Matters.* Boston: Beacon Press, 1993.

Wing, Bob. "Educate to Liberate: Multiculturalism and the Struggle for Ethnic Studies." *Colorlines* 2, no.2 (summer 1999): 1–7.

Youth of the Rural Organizing and Cultural Center. *Minds Stayed on Freedom: The Civil Rights Struggle in the Rural South, an Oral History.* Boulder, CO: Westview Press, 1991.

Contributors

NORLISHA F. CRAWFORD is Assistant Professor, Department of English and Director, African American Studies Program, University of Wisconsin Oshkosh. She is the author of several recent essays on African American detective fiction. Professor Crawford is currently completing a critical biography of Chester Himes and his Harlem-based detective fiction series.

ELIZABETH CRESPO-KEBLER conducts research, writes, and teaches about gender, sexuality, race, ethnicity, and feminism in Latin America, the Caribbean, and the United States. She is Professor of Sociology at the University of Puerto Rico in Bayamón and Dean of Academic Affairs at the Centro de Estudios Avanzados de Puerto Rico y el Caribe. She is co-author of *Documentos del Feminismo en Puerto Rico: Facsímiles de la Historia, Vol. 1, 1970–79.* She is author of "Y las Trabajadoras Domésticas, ¿Dónde Están? – Raza, Género y Trabajo," in *Contrapunto de Género y Raza en Puerto Rico,* Centro de Investigaciones Sociales, Universidad de Puerto Rico.

ISABELL CSERNO is a PhD candidate in American Studies at the University of Maryland, College Park. Her dissertation is entitled "The Aesthetics of Race, Gender, and Nationhood in Consumer Culture: Advertising for Food in the United States and Germany, 1890s–1930s." Currently she serves as the graduate student representative on the Board of Directors of the National Association for Ethnic Studies. Her work has been funded by the Smithsonian Institution, The Winterthur Museum and Country Estate, and the John W. Hartman Center for Marketing, Sales, & Advertising History.

SARAH DAYNES is a visiting professor at the New School for Social Research in New York City. Her book *Desire for Race,* written in collaboration with Orville Lee, is forthcoming.

LAN DONG is Assistant Professor of English at the University of Illinois at Springfield, where she teaches Asian American literature, world literature, and composition. She has published articles on Asian American memoir, fiction, and films, and on Chinese films. She is currently working on a book project on the cross-cultural journey of the woman warrior Mulan from pre-modern China to Asian America.

CARMEN R. GILLESPIE is an Associate Professor of English at the University of Toledo. She is a scholar of American, African American, and Caribbean literatures and cultures and is also a creative writer. Her articles and poems have appeared in numerous literary journals and anthologies. Her book, *A Critical Companion to Toni Morrison*, is scheduled for publication in 2007. In 2005, Prof. Gillespie was the recipient of an Ohio Arts Council Individual Artist Fellowship for Excellence in Poetry. She has been a Fulbright scholar and a Cave Canem Fellow and has received awards from the National Endowment for the Humanities, the Mellon Foundation, the Bread Loaf Writer's Conference, and the Fine Arts Work Center in Provincetown.

GLYNE GRIFFITH is Associate Professor of English and Chair of the Department of Latin American, Caribbean, and U.S. Latino Studies at the State University of New York at Albany. He is the author of *Deconstruction, Imperialism and the West Indian Novel* and is completing a book about the BBC "Caribbean Voices" radio program and the development of literature in the English-speaking Caribbean.

LINDEN LEWIS is Professor of Sociology at Bucknell University. He is the editor of *The Culture of Gender and Sexuality in the Caribbean*. Dr. Lewis has published widely in the areas of race, gender, labor, the state, issues of globalization, and neo-liberal economic policies. He is currently completing a book on Caribbean masculinity.

ANDREA O'REILLY HERRERA is a Professor of literature and director of the Ethnic Studies Program at the University of Colorado at Colorado Springs. In addition to being a published poet and the author of the novel *The Pearl of the Antilles*, she is the editor of several collections, including *ReMembering Cuba: Legacy of a Diaspora* and the forthcoming work *Cuba: "Idea of a Nation" Displaced*. She is currently completing a manuscript entitled *"Setting the Tent Against the House": Cuban Artists in the Diaspora*.

UTA KRESSE RAINA is a PhD candidate in the History Department at Temple University. Her dissertation is entitled "Intellectual Imperialism in the Andes: German Anthropologists and Archaeologists in Peru, 1870–1930."

THEDA WREDE, PhD, is an Assistant Professor of English at Dixie State College of Utah, where she focuses her teaching and research on the intersection of ethnicity, gender, and geography in contemporary American literature. She has published an article in *Interdisciplinary Humanities* and a book review in *South Atlantic Review* and is currently working on *Critical and Personal Perspectives on James Dickey*, a book of essays co-edited with Dr. William Thesing.

Index